CRITICAL CONDITION

Gender and Culture

A SERIES OF COLUMBIA UNIVERSITY PRESS
Edited by Carolyn G. Heilbrun and Nancy K. Miller

In Dora's Case: Freud, Hysteria, Feminism
  Edited by Charles Bernheimer and Claire Kahane
Breaking the Chain: Women, Theory, and French Realist Fiction
  Naomi Schor
Between Men: English Literature and Male Homosocial Desire
  Eve Kosofsky Sedgwick
Romantic Imprisonment: Women and Other Glorified Outcasts
  Nina Auerbach
The Poetics of Gender
  Edited by Nancy K. Miller
Reading Woman: Essays in Feminist Criticism
  Mary Jacobus
Honey-Mad Women: Emancipatory Strategies in Women's Writing
  Patricia Yaeger
Subject to Change: Reading Feminist Writing
  Nancy K. Miller
Thinking Through the Body
  Jane Gallop
Gender and the Politics of History
  Joan Wallach Scott
The Dialogic and Difference: "An/Other Woman" in Virginia Woolf and Christa Wolf
  Anne Herrmann
Plotting Women: Gender and Representation in Mexico
  Jean Franco
Inspiriting Influences: Tradition, Revision, and Afro-American Women's Novels
  Michael Awkward
Hamlet's Mother and Other Women
  Carolyn G. Heilbrun

CRITICAL CONDITION

Feminism at the Turn of the Century

Susan Gubar

 Columbia University Press   New York

COLUMBIA UNIVERSITY PRESS
Publishers Since 1893
New York   Chichester, West Sussex

The author and the Press wish to thank Indiana University
for its contribution torward the cost of reproducing the book's
illustrations.

"Eating the Bread of Affliction: Judaism and Feminism" was
originally published in *Tulsa Studies in Women's Literature* 13, no.
2 (Fall 1994): 293–316 and is reprinted by permission of the publisher, *Feminist Studies*, Inc. It was reprinted in *People of the
Book*, edited by Jeffrey Rubin-Dorsky and Shelley Fisher
Fishkin, University of Wisconsin, 1996.

"The Graying of Professor Erma Bombeck" was originally
published in *College English* 61, no. 4 (March 1999): 431–47.
Copyright 1997 by the National Council of Teachers of English.
Reprinted with permission.

"What Ails Feminist Criticism?" was originally published in
Critical Inquiry 24 (Summer 1998): 878–902, and is reprinted,
along with portions of "Notations *in Medias Res*," CI 25 (Winter
1999): 380–96, by permission of the publisher, the University of
Chicago. All rights reserved.

"Feminist Misogyny; or, The Paradox of 'It Takes One to
Know One'" originally appeared as "Feminist Misogyny: Mary
Wollstonecraft and the Paradox of 'It Takes One to Know One'"
in *Feminist Studies* 20, no. 3 (Fall 1994): 453–74 and is reprinted
by permission of the publisher, *Feminist Studies*, Inc. It was
reprinted in *Feminism Besides Itself*, edited by Diane Elam and
Robyn Wiegman, Routledge, 1995.

Library of Congress Cataloging-in-Publication Data
Gubar, Susan, 1944–
    Critical condition : feminism at the turn of the century /
Susan Gubar.   p. cm.— (Gender and culture)
    Includes bibliographical references and index.
    ISBN 0–231–11580–6 (alk.paper)
    1. Feminist literary criticism. 2. Feminism in literature.
3. Women and literature. I. Title. II. Series
PN98.W64G83 1999   99–16564
801'.95'082—DC21

For Marah and Simone

Contents

Acknowledgments

As my references to Sandra Gilbert throughout this book indicate, I remain indebted to a collaborator whose creativity enriched my life and love of literature for more than twenty-five years, though she should in no way be held accountable for any of the views I put forward in this book. Thanks go as well to other colleagues who have been generous about reading and reacting to my writing: Elizabeth Abel, Vereen M. Bell, Mary Burgan, Linda Charnes, Thadious Davis, Jonathan Elmer, Judith Kegan Gardiner, Marianne Hirsch, Ilinca Johnston, Tricia Lootens, Alyce Miller, Carolyn Mitchell, Judith Roof, Janet Sorensen, Martha Vicinus, Sandra Zagarell, and Bonnie Zimmerman helped me immeasurably with their honest responses to work in progress. Stimulating conversations with Mary Favret and Andrew H. Miller, as well as bracing exchanges—in print and in person—with Robyn Wiegman ignited my thinking on many of the subjects broached in the new essays. On the phone and e-mail, Nancy K. Miller literally invented the idea of this book and Carolyn Heilbrun gave me the courage to pursue the most unpopular opinions expressed in it. Their wonderful friendship with each other and with me has energized and heartened me. The editor of their series at Columbia University Press, Jennifer Crewe, and my agent in New York, Diana Finch, helped from afar, as did Kenneth

Gros Louis, Morton Lowengrub, and Kenneth Johnston back home in Bloomington. For research assistance, I am indebted to Johanna Frank, Will Murphy, and Alice Rutkowski. Susan Heath did a fine job copyediting this manuscript, and my responses to her queries benefited from the hospitality proffered by the community of people at the Virginia Foundation for the Humanities in the spring of 1999.

In their willing suspension of disbelief at my frequent follies, some friends are like family: Shehira Davezac, Julie and Susannah Gray, John Lyons, Jan Sorby, and Jayne Spencer especially. On a daily basis, conversations with Mary Jo Weaver keep me grounded in the spiritual and ethical perspectives she makes palpably real. I am blessed, too, by the kindness of my dear mother, Luise David, whose regimen at the computer bests my own efforts. As always, Donald Gray, first and finest editor, has greatly improved my work. How, as friend and companion, he enhances my life, I can barely grasp without feeling buffeted by alarming bouts of affection. Since this is a book about my fears and hopes about the future of women, I have dedicated it to my daughters, Marah and Simone Gubar. My love for them is fostered by my delight in the intrepid wit and tenderness they generously bestow on me and periodically lavish on each other.

CRITICAL CONDITION

PART I

Enormous Changes at the Last Minute

1

Introduction

The last two years of the twentieth century were troubled by journalistic intimations of feminism's mortality and immorality. "IS FEMINISM DEAD?" queried *Time Magazine*'s June 29, 1998, cover on which four severed heads—a grim Susan B. Anthony, an ageing Betty Friedan, a jaunty Gloria Steinem, and a perplexed Ally McBeal—floated eerily in a lineup against the dark background. That this lineage presented the first three women in documentary black-and-white while the TV character Ally McBeal emerged in sitcom living color illustrates Gina Bellafante's point in the accompanying article that "much of feminism has devolved into the silly" (58). Although female workers still earn less than their male counterparts, although the glass ceiling remains impenetrable, although the problems of inadequate day care, domestic violence, and increases in the incidence of anorexia have not been solved, "frazzled, self-absorbed girls" dominate a movement "divorced from matters of public purpose" and therefore moribund (58, 60).

Whereas *Time* castigated a feminism commodified through self-indulgent, self-promoting icons and pundits in popular culture, *LinguaFranca* brought these same charges against the most visible spokesperson for feminism within the academy, the then president of the Modern Language Association. Its September cover, asking "WHO'S AFRAID of Elaine

Showalter?," featured Emily Eakin's article about Showalter's passion for shopping, her acquisition of a London flat and a publicist, her blaming female patients for hysterical symptoms she had previously diagnosed as the product of misogyny, and her noblesse oblige toward unemployed graduate students (advised to retool for work in the media and business), all of which left her open to the accusation of being motivated by nothing but "crass self-interest" (35). Like Bellafante's, Eakin's piece could be said to have constructed the image of a co-opted feminism it then derided; however, more troubling for Elaine Showalter's friends and colleagues was her admission that she had been "devastated" by the attacks she received from feminist critics ("I was very shaken by Toril Moi's book. She makes me the enemy"), a shock that may illuminate the most disturbing comment in the piece: "I don't care what the latest development is in feminist theory or gender theory," Showalter was quoted as saying. "It's completely irrelevant to me" (34).

As if widening the grounds of that irrelevance beyond the personal pain it produced in Showalter, half a year later Martha C. Nussbaum deplored "the great tragedy in new feminist theory," which she identified with the "loss of a sense of public commitment" (44). "Something more insidious than provincialism has come to prominence in the American academy," she declared about feminism in *The New Republic*. "It is the virtually complete turning from the material side of life, toward a type of verbal and symbolic politics that makes only the flimsiest of connections with the real situation of real women" (38). Nussbaum's belief that the "quietism" of academic feminists "collaborates with evil" (45) might seem draconian, were it not for the fact that a woman is raped every five minutes in America today and the sexual abuse of children has reached epidemic proportions. Whether disavowed as silly by a journalist of popular culture or as immaterial by some of its earliest and foremost academic advocates, feminism and gender studies were getting a lot of bad press. But, then, they always have.

When I shoved a copy of the table of contents for this project under the eyes of a good friend in Bloomington, she immediately confirmed its pertinence by informing me that books about "the F word" don't sell. "Why not refer to 'women' or (better yet) 'sex' instead," she cautioned, since feminism has been so tarnished by media hype identifying it with humorless, antediluvian man-haters. "I'm not a feminist, but . . ."—the sentence we and many of our colleagues repeatedly hear from undergraduates—may often be followed by a litany sounding suspiciously like what we would ordinarily call feminism: that is, these students want equal pay for equal work, the possibility of rewarding professional and personal lives, the right to obtain abortions as well as contraception, and freedom from sexual harassment. Yet they do not define feminism as equity for women or an awareness of the social construction of gender or reproductive control or political agitation for the ending of sexual violence. Where had we failed, I wondered—"we" here meaning those of us working with feminist methodologies in college courses devoted to studying the historical evolution and psychological dynamics of the relationship between the sexes.

But if the discrediting of the word "feminism" seems like a cause for alarm, what of the indisputable fact that the situation of women in higher education has completely changed for the better? When, back in the sixties and early seventies, I attended City College, the University of Michigan, and the University of Iowa, I never had a female professor. Granted there were a few, but not enough to go around. Now most undergraduates in the humanities, at least, are surely taught by several female professors, and not only in the newly installed Women's Studies courses in which they may have enrolled—classes that did not exist during my days as a student. Indeed, they might know women administrators at their universities or hear female public intellectuals, state department officials, and cabinet members at graduation ceremonies—an uncommon event in the sixties. As important, many of today's students were brought up by mothers who combined rewarding professional and personal lives, and had access to abortions as well as contraception, although the standard of equal pay for equal work is still an ideal to be fought for, and sexual harassment at work still a custom to be fought against.

"The more things change, the more they stay the same"—or—"We've come a long way, baby" (this last slogan, alas, a cigarette ad that paradoxically undercuts itself by attesting to the commercial misuses of feminist bravado)? Friends and colleagues debate the point endlessly, trying to assess the impact of the movement that shaped our lives. In the public arena, current events repeatedly baffle an easy conclusion. What does it mean that the most feminist-friendly president to date occupied the White House during the nineties, but that he was a philanderer (to use an old-fashioned word), a sex addict (to use a new-fangled concept)? Take, for instance, the infamous incident of the cases made on the behalf of Paula Jones, Kathleen Willey, and Monica Lewinsky's against President Clinton.

On the positive side, early signs of the brouhaha were brought to the attention of TV viewers by female reporters like Cokie Roberts and Jackie

Judd. Soon Clinton's secretary of state and of education (both women) staunchly defended him before the cameras. The language of public debate over where and when a sexual advance constitutes an actionable violation relied on discourses established by feminist scholarship and was used by the female judge, Susan Webber Wright, who dismissed the harassment case against the president. When Paula Jones, who was suing Clinton, underwent a major make-over—new hairdo, cosmetics, wardrobe, even teeth and nose—did she give inspiration to the less prepossessing viewers of talk-shows or did she signal the continued fetishization of the female body? A comparable question about fetishized female roles could be posed about the packaging of Hilary Clinton, who had incurred the public's wrath with her liberal views on health insurance yet now reigned supreme as a wronged but patient Griselda, standing by her man. Once again, too, male prosecutors, lawyers, and senators in the public sphere used women's private experiences as grist for a partisan political mill. Embarrassing in its detailed recounting and shocking in its deceitfulness, the misconduct of the president—though it may have involved neither harassment nor "high crimes and misde-meanors"—left many feminists reeling between their abhorrence of Clin-ton's sleazy sexcapades and their historical commitment to rights of privacy and consensual relationships between adults.

Just as it is difficult to decide if the *Time* magazine obituary about femi-nism's devolution into narcissistic frivolity fairly characterizes the Clinton years, it is hard to assess Elaine Showalter's and Martha Nussbaum's disillu-sionment about the irrelevance of feminism as an academic enterprise. For those of us inside colleges and universities, should we be heartened or dis-heartened by the media hype of pop-feminists and pop-antifeminists whose sound bites grotesquely caricature our ideas? Do they reflect widespread recognition of the importance of our subject or a commodification that drains feminism of its intellectual panache? Should we worry or rejoice over the fact that feminist critics used to stress the first term in their appellation (their ori-gins in the politics of social change) but now emphasize the second (their contribution to academic scholarship)? What are we to make of the well-pub-licized diatribes against Women's Studies programs, as well as their growth across the country? Have the proliferating disciplines and competing method-ologies in our field—African-American, Postcolonial, and cultural Studies; poststructuralist, new historicist, and queer theories—demonstrated its vital-ity or its capitulation to a divisive specialization? And will the propagation of differences among feminist teachers in academe—in race, sexual orientation, religion, national origin, and professional rank—prove our resilient exten-sion of the field or the end of our common enterprise?

To rephrase a famous passage in Wordsworth's *The Prelude*, has feminist knowledge been purchased at the price of power? In the essays collected in this book, I explore the sometimes bumpy evolution of feminist criticism dur-ing the turn of the twentieth century, paying special attention to those contro-versies that threaten its unity, even as they prove its vigor. After feminist intel-lectuals entered the humanities in numbers, some began decrying a feminism horrifically balkanized, while others welcomed the opportunity to address those conflicting loyalties and internal disagreements wherein women's mean-ings reside. Do our disputes prove that feminist criticism is self-destructing or that it is going through a transition that will issue in innovative modes of inquiry? While working on this manuscript, I found myself oscillating between discouragement at evidence that feminist scholars remain immured in self-destructive maneuvers and elation over the energy with which women artists, critics, and theorists manage to continue redefining feminist studies. I eventually realized, during the process of organizing the essays on the table of contents, that my mood was swinging from pessimism to optimism about the state of feminism at the turn of the century, a shift to which my succession of titles for this project testifies.

When I first proposed the collection to Columbia University's editor Jennifer Crewe, it was called *Will the Hive Survive?* A quotation from the final poem in Sylvia Plath's brilliant Bee Sequence, this title used the question she posed about her chances at personal survival to speculate on the prospects of feminist criticism. At the conclusion of "Wintering," Plath wonders about her own future as a woman and a poet, ending equivocally, but with a gesture toward perseverance at odds with her subsequent suicide:

> Will the hive survive, will the gladiolas
> Succeed in banking their fires
> To enter another year?
> What will they taste of, the Christmas roses?
> The bees are flying. They taste the spring.   (*CP* 219)

The female hive—"The Bees are all women"—could serve as a metaphor for the female academic community that assembled during the last few decades of the twentieth century. Plath's phrase provided me an opportunity to spec-ulate on the issues of gender and education because I like the sound of the hive busily buzzing, the fact that there are such regal creatures as queen bees, that the bee was a symbol of artistry for writers from Jonathan Swift to Emily Dickinson, that its products evoke the "sweetness and light" Matthew Arnold revered, that the bee sounds like the word "be" and can sting, that in the nineteenth century a woman with a "bee in her bonnet" was a woman with ideas—even that the "beehive" was a hairdo back in the murky days before the dawning of feminism's second wave. Taking my cue from Plath, I remained expectant but not for a moment certain about the regeneration made possible by women's multiple ways of being feminist.

Still, given Plath's fate, that first title ominously gestured toward the potential extinction of feminist criticism and thus spotlighted the sorts of predicaments I had detected in two of the most polemical pieces included here, "What Ails Feminist Criticism?" and "Feminist Misogyny." Composed first but placed last in this volume, these essays reflect my dismay at mind-numbing battles in which so-called social constructionists faulted so-called essentialists for their naive totalizing, feminists of color blamed white scholars for their racism, lesbian critics accused straight thinkers of homophobia. Contempt for those whose speculations did not conform to the prevailing notion of the properly radical position in the field spilled over into self-righteous, routinized posturing. Ironically, however, those very terms used as categories of critique themselves underwent a sort of spectacular unraveling. Because of their propensity to challenge fixed terms of origins and reality, some poststructuralists became aware of their own tendency to totalize; many African-American and postcolonial writers emphasized the diversity among black and third-world women's experiences; and a host of lesbian thinkers addressed a variety of queer experiences. The best work in the field began to attend to the perplexity of women's fractured, divided, multiplied, and contradictory modes of identification.

My next try, *Reinventing Feminist Criticism*—besides containing a well-earned *hommage* to Carolyn Heilbrun, the author of (among other works) *Reinventing Womanhood*—kept a nice ambiguity in play between the adjectival and verbal forms of its first term: feminist criticism has always been in the process of reinventing itself and now we must reinvent it for the twenty-first century. Even for a traditionally trained, older scholar like myself, the sometimes irksome challenges issued by iconoclastic voices coming from African-American, postcolonial, lesbian, religious, materialist, and poststructuralist methodologies recast our enterprise. But this title erased my earlier obstinate questionings even while it sounded too grandiose, as if I were personally taking credit for reinventing feminist criticism. Worse yet, its cheerfulness tottered on the edge of the sort of sound bites administrators coin in an age of diminishing financial support.

So I settled on a title proposed by a friend, *Critical Condition*: the condition of feminist studies—less an activist, more a scholarly enterprise—has itself become critical because of a number of heated disputes that have put its proponents at odds. It somehow sounded right, but might it give the impression that I was pathologizing work being done in the profession simply because I did not agree with its practitioners' methodologies? I hardly wanted to be placed in the discomforting role of hapless diagnostician of a potentially incurable malady. Plus, I had come to believe that simply to decry contention inevitably means replicating it; to repress disagreement spells regression. From this perspective, what made *Critical Condition* seem honest was its equivocation, which captures my sense of being poised between causes for regret and for celebration: now institutionalized in a variety of humanities departments, feminist studies have multiplied into various forms of inquiry in which every category linked to gender so as to make our investigations more sophisticated has itself undergone critical redefinition. Just as proponents of identity politics enlarged the meaning of the term "women" by combining such categories as race and sex with gender analysis, poststructuralist thinkers used gender analysis to display the instability of such categories as race and sex. In other words, the terms that happen to interest me in the first four chapters—race, sex, religion, caste—started out as fixed phrases vis-à-vis gender, but considerations of gender quickly complicated their meanings.

Similarly, in our current critical condition, centrifugal forces spin us away from what used to be a more integrated undertaking, toward a vertiginous variety of tasks. Just as an erupting star, a supernova, creates new matter and energy, explosive clashes in feminist conversations issue in exciting modes of thinking. For this reason, whole fields have sprung up around race and gender, sex and gender, religion and gender, caste and gender (scholarship upon which I draw in the first part of this book). Nor are our proliferating specializations limited to such critical categories, for many feminist critics define their studies around historical lines (Medieval Studies, modernism), social issues (women and trauma, maternity), nation (gender arrangements in Middle-Eastern countries), a multiple of disciplines (law, medicine, computer technology) as well as genres (film, photography, opera). Albeit at times irritating, at times chaotic, proliferating critical conflicts, contentions, confrontations have nevertheless taught us how to propagate differences and thereby produce invigorating scholarly venues.

To reflect this more sanguine framing of the topic, I reversed the order I had expected to use to organize the table of contents. Instead of beginning with (and thus emphasizing) my distress, I move "forward into the past" (the phrase is May Sarton's), starting with the stimulating types of thinking made possible by combining gender with other conceptual lenses and moving back to the impasses that have generated this evolution. Whereas part 2—"Contending Forces"—takes its title from a powerful turn-of-the-nineteenth-century novel by Pauline Hopkins about conflicting societal forces that combine to create regulatory mechanisms of oppression, part 1—"Enormous Changes at the Last Minute"—comes from a contemporary collection of Grace Paley's marvelously buoyant short stories. Together, the four essays in the first section deal with the enormous changes effected when the concept of gender is put to use in understanding shifting and shifty racial, sexual, religious, and caste contexts. Each of the typologies proposed in part 1 of this volume—African-American women artists, lesbian writers, Jewish-American feminists, female professors—spawned a quite variegated assortment of characters, a sign of the volatility of identity categories under the pressure of poststructuralist inquiries. Distressing though they may be, feminist altercations have produced significant alterations in our critical practices. When coupled with other categories of difference, gender continues to generate new insights.

In the first two essays I demonstrate how the racial and sexual challenges posed by African-American, Postcolonial, and Gay Studies scholars have stretched the boundaries of feminist criticism, subverting the presumed whiteness and heterosexuality of feminists's constituencies. By emphasizing the intertwined roles of race and gender as well as sexuality and gender, African-American, postcolonial, and lesbian feminists have taught many of us how to engage in comparative forms of ethnic analyses, transnational as well as transgeneric inquiry, and sexual studies. Though scholarly fashion deems modish a discourse of abstract arguments about philosophical texts (composed, for the most part, by French men), I put the creative and critical accomplishments of women back into conversation, to highlight the theoretical work achieved in the aesthetic realm populated by contemporary poets, fiction writers, dramatists, performance artists, and painters. Though feminist criticism has been nudged by cultural studies advocates toward important popular forms ranging from TV programs to sporting events, I attempt to underline the ongoing relevance of the so-called "high" arts.

In "Women Artists and Contemporary Racechanges"—linking my last book, *Racechanges: White Skin, Black Face in American Culture*, to the feminist work that preceded it—I marvel at the dazzling dismantling of the category of race achieved by performance and visual artists of color. By disclosing the inadequacy of integrationists' touting of assimilation and multiculturalists' advocacy of identity politics, such feminist performers and painters as Adrian Piper, Anna Deavere Smith, and Faith Ringgold render race itself obsolete, in the process making concrete not only the procedures through which other Americans can jettison this bankrupt idea but also what new metaphors might replace anachronistic racial paradigms. Philosophically astute, the women artists in the first chapter participate in a dialogue with theorists so their art acts in a quasi-theoretical way, actually setting the stage for new conceptualizations of color. In the second chapter, too, I consider how artists participating in theoretically resonant discussions make palpable the ideas debated in more academic forms of criticism. "Lesbian Studies 101 (As Taught by Creative Writers)" uses a poem by Marilyn Hacker along with short stories by Jeanette Winterson and Rebecca Brown to survey the historiographic, aesthetic, and psychoanalytic speculations of lesbian thinkers actively engaged in Gay Studies. What functions were performed by the image of the lesbian as a woman-identified-woman and then as a feminist-separatist, and why these figures were followed by the queering of homosexuality: these are the subjects that emerge from the juxtaposition of Hacker's historical inquiry, Winterson's separatist manifesto, and Brown's critique of Freud and Lacan.

From what personal background, with which sort of investment, with whose imprimatur do I approach such subjects as African-American and lesbian modes of expression? Implicitly this collection asserts for the critic what many creative artists have always claimed, namely that interest and imagination provide sufficient license for intellectual scrutiny—besides doing the requisite homework, of course—investigations that ought not be and really cannot be policed. That you don't have to be a black to write about blacks or a lesbian to write about lesbians follows logically from these two essays, which demonstrate exactly how unstable, how slippery those terms ("black" "lesbian") are, especially as identity categories. Shaped by my commitment to making scholarship activist in the dismantling of racist and homophobic mindsets, my stake in writing about African-American and lesbian art also derives from a passionate belief that the pedagogic function of feminist studies depends on abrogating scholarly ghettoization and that its future vitality hinges on our ability to bring gender into play with different sorts of differences.

Though racial and sexual modes of inquiry fueled enormous changes in feminist criticism, so have analyses of the religions that confuse and enrich women's lives and practices. "Eating the Bread of Affliction," which considers the contradictory roles religion has performed in feminist methodologies too often oblivious to the importance of such affiliations, describes how troubling and yet also how empowering Judaism has been for a prominent proportion of the academic feminists writing during the seventies. A postscript, composed several years after this piece was originally published, discusses what propels, what inhibits the recent emergence of new conversations between feminist studies and Jewish Studies scholars. The complications resulting from a range of beliefs (even in one religious group) set the stage for confronting the aging of feminists placed in various ranks with diverse degrees of status, a fall-out from the process of feminism's institutionalization. By drawing on the tradition of American women's humor, in the next chapter I transform Erma Bombeck's frazzled housewife into a harried professor to produce a parodic conduct book for women teachers. In the process of dealing with mid- and later-career stress, this essay—which profits from many scholars' recent attempts to understand the politics at work in academic and disciplinary settings—addresses the material conditions attending the institutionalization of feminist studies during a period of retrenchment as well as the ways in which our diverse relationships to establishments of higher education will stretch and transform our feminism. Astonishing as our success at integrating women into the academy has been over the past three decades, it can strain our relationships to each other.

After this segment on the powerful modifications staged in feminism at the end of the twentieth century, I return to some of the disputes that generated them. I begin part 2 with "What Ails Feminist Criticism?" because this piece opens with an historical overview of the development of feminist literary criticism and because it outlines the contentiousness that paradoxically accompanied and helped to activate the transformation of feminist criticism, but also because it cost me a job offer, a rejection that perversely intensified my incentive for working on this subject. As a candidate for a senior position at a school to remain nameless, I delivered an early draft of this piece, then melodramatically called "Who Killed Feminist Criticism?" The department chair had been worried that the right wing of his department might be alienated by my feminist credentials; however, I confided my fear that it would be the left wing my talk would trouble. Unfortunately, I turned out to be correct. For I was taking to task writing practices that I felt undermined our common project, much to the chagrin of exactly those feminists in the audience with whom I identified and from whose scholarship I had profited.

Probably written in too bellicose a manner, the lecture that cost me a job offer nevertheless engaged an issue close to my heart: namely, my feeling that some of the prevailing languages of feminist criticism alienated feminist academics from each other and from women shut out of theoretical discourses that had hardened into orthodoxies. A yearning for textual pleasure, but also a revulsion against what Toni Morrison calls the "calcified language of the academy" animates this piece and in particular an abhorrence of the hostile putdowns that so hurt Elaine Showalter. For, as Morrison explained in her Nobel lecture, "Oppressive language does more than represent violence; it is violence; does more than represent the limits of knowledge; it limits knowledge" (16). Now entitled "What Ails Feminist Criticism?," this essay looks at predominant areas of contention during the eighties and nineties to pose its own highly contentious query: To what extent have certain sponsors of African-American, postcolonial, and poststructuralist studies subverted the term "women" that feminism needs to assure its political agency as an intellectual and social movement? Because even the published version of this meditation was misinterpreted as an instance of generational fury at poststructuralist theorists or as a racist rejoinder to the fields of African-American and Postcolonial Studies, I have revised and expanded its conclusion. Not race-related scholarship, but identity politics; not poststructuralism per se, but poststructuralist pieties about the assumed fictitiousness of subjectivity and collectivity: these were the objects of my critique.

This was not a fight I set out to pick, I felt during the composing of this piece, but one thrust upon me by the barrage of criticism Sandra Gilbert and I (as well as many of our peers) received throughout the eighties and nineties. "There is a certain generation of feminist theorists who have really gotten it from all sides," Marianne Hirsch has explained about us; "and I don't just mean criticized, I mean trashed" (364–65). About that curious entity called "Gilbert and Gubar," Carla Kaplan declared, "no other American feminists have been so badly caricatured as advocates of illusory and essentialistic notions of sameness and identification" (32). Gayle Greene, Janet Todd, and Susan Bordo also recorded what Bordo called "the raw hostility" some feminist speakers exhibited toward the work of earlier scholars such as Carol Gilligan and Nancy Chodorow (*UW* 233). In her introduction to the republication of *A Literature of Their Own*, "Twenty Years On," Elaine Showalter contrasted the respectful reception the book originally earned from men with attacks "from virtually every point on the feminist hermeneutic circle" by scholars who labeled her "separatist, careerist, theoretical, antitheoretical, racist, homophobic, politically correct, traditional, and noncanonical" (xv–xvi).

Regardless of the terms in which they were castigated, the first generation of feminist critics felt deluged by the hostility of our successors. Yet, looking back at my own intellectual trajectory, I realize how much I wanted to disentangle my critique of the field from a purely defensive posture. Yes, it was painful to be derided, but I did not then and do not now want my personal discomfort to be used to discount what I believed and still believe to be a just representation of a generalized chagrin among many other feminists about an unproductive divisiveness in feminist scholarship.

Although I reproach the advocates of identity politics and of Derridean and Foucauldian theory for the debilitating atmosphere they spawned, it sometimes seems impossible for feminists not to slip into suppositions or arguments that maintain ideas deleterious to women. The self-subverting tendency of even the most radical writers—from Mary Wollstonecraft to Hélène Cixous and Andrea Dworkin—is the subject of the last reprinted essay, "Feminist Misogyny," which considers the curious dialectic between feminist and misogynist intellectual history. In our effort to counter degrading social constructions of womanhood, are feminists destined to collude with or perpetuate such constructions? If feminists are products of masculinist histories, how can there be any place from which they can launch a philosophical rejoinder to male-dominated definitions of femininity? By placing "What Ails Feminist Criticism?" and "Feminist Misogyny" at the back of this volume, I gesture toward the hope that we are moving beyond contention, but I also try to avoid dating myself and my generation as a bunch of has-beens nostalgically lamenting our lost origins and pinning the blame on the strange doings of the young. Instead of marking the nineties as the death date of feminist studies, we should see the decade as a rite of passage into a maturation that requires us to answer the question with which I ended "Feminist Misogyny," namely, what happens when feminists turn away from our differences with men to attend to our complex relationships with each other.

I therefore decided to background my grousing, hoping that a positive engagement with the insights of African-American, postcolonial, and poststructuralist thinkers in what are now the opening chapters on the table of contents would free me from the allegation that I had dismissed or calumniated their labors. By foregrounding my efforts to devise a way of coping with the challenges of racial and poststructuralist discourses, I hope to tap their powerful epistemologies for an inquiry more congenial to my sensibilities than the work I had been bewailing, a feminist approach turned more resolutely toward the creative arts, on the one hand, and toward activist goals, on the other. My personal struggle against cynicism—always a challenge in later life—convinces me that feminist critics of all ages can and will reinvent themselves in the coming years. So do the comments of my contemporaries, whom I canvassed for the epilogue for this book. Here I borrow a project proposed but never composed by Virginia Woolf because, like her, I want to glimpse the future, to press "as closely as can be upon the massy wall of time, which is forever lifting and pulling and letting fresh spaces of life in upon us" ("JMJM" 48). What the forecast holds for feminist critics: this was a subject I only dared approach through the chorus of voices I assembled through a questionnaire sent to my peers.

Besides my wish to disrupt learned configurations of knowledge by splicing academic with artistic practices and by participating in many other people's efforts to bring racial, sexual, religious, and institutional speculations (as well as their activist agendas) into the purview of feminist criticism, part of my impetus throughout this undertaking springs from dissatisfaction with the currently available histories of feminist criticism. Though we need accounts of its development so as to preserve our intellectual past, K. K. Ruthven's *Feminist Literary Studies* (1984), Toril Moi's *Sexual/Textual Politics* (1985), Janet Todd's *Feminist Literary History* (1988), and Jane Gallop's *Around 1981* (1992) appear either oddly skewed or weirdly hostile to the subject they address. So Sandra Gilbert and I thought when we broached this topic in our collaborative talk at a 1994 "Feminist Criticism Revisited" panel we organized for the Modern Language Association convention, and so I still think today. Ruthven, convinced that feminists are "excessively fond of 'underdetermined' theories" (7), argued that "the female 'problematic' . . . is too important to be left in the hands of anti-intellectual feminists" (9). Ignoring cross-Atlantic interaction, Moi invariably set American against French feminists, to find the former wanting in epistemological savvy (*pace* Elaine Showalter). Although she sought to redress that wrong, Janet Todd focused so extensively on Showalter as a representative figure that she flattened out the plethora of opinions jostling for space in periodicals and books, especially those expressed by African-American and lesbian thinkers. Because Jane Gallop dealt with anthologies of criticism, she neglected single-authored works by such important writers as Kate Millett, Carolyn Heilbrun, Adrienne Rich, and Audre Lorde.

Unlike these earlier accounts, *Critical Condition: Feminism at the Turn of the Century* is not organized chronologically as a history of feminist criticism. However, its sundry essays attempt to locate important sites of knowledge that drew scholars into dialogues. There is no plot to the book, no master metaphor or narrative, because a number of these chapters originated as independent articles, because we are still too close to the history through which we just lived, and because I am obviously so personally and professionally implicated in it. Yet it would be nice to believe that the monotonous litany of "race, class, sex, and nation," as well as the policing for which identity categories were used and the professional certification for which poststructuralist vocabularies were employed, are being dislodged by the more risk-taking, stimulating scholarship those very ideas generate. Readers feeling gloomy (will they be first-generation feminists?) can begin at part 2; readers feeling upbeat (will they be second- or—for that matter—third-generation feminists?) should begin at the beginning (where upbeat people usually start in any case). Just the fact that we now have several generations of feminist scholars seems like a fine excuse to party.

Whether glum or cheerful, most participants in the enterprise would agree that feminism has undergone astonishing modifications during the turn of the century, that it cannot be judged "divorced from public matters" and moribund, as *Time* magazine claimed, although (as I hope to show in the pages that follow) it must begin to deal directly with the charges of irrelevance leveled by Elaine Showalter and Martha Nussbaum. When, in a television show subsequent to the publication of the *Time* cover story with which I began, a baffled Ally McBeal experienced a minatory vision that someone was trying to make her into an icon of the death of feminism, the episode reflected the ways in which the popular arts imitate journalism in postmodern spin-offs many of us watch with amusement. A more alarming recycling of gender politics occurred during the Senate impeachment investigation of President Clinton, when antichoice, Christian Coalition, and "family values" Republicans stood up to pledge their allegiance to a feminist agenda—championing the rights of victims of harassment in the workplace—so as to legislate against private sexual conduct in a puritanical proceeding some observers likened to the Salem witch trials. If feminism is not dead, one might understandably wonder, has it been curiously kidnapped? Paradoxically, however, even media and govern-mental manipulations of feminism prove its centrality to the culture at large. What the thrilling evolution of feminist inquiry within the academy suggests is that feminism as it used to be defined may be defunct, but long will its per-mutations thrive. Given recent scholarly expansions of the field, the *Time* magazine line-up—Susan B. Anthony, Betty Friedan, Gloria Steinem, Ally McBeal—constitutes a white, American, middle-class, heterosexual cast made anachronistic by the incursions of race, nation, class, religion, and sexuality into gender analyses increasingly sensitive to the ways in which all rhetorics—including those dedicated to social justice—can be used and abused under a variety of complex circumstances. While the diversity of feminists raises prob-lems about future bridge-building between various constituencies, it also attests to feminism's versatility.

Certainly what has led many people to reject the term "feminism" has been what Linda Williams calls "the association of feminism with an all-or-nothing understanding of what *is* good for women, with often self-righteous positions that know for sure on which side of any binary opposition a 'prop-er' feminism belongs" (362). Although I disagree with a number of the femi-nist theorists I discuss in the pages to come, such disputes certify our libera-tion not only from discourses that previously had to attend to our common resistance to masculinist formations but also from complacent pieties assumed to be programmatically and politically correct. Quite astonishingly, in a mere three decades we feminists have generated an enormous amount of conse-quential scholarship and teaching in the humanities. Instead of squabbling, we should be honoring each other at those parties I'm envisioning (in a host of eccentric ceremonies that would be fun to imagine). While we move from our original struggles against patriarchal structures to our current conversa-tions with each other, we need to remember how weirdly recalcitrant, how exceptionally tenacious those structures have proven to be and yet how much we have already achieved. Thinking about how much has been accomplished may point us toward what still needs to be done in the society at large and within the academy, not only inside the confines of intramural criticisms.

The reproduction of feminism, which remains my concern throughout the pages to come, will depend upon my daughters' and my students' genera-tion of young women. "Will the hive survive," I continue to wonder, even in the midst of my newfound engagement with emerging modes of inquiry, since feminism as a political movement appears to be imperiled, while the social problems it addresses remain intact. In the poem she wanted to conclude *Ariel*,

Plath hints that, although the female workers she calls "honey-drudgers" may subsist on a diet of syrup "instead of flowers," the queen cannot extricate her creative potential from self-destructive powers: even when she flies out of the wax house, she is consumed like a "red comet / Over the engine that killed her." Plath's readers have worried that the "Christmas roses" the bees taste might be poisonous, that the poet immobilized and "too dumb to think" during one of the coldest of London's winters knew she could not last until the spring, that the very word "spring" may refer to a season of renewal she could only achieve by leaping outside of life itself, that her despair appears in drafted lines which read something like a riddle, something like prayer: ("Impossible spring?) / (What sort of spring?) / (O God, let them taste of spring)" (Van Dyne 115). Resonantly enigmatic about her powers of endurance, Plath wrote before the emergence of feminism's second wave, reminding us how brief a time it has had to make its mark.

Born before Plath, Adrienne Rich has lived long enough to bring her feminist eye to Plath's "fascination" and "terror" of "Man's power—to dominate, tyrannize, choose, or reject the woman" ("W" 36). For Plath's most ambitious successor, the "dynamic charge" of the Bee sequence derives from "the woman's sense of *herself*—embattled, possessed—" by a "furious awareness" of this masculine power and thus profoundly devoid of sustaining female companionship. That Ted Hughes managed to get the final published word into the poetic dialogue Plath maintained with him in *Ariel* underscores her vulnerability. The hive Plath could only envision as a female colony haunted by the wounding abandonment of a magisterial man emerges as a feminist community in Rich's brilliant verse. Indeed, the last poem in Rich's volume *An Atlas of a Difficult World* seems to ruminate on the repercussions of that transformation of the swarm. The lines "it will not be simple, it will not be long / it will take little time, it will take all your thought" can be read in a number of ways: as an analysis of the conditions of reading her book, for instance. But I want to interpret one of its stanzas as an address to future generations of feminists about their encounter with a past that was my present.

How often, in the ever recurrent mappings of the world, have women's difficult achievements in the public sphere been forgotten, misremembered, depreciated? Will future generations of academic feminists be able to counter that tendency by preserving our intellectual heritage? "Gazing across at the next generation," Catharine Stimpson exclaims in a recent essay, "I feel enormous relief that they are there. For who wants to say something, *as if it were new*, and then have it disappear before it has a chance to get old? Moreover, women's studies began as a revisionary act. So doing, it provided a model of thought as persistent revision, consistent correction" ("WAI" 63). People of my generation—though we dislike being put into either the doddering elderly or the know-it-all elder box—necessarily depend on the young to dispute, augment, and thereby extend what we have produced so as to create new forms, innovative contents:

> You are coming into us who cannot withstand you
> you are coming into us who never wanted to withstand you
> you are taking parts of us into places never planned
> you are going far away with pieces of our lives.   (Rich, *ADW* 57)

Whereas Plath worried about the generational rivalries between the queen and the new virgins (who "Dream of a duel they will win inevitably"), whereas she brooded over the antagonism between the royal queen and the female workers ("Will they hate me?"), between herself as owner of the bee box and the anarchic swarm inside ("I am no source of honey / So why should they turn on me?"), between the furious bees and the man they "found . . . out" ("They thought death was worth it"), Rich moves toward a sense of herself and other women no longer fascinated or terrified by "Man's power" and therefore no longer necessarily embattled in lonely isolation. In so doing, Rich can relinquish control over the hive in the hope that it will make of her work something she could not anticipate. That those being trained now in feminist modes of inquiry will transform our endeavor in ways none of us can foresee tells us exactly how dependent we remain on their ability and willingness not to submit to the cultural amnesia and divisiveness that have for too long marked and marred women's history.

2

Women Artists and Contemporary Racechanges

*I believe that racism's hardy persistence and immense adapt-
ability are sustained by a habit of human imagination, deflective rhetoric, and hidden license. I believe no less that an optimistic course might be charted, if only we could imagine it.*
—Patricia J. Williams, *Seeing a Color-Blind Future*

*I have . . . [worried] about too hearty an endorsement of racial
identification. . . . So here are my positive proposals: live with
fractured identities; engage in identity play; find solidarity,
yes, but recognize contingency, and, above all, practice irony.*
—K. Anthony Appiah, *Color Conscious*

More than any other field, African-American and
Postcolonial Studies have transformed the work of
feminist critics in the past three decades. Besides
bringing black women writers into the literary
canon, subverting the earlier propensity of thinkers
to universalize whiteness, extending our understanding of the psychological dynamics of racist
stereotyping, and historicizing the impact of slavery
as well as imperialism on Americans from diverse
ethnic backgrounds, feminists of color play such an
influential role that they have effected a virtual
racechange in Women's Studies. Paradoxically, race
takes center stage in feminist criticism at precisely
the moment when its fictiveness as a biological category has been fully demonstrated but also when its
malevolence as a barrier to social justice has been

fully documented. Perhaps this is why so many people have begun to sabotage even the most apparently libertarian models we have previously used to fathom the impact of race on gender, of gender on race. Such saboteurs wonder: Has multiculturalism become as inoperative a racial paradigm as the earlier model of integration? At least partly inspired by their feminism, many critical as well as imaginative writers, performance artists, and painters seek to move us beyond integrationists' advocacy of assimilation and multiculturalists' of identity politics to a more nuanced understanding of race that might, in turn, lead to the post-racist society many people wish to inhabit. What I am calling feminism's "racechanges" are not simply those steps taken by contemporary thinkers to enlarge the sphere of feminism beyond what Adrienne Rich called "white solipsism"[1] but also their imaginative efforts to enlist all of us more effectively in making racism as well as racial categories obsolete.

A sort of shorthand on the detriments of twentieth-century racial paradigms is provided by two brilliant paintings by Faith Ringgold. As its title suggests, *We Came to America* (1991) addresses the melting pot ideal many of us were taught as children (see illustration 1), the fairy tale that told us most folks came to America in boats, though the vessels varied. Some people paid for their tickets in first-class cabins, while others were purchased as cargo—but hey! once on these shores, we immigrants were all equal. From the 1920s until the Civil Rights movement of the sixties, the story presented assimilation as the key; color blindness as the ideal. Differences were supposed to melt away in an alchemical bowl or vat of steel, homogenized dross transmuted into gold or iron, carbon, nickel, chromium, and manganese toughened into one resistant substance, although the melting pot also summoned to some minds the image of a soup so long cooked that all the ingredients dissolved into each other.

Increasingly after the post WWII period, of course, the inequality of various ethnic groups made the melting pot metaphor suspect. Faith Ringgold had only to perform a racechange on the Statue of Liberty to demonstrate the horrific fate of Africans in the land of the free, the home of the brave. *We Came to America* depicts the tired and poor tempest-toss'd: a slave ship burns on the horizon (did a rebel set it ablaze?); castaways drown in the surf (or are their mouths open, their arms raised in exultation at a baptism repudiating a degraded life of captivity?); only a lonely baby survives (will the child in Liberty's arms grow up to be crucified on the cross of slavery?). As Moira Roth observes, "the scene blends exhortation, jubilation, and an almost biblical promise of deliverance" (58), but it also fuses these to a vision of apocalypse now. An America symbolized by a white Liberty white-washes the devastating past her dark double memorializes. The connection between the red-rimmed (rising or setting) sun on the horizon and the bloody waves, the ill wind that links Liberty's foregrounded torch with the smoke and fog of the backgrounded flames declare that the wretched refuse of America's teeming shore may be doomed rather than exalted. In the roiling waters of the Atlantic, African Americans will be forced to melt out of existence.

With the demise of the melting pot/assimilation/color blindness script by midcentury, multiculturalism emerged as a commitment to racial diversity, and it quickly became associated with identity politics. Not racial integration but racial pride; not assimilation but separatism; not differences neutralized but differences naturalized; not color blindness but color consciousness; not a melting pot or soup but a mosaic or salad bar: these would assure our respect for the jostling ethnicities that had to be understood, each in and for its own integrity.[2] To counter insulting images of Aunt Jemima or Shylock, positive valuations of blackness or Jewishness were embraced as sources of pride. Awareness of shared racial (or, for that matter, sexual or ethnic or class) backgrounds could function to unite people struggling against prejudice. Since one's origins presumably authenticated one's political attitudes, discussions of subjectivities were replaced by attention to the position from which subjects wrote or spoke. Just as important, racial or ethnic identity provided certified credentials to representatives who claimed the right to stand for particular groups.[3]

Recently, this type of identity politics has come under attack by feminists who chafe against its pigeon-holing, but who also refuse to return to the wornout assumptions of assimilation. Using shorthand to explain the problem of identity politics, Nancy K. Miller calls it a form of "as a" speaking: "if 'identity politics' has challenged bourgeois self-representations—with all its unself-conscious exclusions—speaking 'as a' has emerged as an equally problematic *representativity*" (*GP* 20). How can any one individual—with all the eccentricity life affords each human being—possibly represent a group so heterogeneous as, say, African-American women or Asian-American men, when even these composite categories hide multifaceted variants? According to Diane Elam, in some instances "identity politics promote the very stereotyping and tokenism that they allegedly fight against by trying to solve complex problems by merely invoking oversimplified labels" ("SA" 65). Equally skeptical, Nancy Fraser condemns "the balkanizing tendencies of identity politics" ("MA" 181), which "fail to connect" with "the social politics of justice and equality" (175). Valerie Smith has pointed out that "the circumstances of race and gender alone protect no one from the seductions of reading her own experience as normative and fetishizing the experience of the other" (57).[4]

Once again, a Faith Ringgold canvas crystallizes the problem of hegemonic racial paradigms, in this case the difficulty of multiculturalism's allegiance to identity politics. In her 1967, six by eight feet *U.S. Postage Stamp Commemorating the Advent of Black Power* (see illustration 2), one hundred masklike faces are presented in a grid, 10 percent of them the darker ones that mount like steps from the lower-left toward the upper right side of the painting. The black letters spelling out BLACK POWER form an X with these faces (as in Malcolm X perhaps) since the word's letters descend from the upper-left to the lower-right side of the canvas. Containing all colors, black stands out as a positive identity for some 10 percent of the nation's population against the remaining 90 percent, who have less color here, unless one turns the work on its side so as to read its horizontal (instead of its vertical) letters. Then what surfaces (though previously invisible) are the huge, all-pervasive words "WHITE POWER." Identity politics, this image seems to hint, are well and good, directing our attention to minorities uniting to seek rights in American society; however, they disregard the universalized default position of a whiteness so pervasive it cannot be seen, a whiteness synonymous with the cultural air we unconsciously breathe in and out every minute of our lives.

To the extent that the X marked by African-American faces and the letters of black power on Ringgold's canvas does not topple but depends upon the all-pervasive whiteness on which it is inscribed, the ideology of black power calls for social justice without revealing the ubiquity of white power or subverting it. That some viewers of Ringgold's canvas see the X of black faces as a shadowy replication of the crossed bars on the Confederate flag, that others perceive all the images as male: these reactions multiply the ironies at work here. Do identity politics require African Americans to situate themselves in a preexistent pattern, the X-grid, regardless of their private desires? Does the Black Power movement commemorated on this *U.S. Postage Stamp* stamp out the individuality of blacks (as well as whites)? If human beings demand respect *as* blacks, will prescribed ways of being black become yet another tyranny? Ringgold's misgivings about the sexual politics of Black Power advocates suggest as much:

For me the concept of Black Power carried with it a big question mark. Was it intended only for the black men or would black women have power, too?

(*WF* 158)[5]

Because of her gender, Ringgold is especially sensitive to what Anthony Appiah calls the "imperialism of identity" (*CC* 103); a politics based on one identity marker risks making human beings forget the multiplicity of their various modes of identification.[6] Just as important, the various shades of yellow, pink, and tan faces complicate the majority, reminding us how the vocabulary of "black" and "white power" obscures the presence of Chicanas, Indians, Asians, or people of mixed backgrounds.[7] Thus the image broods over the tension between multiple skin colors and a dualistic black-and-white racial language, encouraging us to question the efficacy of racialized identity politics, which may not be able to dislodge white privilege or foster the interracial sensitivity and compassion this society needs so badly.

Exactly the contrast between Faith Ringgold's foregrounded "BLACK POWER" and her backgrounded "WHITE POWER" constitutes the combination of "deflective rhetoric" and "hidden license" that Patricia J. Williams diagnoses as the basis of racism's "hardy persistence." Yet, Williams cautions, "one of the greatest obstacles to progress at this moment [is] the paralyzing claim that racism *has* no solution" (*SCB* 67). A number of contemporary women artists, seeking to confound bigotry's resistance by envisioning solutions to it, extend our racial vocabularies, proposing new images beyond those provided by assimilationists and multiculturalists. For if, in the melting pot, racial difference is conceived as a kind of boundedness that must be relinquished (the nickel fuses with the carbon, the onion mixes with the celery); if, in the mosaic or salad bar, race is imagined as a distinct border that ought to be respected (the green tiles surround the yellow, the cauliflower sits next to the spinach); both models nevertheless envision race in terms of contours or perimeters, not unlike the "color line" W. E. B. Du Bois viewed as the central problem of the twentieth century (vii). Antithetically, contemporary feminists of color surface new images based on permeable boundaries to underscore the obsolescence of earlier racial lexicons, the need for fresh paradigms emphasizing the contingency of color, the idiosyncratic and incidental volatility of traffic across a shifting, blurred, multiplied, invisible, or nonexistent color line.

Although in the past most cross-racial representations have mocked those deemed Other, recent feminists—aware of the mutability of gender roles—deploy racechanges to exhibit the social construction of race.[8] Perhaps performance artists and painters play a particularly important role in this undertaking because they address so directly the issue of the embodiedness of sex and color within a culture that increasingly invests visual symbols with powers previously paramount in language. Experimentalists such as Adrian Piper, Anna Deavere Smith, and Faith Ringgold employ the visual power of representation to confront the physicality upon which psychologically damaging classifications hinge.[9] As performance artists and painters, in other words, these thinkers have privileged access to the process Richard Rorty terms "the literalization of selected metaphors" by which (he believes) social thought progresses (44). Located inside what Audre Lorde called "the very house of difference rather than [in] the security of any one particular difference" (Z 226), Piper, Deavere Smith, and Ringgold endorse, like Anthony Appiah, living with "fractured identities," engaging in "identity play," recognizing "contingency" within solidarity, and practicing "irony" (CC 104). As feminists, their contribution to racechange takes many forms, ranging from Piper's sensitivity to racism's peculiar assault on African-American men to Deavere Smith's exhibiting herself as a medium or spiritualist, and Ringgold's realization that race (given the multiplicity of colors) can be more easily scrapped than gender (given the binarism of male and female). But because, as Williams suggests, "we dream our worlds into being" (SCB 16), all these artist-theorists have begun to literalize new metaphors to generate the words needed to usher in post-racist as well as post-race worlds.

Playing the Race Card

In 1986 one of Adrian Piper's performances sought to surface racist misconceptions in a specific setting, namely when the light-skinned artist found herself in an otherwise exclusively white social event where she was presumed to be white herself. If racist remarks were made in her presence, she simply handed out her printed card:

Dear Friend,

I am black.
   I am sure you did not realize this when you made/laughed at/agreed with

that racist remark . . .

I regret any discomfort my presence is causing you, just as I am sure you regret the discomfort your racism is causing me.

Sincerely yours

Adrian Margaret Smith Piper   (*OO* I:220)[10]

As with another card meant to protect Piper's privacy in public spaces (when men approach assuming she wants to be picked up), the action is intended to draw attention toward and ward off repercussions of singularity by redirecting an insult back on the insulter. In the all-white setting, various alternative options remain available to her: saying nothing at all; denouncing the culprit; announcing on arrival her race; abdicating her black identity after the slur. But these would have tangled her up in psychologically harmful processes. The card, according to Piper, has the benefit of "a semiprivate context" with a specific person guilty of having made a prejudiced remark and it might actually facilitate dialogue (*OO* I:219–20). As Judith Wilson has explained, "Both the card's association with antique forms of etiquette and its tone of exquisite civility underscored the artist's view that 'racism or sexism are not only unjust and immoral, they are also boorish and tasteless . . .' " ("IMN" 55).

The resonant title of Piper's performance—*My Calling (Card)*—contains at least four suggestions about the disposition of the race card: first, as Wilson asserts, it functions like an anachronistic visiting card containing the name of a person who has not been received, just as Piper's full identity has not been fully perceived; second, it hints that the card constitutes Piper's spiritual "calling"—the sanctified work she is meant to do to right the wrong of racism; third, it "calls" a form of behavior by its right name, not letting it slide by; fourth, it operates like a parodic business card. To take the old-fashioned visitor's card first, Piper's announcement dramatizing her presence—in this case, as a black person—remains at odds with the visual appearance of her features. Displaying the unreliability of ocular perceptions in the area of race, Piper's "female impersonation" of a prim, proper Victorian lady extricates corporeal signs from racial categories, proving how easily duped white people can be.[11] No wonder, then, the playing of the race card constitutes Piper's spiritual calling, for with it she proves that race is merely a flimsy, nonsensical house of cards that can be blown away with the breath it takes to say a monosyllabic word. Reversing highly popular "passing" narratives, from Mark Twain's

Puddn'head Wilson to Fannie Hurst's *Imitation of Life* to *Showboat*, all of which assume that power and privilege require a white camouflage, Piper rejects the racial closet and conspicuously, voluntarily "outs" herself.

Though a "call" often invites a response, Piper appears "genuinely surprised" that "No one who got this card ever initiated dialogue" with her (Shatz 52). Perhaps no response occurs because the card "calls" racism just that, protesting against its irrational but painful wounding. In this respect, playing the race card functions something like dispensing a traffic ticket; that is, issuing a violation against the offender. Besides "calling" an act of incivility (instead of letting it go), Piper's riff heralds a businesslike exchange of goods or services by initiating a series of interesting racechanging deals. What the card's "I am black" proclaims to its recipient is "you are white." The newly raced reader experiences the shock of being an Other to the previously-thought-to-be confederate. Inducted into a consciousness of his or her whiteness, the receiver of the card may feel the jolt of being raced for the first time since whiteness so often remains disguised as a universal category of humanity.[12]

Reversing the relation between self and Other in exactly the way Maurice Blanchot describes, Piper as "the Other relates to me as if I were the Other and thus causes me to take leave of my identity. . . . When thus I am wrested from myself, there remains a passivity bereft of self (sheer alterity, the other without unity)" (18). This trauma of alterity (generated by being racially marked) is one that many African Americans can remember in their own lives: one has only to think of Zora Neale Hurston's famous "I remember the very day that I became colored" (152) or Patricia J. Williams's recollection, "Three was the age when I learned that I was black" (*SCB* 7). The embarrassment at having made a racial slur that the card's white reader then undergoes also parallels the earlier chagrin of the card-carrying African American who—knowing she had the hidden card on hand in case of need— endured her unperceived racial identity as something about which she ought not speak, a secret infirmity perhaps or clandestine source of embarrassment. In this regard, the card curiously recalls the sorts of notes handed out by those who used to be called the "deaf and dumb" on subways and sidewalks to elicit financial or physical help. It signals, after all, the impossibility of speech in a particular setting where Piper's articulation of her feelings would certainly disconcert either herself or a roomful of people.

Piper's "I am black. I am sure you did not realize this" card solves the problem the poet Toi Derricotte encountered when "in conversation with a white person who [didn't] know I'm black," she tried to "prepare [herself] for painful distinctions" (25–6). Significantly, Derricotte entitled an early section of her autobiographical *The Black Notebooks* "The Club," not only because she wished to explain how excluded she felt from the whites-only private club her neighbors attended but also because whiteness itself seemed like an exclusive membership to her.[13] "Whiteness is a kind of clubhouse" Patricia J. Williams believes (52), as does Marilyn Frye: being white "is like being a member of a political party, or a club, or a fraternity—or being a Methodist or a Mormon" (149). Frye goes on to advise those who don't relish the arbitrariness of the club's privileges to resign their membership or figure out ways to get kicked out.

Although race is "*constructed as* something inescapable," according to Frye, what antiracist people require may be "conceptual creativity, and perhaps conceptual violence" (131). If you are a member of the white club and you wish to draw upon Piper's creativity to resist assimilationist as well as multicultural models of race, you could resign by obtaining and distributing the race card at moments when bigoted pronouncements are made in your vicinity. Remember, elsewhere Adrian Piper has urged more white people to acknowledge the black ancestors who populate most Euro-American family trees in this country.[14] Whether or not individuals can find such progenitors, what is to stop them from not exactly false, but perhaps slightly misleading advertising? Jane Lazarre, the Jewish mother of black sons, once received a compliment in the form of the following description given to her children: "Your mother isn't really white. She's a Black person in disguise" (25).[15] Espousing this appellation and thereby engaging in precisely the "identity play" that Appiah prescribes, you might discombobulate racist relatives or colleagues by simply decking them with a copy of Piper's calling card.

Needless to say, this suggestion constitutes a somewhat disturbing piece of advice, given the long history in which white mimicry of African Americans has remained contaminated in and by the degradations of minstrelsy. But it gets at Piper's efforts to rob race of a fixed or essential status. After all, at the all-white social event, Piper herself remains "white" to most partygoers, "black" to one or two others. Not an ontological statement of being, her emergence as a person of color is performed only in the context of a racist remark and thus takes on the aura of a personal intervention. Her declaration of difference, in other words, marks not a naturalized physical state but an entrance into a public disagreement about racial ideology; not who she is, but what she thinks—what she *claims* to be—is the issue. The resulting cognitive dissonance, occurring in a highly localized setting, is meant to affect a single person's shift in consciousness and thereby tacitly acknowledges the recalcitrance of those economic and psychological structures that continue to buttress bigotry. Not always deployed, not necessarily believed, the race card also signals the asymmetry of our definitions of black and white, for a dark-skinned person would receive very different results distributing an "I am white" voucher, which might just mark *her* as a "card"; that is, a jester. If to some minds Piper's permit alludes to the racial identity certificates required of South Africans under apartheid, it draws attention to the political repercussions of racial categories that have governed discriminatory social interaction. Given the United States context, many of the issues related to the relative ease with which nonblack immigrants (Jews, Italians, Indians) assimilated into America by becoming white—which James Baldwin called "the price of the ticket"—accrue around Piper's transfer, a "pass" that challenges the involuntary nature of racialized group identities.

"We no more choose our color than choose the language by which we communicate," Amy Gutmann believes (168), and the fact that "we are not free" to pick "a racial identity is morally troubling" because "it has the effect . . . of dividing human beings against the cause of social justice" (169). Yet in the case of fiction, of course, writers *are* free to select a racial identity at odds with the one they were assigned at birth. That the best-selling Native-American classic *Education of Little Tree* was actually composed by the KKK author of Governor George Wallace's famous "Segregation now . . . Segregation tomorrow . . . Segregation forever" speech proves that authorial instances of cross-racial impersonation (which scholars term "racial drag" or "ethnic transvestism") may not have been undertaken to serve "the cause of social justice."[16] Such hoaxes abound in American literary history, with non-Jews masking their roots to pen purportedly "Jewish novels," non-Chicanos publishing what are advertised as "Chicano memoirs."

More pointedly libertarian in purpose, however, are recent texts such as Toni Morrison's *Paradise* as well as her earlier story "Recitatif" in which ambiguous racial markers make readers conscious of the (curiously gratuitous, idiosyncratic) basis upon which they apply racial labels. How we interpreters determine that an indeterminate character is "really" white or black speaks volumes about the assumptions brought to such societally formative language. That Morrison titled her short narrative about a "salt and pepper" pair of girls "Recitatif"—the boring, prosey parts of an opera's narrative—suggests that the reader's quest to ascertain which character is black, which white constitutes a silly script decidedly subordinate to the dramatic arias worthy of attention.[17] When she opened her later novel *Paradise* with the sentence "They shoot the white girl first" and closed it without ever revealing which character that was, Morrison explained that she "wanted the readers to wonder about the race of those girls until those readers understood that their race didn't matter." The mystery remains unsolved to prove that "Race is the least reliable information you can have about someone. . . . it tells you next to nothing" (Gray 62).

While a select number of ambiguous characters and light-skinned people can deploy the race card in a variety of playful ways, Adrian Piper understands full well that the metaphor has another significance for darker-skinned men. When an allusion to it appears in Piper's photomontage *Forget It*, the race card ominously materializes in the central panel as an application for a credit card superimposed on an image of a black man with an erect penis as well as heavy testicles, the hypersexualized rapist of racist lore, the same figure she herself impersonated in her *Mythic Being* series of performances. Executed during the early seventies, this instance of street theater featured Piper sporting an Afro, bell bottoms, and dark glasses, which helped her "swagger, stride, lope, . . . sit with my legs wide apart on the subway, so as to accommodate my protruding genitalia" in an effort to "embody everything you most hate and fear" (Golden 26). Clearly, this man need not apply; he should simply "forget it." Credit—be it financial or moral, monetary or ethical—will not be given to him in our society. Carded, he will be denied entrance into the club of privilege, or so Piper insinuates in an allegation against American culture justified by the grotesque statistic that by the year 2000 one out of every three African-American men will spend time in American prisons.[18] Though the race card seems flimsy, it can turn up in a number of power games that arbitrarily assign gratuitous values to the faces of differently colored suits, playing havoc with people it reduces to "spades."

"What does it mean that the deep wound of race in this country has come to be euphemized as a card," Anne Anlin Cheng asks about the deployment of this rhetoric during the O. J. Simpson trial (49). According to Cheng, "one would 'play' a card only because one is already *outside* the larger game, for to play a card is to exercise the value of one's disadvantage, the liability that is asset" (50). In other words, the "I am white. I am sure you did not realize this" card deployed by a light-skinned man or woman would not work exactly the same way as Piper's since the person whose whiteness automatically trumps other suits need neither shuffle nor deal to win. Transmuting liability to asset and back again into liability, Piper's race card confronts the perplexing conjunction between minority identity and injury for people who know they haven't been dealt the "full deck" that would make playing the card unnecessary. Taken together, *My Calling (Card)*, *Mythic Being*, and *Forget It* demonstrate how Piper's feminism shapes her sensitivity to the engendering of racism that robs all African Americans of respect but reserves a particularly vicious form of representational violence for black men. A singular anomaly as an African-American woman in the departments of philosophy and fine art that hired and fired her, Piper could use both her race and her gender to make herself what she calls "a cognitive anomaly"—a Euro-looking black, a macho-looking female (Shatz 46).

A Bridge of Moving Identifications (With—Not As)

Since, as Piper knows, there is no biological basis for racial language, why can't individuals in quest of a consciousness that takes color as accidental and inessential escape the Manichean divide between black and white?[19] Although sociologists, ethnographers, and anthropologists keep on explaining that "nobody has a race" (Appiah *CC* 37), it remains a recalcitrant category in many people's minds, one that literary and visual artists have begun to undermine by means of identification. Whereas historically African Americans have been socialized to identify cross-racially with the mainstream culture in which they have had to survive, Euro-Americans have deformed or deflected identification with various modes of mockery. Attempting to detonate such disavowals, some contemporary artists convert the one-way traffic jam across the color line into a two-way street. Because they multiply differences, moreover, *inter*racial (not *cross*-racial) identification constitutes their goal; or, if we attempt to take the deconstruction of "race" seriously, moving identifications with people of various colors.

Yet according to Toni Morrison and Adrienne Kennedy, the effort to detach color from race—commendable as it may be—labors ineffectually under the burden of the past. A quest for color without race impels the wonderfully named Baby Suggs in Morrison's *Beloved*, for example, who finds herself so horrified with the cruelty of the slave system that she takes to her bed to study the harmlessness of lavender, pink, blue, yellow, and green. But Baby Suggs's "appetite for color" (4) is less than wholesome, for it attends her relinquishing of the Word, her refusal to preach, and she dies soon after taking to her bed. Color without race cannot sustain the fading, silenced Baby because race—inscribed in black and white on all the legal, religious, scientific, literary documents of print culture—reigns supreme, despite either its fictiveness or Baby's desires. Elsewhere in Morrison's novels, color without race functions destructively, promoting gender bonding at the expense of racial adhesion. A fascinating scene in *Paradise* dramatizes the effect of switching the lens from color to race on a character named Elder, when he witnesses two men arguing with a woman:

> From her clothes, Elder said, he guessed she was a streetwalking woman, and registering contempt for her trade, he felt at first a connection with the shouting men. Suddenly one of the men smashed the woman in her face with his fist. She fell. Just as suddenly the scene slid *from everyday color to black and white*. Elder said his mouth went dry. The two whitemen turned away from the unconscious Negro woman sprawled on the pavement. . . . He never got the sight of that whiteman's fist in that colored woman's face out of his mind. Whatever he felt about her trade, he thought about her, prayed for her till the end of his life.
>
> (emphasis mine, 94–5)

Everyday color-vision causes Elder to identify with the respectable men against the streetwalking woman, but the raced-perspective of black and white leads him to ally himself with the hurt Negro woman against the abusive whitemen. Efforts to substitute color for race remain doomed for Baby Suggs, for Elder, because they inhabit a rigidly raced world.[20]

By linking the black-and-white mindset to the flimsy unreality of celluloid film and then exhibiting the stranglehold of Hollywood movies over the material and psychological realities of African-American lives, Adrienne Kennedy dramatizes the supreme power of the destructive fictions of race over the physiological facts of color. In one of Kennedy's most formally innovative plays, *A Movie Star Has to Star in Black and White*, the doomed African-American heroine, Clara, has so internalized the images of Hollywood that white stars of the screen tell the story of her life. A *"Negro woman of thirty-three"* (according to the stage directions), Clara ignores her surroundings, writes in her notebook, and lets *"Her movie stars speak for her"* (2086). Those movie stars, played by actresses who *"look exactly like their movie roles"* (2081), are Bette Davis in *Now Voyager*, Jean Peters in *Viva Zapata*, and Shelley Winters in *A Place in the Sun*.

Glamorous white actresses articulating Clara's depression about the conflicts between her dark-skinned father and light-skinned mother, her bleeding after a miscarriage, and her eventual sense of drowning in an unhappy marriage accentuate the surrealism of a life shaped by a culture assigning the African-American woman writer a bit part. The allure of Hollywood's black and white pictures drains Clara of any color so her famously seductive white avatars express her interiority. In other words, her subjectivity has been undermined by an industry that has colonized her consciousness.[21] Unlike the voiceless white actors, the white actresses can speak "for" Clara precisely because they suffer the wounds of gender, menstrual and miscarriage bleeding she endures as well. As the black blood of movie stars spatters on sheets exhibited on the stage, as the black letters of Clara spill out on the sheets of her pages, Kennedy insists on the persistent tensions between maternal procreativity and aesthetic creativity. Lest we assume that menstruation, pregnancy, and miscarriage are a cross-racial problem for all women, however, the audience is constantly reminded that the actresses' obsession reflects the personal suffering Clara has projected onto them, a projection that robs Bette Davis, Jean Peters, and Shelley Winters of Otherness. Merely doubles, the film stars remain images, as if whiteness itself is only a fetishized mirage or simulacra (Diamond 138). They therefore cease to provide an escape from or alternative to Clara's pain, merely reflecting it back to her.

It seems fitting that the brilliant performance artist Anna Deavere Smith began the research that issued in her ongoing series of dramatic creations—*On the Road: A Search for American Character*—in 1982 when she was directing a production of *A Movie Star Has to Star in Black and White* (Richards 40). Cross-racial identification, which both Morrison and Kennedy study, combines with the multiplication of categories of alterity in Deavere Smith's work to generate forms of empathy that do not usurp the Otherness of people from unassimilated immigrant groups. For *Fires in the Mirror* (1993) and *Twilight* (1994), Deavere Smith conducted interviews with participants in racially charged conflicts and then she learned to replicate their words, mannerisms, and appearances in theatrical performances of people who become her varied cast of characters.[22] Murderous moments of violence witnessed by private citizens, rioting, name-calling, internecine disputes between judicial, police, political, and community spokespeople fuel what Cornell West calls the "xenophobic frenzy" behind the testimonies that are given and then performed verbatim in what he terms a "kind of polyphony of perspectives" (*F* xviii–xix).

To the extent that Deavere Smith becomes an "empty vessel, a repeater" (*F* xxv), she hopes that "the reenactment, or the reiteration of a person's words would also teach [her] about that person" (xxvi): "The frame of reference for the other would *be* the other," she declares; "Learning about the other by being the other requires the use of all aspects of memory, the memory of the body, mind, and heart, as well as the words" (xxvii). No one is more self-conscious than the artist herself about how her work rebuts the premises of identity politics:

> If only a man can speak for a man, a woman for a woman, a Black person for all Black people, then we, once again, inhibit the *spirit* of theater, which lives in the *bridge* that makes unlikely aspects *seem* connected. The bridge doesn't make them the same, it merely *displays* how two unlikely *aspects* are *related*. These relationships of the *unlikely*, these connections of things that don't fit together are crucial to American theater and culture if theater and culture plan to help us assemble our obvious differences (xxix).

Because she displays the dissonance between herself and, say, a white male personage she plays, Deveare Smith neither expects her audience to identify her *as* a white man, nor identifies herself *as* a white man. Besides being delusive, such a form of identification—mentally becoming what one is not—could be viewed as a form of arrogation. Instead, she fosters the audience's identification *with* her and *with* the white man to whom she relates through her unlikely impersonation.

Recorded on video and therefore easier to analyze, *Fires in the Mirror*, about the 1991 conflict between Lubavitchers and blacks in the Crown Heights neighborhood of Brooklyn, documents reactions to the killing of seven-year-old Gavin Cato by one of the cars in the Hasidic rebbe's procession, followed by the fatal stabbing of the twenty-nine-year-old Yankel Rosenbaum by a group of young black men.[23] Deavere Smith plays Al Sharpton and Angela Davis as well as Letty Cottin Pogrebin and Rabbi Joseph Spielman, Gavin Cato's mourning father as well as Yankel Rosenbaum's grieving brother. No stasis, no fixity, but a volatile assemblage of personae parade before our view, some endowed with an exceptional degree of individuation, others teetering on the edge of stereotype. The "bridge" is Deavere Smith's own body, on which and through which she convenes a host of manifest differences in diction, lexicon, hairstyle, costume, education, body language, physical ease, rhetorical control, temperament, etc.

Blasting racial and sexual essentialism, the multiplication of differences—some classifiable like education, but those related to personality highly intangible—emphasizes divergences among blacks, variations among Jews,
despite the fact that the media presented each group as monolithic. Deavere
Smith, by encouraging her audience to look closely and listen intently to a
diverse assortment of unique beings, demonstrates that "not every yarmulke
is the same kind of yarmulke," that the black men whom she interviewed
talked with "accents which were a mixture of bold Brooklynese with rap hand
gestures, and Caribbean lilts" (xxxvi). If (as Tania Modleski suggests) the
actress conjures up the image of "a spiritual medium" ("DJ" 60), if (as the
actress herself puts it) she manipulates the "spiritual power" of words to
"become possessed" ("WBY" 192), then the bridging presence she herself
sustains amidst her various roles functions something like the reincarnation
that huants the heroines to be found in the novels of Alice Walker or Octavia
Butler.[24] As in those fictions, in which one woman feels herself to be a composite of many people, and as in the more generalized image of the woman as
spiritualist (or medium or witch),[25] Deavere Smith's incarnations emphasize
the links between people who themselves do not feel connected and whose
racism often prohibits any acknowledgment of similitude. This connected-
ness—so evident to the drama's spectator, so indiscernible to the dramatized
participant—promotes what we might call xenophilia (a term strikingly
absent from most dictionaries).

Not the printed word but the physical intonations, accents, and rhythms
of speech enable Deavere Smith to be perceived at one and the same time as
the light-skinned African-American actress embodying all the parts and as a
militant Muslim leader or a Lubavitcher mother. Visual ambiguities defy the
conceptual categories upon which conventional sexual and racial languages
depend. Because an actual, named person has been recreated through each of
the characters' monologues, we see not only the actress playing the part and
the persona she plays but also the shadowy real person being both eclipsed
and evoked, caricatured and characterized by the performance. Each of the
brief narrative skits, then, simultaneously contains three presences—actress,
character, real person—and at least two of these can be male and female,
black and white. Added volatility comes from the abrupt switches between
sketches: sharp dislocations between soliloquies disrupt notions of continu-
ity, emphasizing the differences of the opinions being aired. With no hope of
closure, the spectator shifts through a series of emotionally moving identifications with characters who often cannot relate to each other, no less inhabit

the same settings. An audience member who finds herself sympathizing with people tragically hurt and enraged by the injuries inflicted by racism may simultaneously and distressingly sense herself to be the target of that baffled pain and anger.[26]

While inside the variously located soliloquies (a synagogue, a community outreach center), each character identifies *as* a particular ethnic type, members of the audience may find themselves empathizing *with* a cacophony of conflicting perspectives. Using the language of Richard Rorty, we might say that no "metavocabulary" ("which somehow takes account of *all possible* vocabularies") emerges to allow us "to step outside the various vocabularies" we have heard deployed (xvi). Instead, Deavere Smith teaches her audience how to "juggle several descriptions of the same event without asking which one was right—to see redescription as a tool rather than a claim to have discovered essence" (39). For, as Rorty puts it about the cognitive functions of irony and nominalism, the aim is not some transcendent or final truth but instead "an expanding repertoire of alternative descriptions" (39–40). By shifting the race-color dialogue out of the historical past and beyond the narratives that baffled the characters of Morrison and Kennedy, Deavere Smith's vertiginous drama produces a kaleidoscope of juxtaposed identities sometimes at odds, sometimes in accord, so that spectators can find no stable overview but must instead make room for the jostling registers spoken with such passionate conviction that the actress's impersonations of race and gender paradoxically emphasize for some viewers the recalcitrance of their markings.

The affliction suffered by many of Deavere Smith's characters can convince other members of her audience that no just recompense could ever repair the suffering racism has inflicted, that the very catharsis the theatrical event seeks to prompt may have arrived too late in American history. Yet to the extent that the cast of characters emerges through one body—that of Deavere Smith—and that their composite voices elegiacally mourn and thereby memorialize the dead, this woman artist herself becomes the oracular priestess, the shaman of America's commitment to e pluribus unum, a composite of Walt Whitman and Jack Kerouac on the road to becoming a cosmos.

Patchwork

Whereas Anna Deavere Smith seems especially drawn to communities displaying graphic dissimilarities between individuals from markedly diverse backgrounds, morphing—the computer program that mixes features to produce a composite picture of, say, Queen Elizabeth as a woman of color—concentrates on people of mixed backgrounds who blend into each other.[27] Because morphing dissolves one image seamlessly into another, it evokes the hybridity of mixed race people swimming in an eclectic gene pool and dovetails with the work of a number of filmmakers, artists, and critics who have begun to undercut the anachronism of racial census categories by developing a language to account for children of multiracial backgrounds as well as the aesthetic works they produce.

Honoring the integrity of indigenous ethnic traditions but at the same time discrediting their isolation, purity, or irreducibility, Woody Allen (in his chameleon Zelig), Charles Johnson and Ann Douglas (in their approach to the mongrel), Trey Ellis (in his description of the cultural mulatto), and Salman Rushdie (in his novels about hybrids) invent characters that prove either the inanity or the destructiveness of notions of "cultural apartheid" or "ethnic cleansing."[28] These thinkers tend to deal with narrative representations, for, as Judith Wilson has shown, the popularity of mixed characters and miscegenated plots in American fiction contrasts sharply with their relative rarity in the history of the visual arts ("OI" 90). Recently, however, visual artists have redefined hybridity by dislodging it from the interracial sexual narrative usually situated at the core—as the cause of—such imagery.[29]

Faith Ringgold—the African-American feminist who most brilliantly uses not only the piecings but also the piercings of quiltmaking in the service of hybridity—stresses the juxtaposition of traditions that never could have realistically intersected in the way she wishes they might have. In so doing, she substitutes an emphasis on *cultural* miscegenation for the more conventional *sexual* miscegenation plot. Repelled not simply by the ruthless sexual exploitation of black women under slavery, Ringgold might also object to the uses of the sexual miscegenation script as it comes down to us today (in, for example, a movie such as Warren Beatty's *Bulworth*), for this narrative seems all too cozily entangled with buttressing the vanity of white men while condoning the exploitation of black women for the consciousness-raising of white society.[30] Ringgold's efforts to envision forms of cultural miscegenation quite distinct from sexual miscegenation lead her to visualize two racialized traditions intersecting not in a blended, diluted "morphie" or a biracial, mixed human being but instead in a postmodernist palimpsest or patchwork: a fractured or multifaceted surface on which heterogeneous inscriptions have been stratified or juxtaposed to form a collage of not always congruent meanings.[31]

In the case of one of Ringgold's most ambitious undertakings, the twelve "story quilts" of the astonishingly beautiful *French Collection* (1990–1997), those two legacies are the evolution of French impressionism and the aesthetic artistry we identify under the rubric of The Harlem Renaissance. By splicing these together, Ringgold paradoxically invents the African-American impressionism she may have hoped to inherit.[32] Circumventing what history tried to do to Faith Ringgold as a black woman artist, she employs the idea of cultural miscegenation in a patchwork form to invent a more hospitable past made to bear her own image. With its title evoking not only haute couture but also the 1992 *Paris Connections* exhibit that featured her work along with that of sixteen other African-American visual artists, the specifically black expatriate setting engages what Tyler Stovall terms the powerfully attractive "myth of color-blind France" (xiii). The sheer number of jostling media about Paris, the City of Light, makes it impossible for any one to usurp or contain the others.

On borders inside bindings and external panels composed of pieced together fabrics, most of the quilts display a handwritten script about one Willia Marie Simone, a fictional expatriate who arrives in Paris during the twenties, marries (a man who soon dies), has two children (whom she sends to America to be raised by their aunt), and becomes an artist. Although this *Künstlerroman* sometimes recounts conflicts Willia experiences and sometimes painful stories by interpolated storytellers, the brilliantly colored images painted directly on the central section of the canvas often subvert the text. For instance, its opening panel, entitled *Dancing at the Louvre*, looks like an antic celebration between mothers and daughters within the hallowed halls of culture; however, the text instructs us that the mother of the depicted bouncing girls is a judgmental friend who has informed Willia that she ought to be raising her own children in France too. Beyond the complex interplay of words and images, the latter contain pictures within pictures (Leonardo da Vinci's *Mona Lisa*), allusions to famous paintings (Van Gogh's *Sunflowers*), portraits of celebrated painters and performers (Josephine Baker), depictions of important sites of creativity (Gertrude Stein's atelier).

Criss-crossed by visible lines of quilting (the stitching that holds the batting to the fabric that sandwiches it), the paintings on the story quilts consistently confound normative notions of space and time. So, for example, although Willia's adventure occurs in Paris during the twenties, African-American leaders from earlier and later periods—Sojourner Truth and Rosa Parks—miraculously appear on the Continent. When such realistically impossible personages come from Ringgold's own ancestry, her dead cousins and grandparents, it becomes clear that the line between Willia's fictional story and the artist's autobiography blurs. Psychoanalytically, the sequence can be read as a recuperation of the artist's mother, for Willia resembles the Harlem-based fashion-designer who taught Ringgold the art of quilting through their early collaborative efforts.[33] As in Alice Walker's essay "In Search of Our Mothers' Gardens," however, the sequence can also be interpreted as a recovery of the artist's more broadly defined aesthetic matrilineage, for Ringgold's *The Sunflower Quilting Bee at Arles* links her "art" with the history of anonymous African-American women's "craft" in much the manner Walker does at the end of her essay and in her short story "Everyday Use."

Künstlerroman, maternal biography, autobiography, *The French Collection* gestures at a number of other genres as well. That in interviews Ringgold has called it a "novel" may bring to mind the ways in which it revises Nella Larsen's pessimistic *Quicksand*: unlike Larsen's heroine, who rejects a marriage proposal from a European artist and returns to America where she expires, worn out by maternity, Willia recounts her decision not to return to a racist America and instead to let her sister bring up her children in the States. As a parody, the series produces heteroglossia when passages of Steinese (about Gertrude Stein and Alice B. Toklas, who "were always being together. One was always knowing and being an American but living and being in Paris") alternate with recyclings of Zora Neale Hurston's vernacular ("De donkey is de father of a mule . . . Now what kin be more dangerous dan uh mule bone?") (*DL* 139). To establish itself as an aesthetic statement comparable to that produced by a precursor such as Hannah Hoch in her Ethnographic Museum series, a "Colored Woman's Manifesto of Art and Politics" surfaces in the next-to-the-last story quilt, with a message that might be taken as a miniature motto for the whole sequence: "Modern art is not yours, or mine. It is ours" (*DL* 142).

With sly humor, *The Picnic at Giverny* (see illustration 3) typifies the vertiginous effect of all these layers of meaning. A reinvention of *Le Déjeuner Sur L'Herbe*, it uses Monet's water lily ponds as a backdrop to display the naked Picasso seated where a nude woman appears in Manet's canvas. The master modernist, who had himself recycled Manet's *Déjeuner* in numerous sketches and paintings of clothed men accompanied by nude women, has here been objectified, stripped, and placed on display. In an antithetical subject position, the fully clothed and highly cultivated women include patrons, art historians, educators, as well as the daughter of Faith Ringgold: the critic Michele Wallace is placed closest to her painting mother. Writing just before the composition of this story quilt, Wallace explained that her mother's painterly ambitions meant she grew up knowing "that art making and visual production were . . . deeply problematic in Afro-American culture" ("MPP" 43). In a white dress as resonant as the one Emily Dickinson mythologized, the artist Willia has her brush raised like a baton, but the narrative recounts her commitment to a specifically visual form of artistry: "It *is* only when we see it that we know a transformation has taken place" (*DL* 132). Attentive to the psychological and material conditions that govern the aesthetic marketplace, the painting details the many factors needed for her success: not simply raw talent but also an audience, money, an intellectual community, evocative settings, a reversal of sexual power relations ("I just want to see nude men in the company of fully clothed women for a change") so that the gaze becomes detached from the white man and the black woman need no longer consider herself an object under surveillance.[34]

"Magic, sex, and color" are necessary to achieve eminence in art (*DL* 132), the quilt's script declares, and in interviews Ringgold has explained why color remains so important to her. Sponging her canvases with acrylic to produce a stain, Ringgold likes to apply color to color, layering many glazes over each other so that "each one shines through and helps to create tones you don't even know where they came from . . . mixtures of mixtures." The added amalgam of these brilliant mixtures and words, the variously designed costumes of the chatting picnickers, the Klimptlike and African fabrics on which they sit, the realistic attention to their faces contrasted with the impressionist approach to the garden, the joke that the head of a marginalized Picasso is divided from his body by lines of stitches: Do these factors combine to make him look so askance at the viewer or is it his transmutation from artist to model that so discombobulates? That he remains merely a smudge in Willia's work-in-progress on the easel suggests he might not make it into the final study. A fitting revenge since people like Willia never managed to get into Picasso's final studies, or so the later story quilt entitled *Picasso's Studio* hints (see illustration 4).[35]

Displaying Picasso at extreme left again, now in the act of painting *Les Demoiselles d'Avignon*, Ringgold juxtaposes a realistically portrayed and naked Willia against the figures Picasso drew in order to demonstrate that those experimental stylistic distortions for which he was so famous effectively hid his indebtedness to female and African forms. Like the panel displaying the gorgeously reclining Josephine Baker beside a setting evocative of Matisse's *Harmony in Red*, this episode focuses on the singularity of black women in

Europe, their exotic eroticism within an aesthetic economy of primitivism that promoted what Patricia J. Williams calls "racial voyeurism" (*SCB* 21). While the master modernist will dephysicalize Willia into an angular demoiselle, Ringgold mines a tradition established by Robert Colescott in his *Les Demoiselles d'Alabama: Vestidas* when she fleshes out what Picasso would stylize, in her case by drawing on Horace Pippinlike folk artistry and cartoon conventions for a Picasso dwarfed by the African masks on his studio wall. As a meta-aesthetic, *The French Collection* highlights the relationship between the historically white, male creators of visual culture and their black sources.[36] Reversing the normative line of appropriation—whereby impressionists like Matisse and Picasso adopted African and Asian subjects and techniques for their art, while modernists such as Stein and Hemingway patronized African-American entertainers and languages—Ringgold expresses her affectionate appreciation as well as her righteous resentment by appropriating the appropriators.

Given the decidedly offstage white husband so quickly done in and never depicted, the quilts' dazzling multiplicity demonstrates how Ringgold dislodges miscegenation from the sexual sphere to place it in the cultural field. Amid the jubilant patchwork of a miscegenated modernism, the poignancy of the concluding panel, *Moroccan Holiday*, stands out, for the psychological angst of Willia goes beyond personal uncertainties to the larger issue of feminism's future. In the last, somber quilt, Willia vacations with her daughter, Marlena, in Morocco. Under the watchful eyes of Frederick Douglass, Marcus Garvey, Malcolm X, and Martin Luther King Jr. (portraits she has supposedly produced), the mother torments herself and her daughter with her guilt over her creative career in an ironic conclusion to her triumphant aesthetic progress. Like the heroine of Caryl Churchill's play *Top Girls*, an ambitious executive who can only compete in the business world by pawning her daughter off on her working-class sister, Ringgold's Willia understands that her creative autonomy was purchased by the services of her sister. An independent female life, according to Churchill and Ringgold, remains dependent on class and at odds with maternity. Although Willia knows that there is nothing but bigotry for blacks in America and thus assures her own aesthetic integrity by remaining an expatriate in Paris, she only achieves autonomy by relegating her son and daughter to their aunt and life in the States.

Perhaps Ringgold concludes her *French Collection* with Willia's conflicted emotions because they provide a clue to the asymmetries the artist perceives in the categories of gender and race. Being a woman means that, although Willia inherits the courage of the four male leaders she has painted, she faces

We Came to America, The American Collection #1.
74 1/2" x 79 1/2". 1997 Faith Ringgold.

US Postage Commemorating the Advent of Black Power, 72" x 96". 1967 Faith Ringgold.

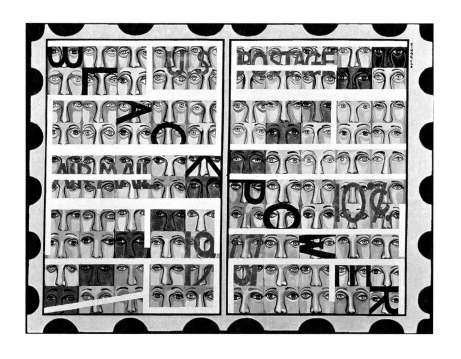

The Picnic at Giverney, The French Collection. 73 1/2" x 90 1/2". 1997 Faith Ringgold.

Picasso's Studio, The French Collection. 73" x 68". 1997
Faith Ringgold

a catch-22. Anger or guilt are her options: anger at relinquishing her art for her children or guilt at sacrificing her children for her art. Though Ringgold's surrogate has chosen guilt (in part because "The world doesn't need another black mother alone with her children"), she remains tormented by what she calls a "futile women's war" (*DL* 144).[37] Pessimistic in its acknowledgment of intergenerational friction, the last story frame nevertheless presents a daughter honoring her mother-artist (not at the expense of her nurturing aunt but along with her). As Marlena intuits, however, anger accompanies her mother's guilt "because despite the fact that you have lived your life exactly as you pleased, you still can't have the power of men. You want it all, Mama, and what's more you deserve it" (*DL* 144). The invention of a woman-friendly African-American impressionism does not achieve the task that would be necessary for Willia to have it all, for that would require "rewrit[ing] the book of life to make men the mothers and women the fathers" (*DL* 144).

Gendered social roles mutate and multiply beyond the dualism of male and female bodies; however, the recalcitrance of biology—the inescapable fact of maternity—contrasts with the fluidity of color in the sequence. Although gender and race are both socially constructed, in other words, the sexual terms "male and female" seem more obdurate than the color terms "black and white." Brooding over this question—does race stand in relation to color as gender does to sex?—the "mother-daughter debates" (*DL* 144) of Ringgold's *French Collection* place the instability of race (given the volatility of color) up against the major obstacle (in the twenties, as in the nineties) to the variability of gender categories. Like Adrian Piper and Anna Deavere Smith, Ringgold uses the commonplace gap between phenotype (a type distinguished by visual characteristics) and genotype (a type distinguished by hereditary traits) to frustrate conventional racial lexicons. Although "what we now understand as racial difference within the human species is easily mutable and erasable through interracial reproduction," Leora Auslander reminds us in a meditation pertinent to Ringgold's, "the vast majority of the world's population is still sexually embodied as male or female" (21).

Yet, as one astute reader of this chapter pointed out, my own construction of the topic—by highlighting the work of feminists with self-defined African-American roots—threatens to reinstate the racial binary Ringgold and her peers try to dismantle. The ambiguously colored—Chicana? Asian? Indian? mixed?—faces on Ringgold's *U.S. Postage Stamp* thematize the disjunction between color and our cultural language of color. "Blackpower and white power, but no yellow power (only peril)" is how this correspondent put it.[38] Still, outside the persistent racism of slavery's inheritance, why would we insist on categorizing Adrian Piper, Anna Deavere Smith, and Faith Ringgold as "African-American," if their genealogies also contain, as they probably do, European, Asian, Hispanic, or Native-American progenitors? Indeed, I was drawn to their work because they address the inadequacies of even hybridized categories of identity for those who are multiply marked.[39] However, given the representational violence bequeathed by America's history of slavery, perhaps only a self-proclaimed woman of color can play all the requisite roles to dramatize that past because—unlike whites and black men—African-American women as a group never used impersonation and mimicry to devalue others but were themselves so devalued. In any case, my quandary reflects a current impasse in feminist thinking, namely, the need to employ identity categories for the purposes of political agency versus the fictiveness of those categories as displayed by poststructuralist and postcolonial theorists.

Despite the limits of my framework, limits related to using racial language to sabotage race, feminism's splitting of gender from biological sexuality, which, in turn, facilitated the divorcing of race from color may eventuate in critical lenses as mobile and nuanced as Piper's playing of the race card, Deavere Smith's bridge of moving identifications, and Ringgold's patchworks. Not Du Bois's "color line" but identity play—deployed to make the politics of identity less smug and exclusionary, more nimble against prejudice—expresses the pleasure current performers and painters reap from a dialogue between gender and race that reinvents the former to annihilate the latter.[40] Drawing upon their passionate commitment to social justice, contemporary artists of racechange exchange race for something more supple than anything we have known before . . . until that day when sex goes the same way, that day when men mother and women father the bright children dancing through the galleries of the future.

3

Lesbian Studies 101
(As Taught by Creative Writers)

Lesbians are the poets of the humanity of women and this humanity is the only one which can give to our collectivity a sense of what's real.

—Nicole Brossard, *The Aerial Letter*

In literature and criticism, lesbian writing has undergone a sort of renaissance from the seventies on. Not since the flowering of lesbian letters during the first few decades of the twentieth century has the vitality of lesbian creativity been so evident. Indeed, if by "lesbian literature and criticism" we mean writing about and by publicly self-proclaimed homosexual women, the contemporary phenomenon remains unprecedented in English and American literary history—a beginning (naissance) rather than a return (renaissance).[1] As they have in the past, though, the poets and novelists of lesbianism today engage in speculations that do not merely illuminate but also contribute to theorizing about women-desiring women.

From Radclyffe Hall, Gertrude Stein, and Virginia Woolf to Audre Lorde, Joanna Russ, Kate Millett, Adrienne Rich, Monique Wittig, Bertha Harris, Gloria Anzaldúa, Cherríe Moraga, and Minnie Bruce Pratt, some of the most important theorists of lesbian sexuality have been its most lyrical advocates. My epigraph from Nicole Brossard hints at the unique importance of the imagination in lesbian history, as does her comment that "in surrounding themselves with women, lesbians constantly pose the question of representation, identity and seduction. The *for women only* that takes shape with each generation of lesbians is a power of dreaming" ("GN" 134).[2] Given their efforts to lend imaginative substance to the collectivity of women that some gay theorists posit, creative writers—many of whom today inhabit the same academic venues as their scholarly colleagues—enter the critical conversation to produce theoretically significant contributions to the field. Proliferating dialogues between creative and critical authors make it difficult to track lines of influence, to determine whether criticism shapes imaginative literature or vice versa, but these discussions simultaneously endow creative texts with notable theoretical import.

Although friends and colleagues would undoubtedly tout other eligible candidates, for me the most optimistic imaginings of the gay eighties and nineties appear in the verse of Marilyn Hacker and the prose of Jeannette Winterson, while the most daring surface in the fiction of Rebecca Brown. Considered along with the speculations of the lesbian theorists to whom their work gestures, Hacker's long poem "Ballad of Ladies Lost and Found" (1985), Winterson's metafictional "The Poetics of Sex" (1993), and Brown's surrealistic "Forgiveness" (1990) summarize key theoretical points that the critics propose in quite different tonalities and therefore can be used to out-line the parameters of current speculations. For Hacker provides a meditation on what it means to historicize lesbianism, while Winterson and Brown engage in the aesthetic and psychoanalytic deliberations that make the study of women's homosexuality so central in feminist thinking. Working in the wake of Audre Lorde's pioneering insight into the erotic as "not a question only of what we do" but "a question of how acutely and fully we can feel in the doing," Hacker, Winterson, and Brown would agree with Lorde that "recognizing the power of the erotic within our lives can give us the energy to pursue genuine change within our world" ("UE" 54, 59). Through the verbal and imaginative genius of their art, these writers make their readers feel how the power of the erotic might change the world; in creative texts readers can sense the emotional resonance of more abstractly framed theoretical debates. For this reason, literature is especially effective in introducing students to the trajectory of discussions swirling around images of lesbian desire.

The lesbian first as a woman-identified-woman, then as a feminist-separatist, and finally as a queer anarchist of the homosexual category itself: Hacker's, Winterson's, and Brown's texts clarify what is at stake in the dialogues staged around these figures.[3] Whereas images of the lesbian as woman-identified-woman served the needs of historical inquiry, whereas portraits of the lesbian as feminist-separatist aligned her with a postmodernist avant garde, the queering of lesbianism opened up conceptual space for resistance to those who fabricate any stable identity from or for lesbian sexuality. Although Hacker's celebrations of woman-identified women and Winterson's paeans to feminist-separatists contrast with Brown's fierce deflation of precisely such mythologizings, the crafty irreverence of "Forgiveness" as a challenge to earlier conceptualizations helps explain the significant emergence of queer theory. In its recent evolution, Lesbian Studies—formed out of a collaborative matrix of creative artists, activists, historians, theorists, critics, and journalists—counters the marginalization of gay women by illustrating Brossard's stirring proposition that "Lesbians are the *poets* of the humanity of women."

Lesbian Historiography

With astonishing precision, Marilyn Hacker's recent publications mark her efforts to mourn as well as protest the losses inflicted not only by her own breast cancer but also by disasters such as the Holocaust and the AIDs epidemic.[4] Earlier in her career, the reclaiming of loss in a lesbian context concerned the poet in "Ballad of Ladies Lost and Found," a work that examines the importance and the difficulty of excavating a lesbian past. Literally meaning a dancing song, the ballad form provided Hacker an opportunity to produce a paradoxically gay dance through the minefields negotiated by the generations of women who preceded her. Though its chorus line consists of the dead, though large portions of their lives have been obscured or obliterated from all record books, their diverse antics and artistry are what entrance the chronicling choreographer. Like historians of lesbian cultures and like theorists who insist on the importance of such historians' work—Bonnie Zimmerman, Lillian Faderman, Adrienne Rich, Esther Newton, Martha Vicinus, Terry Castle—Hacker emphasizes how the historical imagination guards against those forces that have erased lesbianism from public consciousness and wiped out the coherences and inconsistencies of its traditions. Epitomizing one major strand in lesbian scholarship, Hacker's poem finds the lesbian as woman-identified-woman the most hospitable image to serve the needs of lesbian historiography.

The first stanza of "Ballad of Ladies Lost and Found" displays the formal bravura of Hacker's verse. Two technical features of the poem are its repeated posing of unanswerable questions and its reiteration of a final line that becomes a refrain in all succeeding stanzas (which number ten in all):

> Where are the women who, *entre deux guerres*,
> came out on college-graduation trips,
> came to New York on football scholarships,
> came to town meeting in a decorous pair?
> Where are the expatriate *salonnières*,
> the gym teacher, the math-department head?
> Do nieces follow where their odd aunts led?
> The elephants die off in Cagnes-sur-Mer.
> H.D., whose "nature was bisexual,"
> and plain old Margaret Fuller died as well.

With most lines of the poem hovering around the five beats of its final refrain, each stanza consists of two quatrains followed by a couplet, its conclusion always the punctuating clause about "plain old Margaret Fuller." Each quatrain, in turn, organizes itself around an exacting rhyme scheme (of abba) so that in the above lines, for example, "*guerres*" is echoed by "pair" and "trips" chimes with "scholarships." Hardly folksy, the people Hacker mentions seem as sophisticated as her deployment of the usually simple, even sentimental ballad genre.

This is the same poet, then, who is drawn to the technically challenging work of Elizabeth Bishop, a precursor much more guarded about expressing her love of women.[5] And just as Hacker revises Bishop's villanelle "One Art" in the far more upbeat "From Orient Point"—Bishop's opening "The art of losing isn't hard to master" becomes Hacker's "The art of living isn't hard to muster"—"Ballad of Ladies Lost and Found" contains a jaunty, buoyant tone bespeaking a survival quite at odds with its repeated insistence on the death of "plain old Margaret Fuller." On the one hand, the question "Where are the women" can only be answered with the dead-as-a-doorknob "plain old Margaret Fuller" because all of the players in the poem are over the hill or under the ground—except maybe the "butch drunk on the IRT / who used to watch me watch her watching me." On the other hand, as this last line illustrates, the hilarity of the poem is sustained by its verbal inventiveness about the "ladies" who "came out" or "came to." But in what is it grounded, from where does it spring?

Part of the fun of the ballad resides in the historian's quest to gather together in the name of lesbianism women near and far. What the collection exhibits is the diversity of gay experience, for Hacker echoes many social historians by warning against any monolithic conceptualization of a unified lesbian community or identity. Even in the first stanza, one cannot equate the lesbianism of frequenters of early twentieth-century expatriate salons (Natalie Barney's, for instance, or Gertrude Stein's) with that of contemporary math-department heads in the States, just as one cannot liken in the third stanza the nineteenth-century, French, realistic painter Rosa Bonheur and the twentieth-century, Mexican surrealist Frida Kahlo. Consider the erotic range of the personages invoked by Hacker: a female impersonator (the Chevalier d'Eon), a bisexual (H.D.), a married woman with passionate female friendships (Margaret Fuller), a woman wearing trousers who pronounced herself pure (Rosa Bonheur), a declared witch (Anne Hutchinson), an activist whose erotic preferences remain unknown (Sojourner Truth), a novelist noted for not engaging in any sexual experiences (Jane Austen), a dramatist infamous for indulging in many (Aphra Behn), a Mexican nun (Juana Ines de la Cruz), an Aztec given as a slave to Cortes (Malinche)—to name a few.

Any collectivity purchased at the price of diversity would diminish this group, Hacker suggests. The product of a distinctive time and place, each individual needs to be located through historically specific letters, diaries, portraits, legends, or biographical accounts. Yet lesbianism itself is a transcultural, transhistorical phenomenon that metamorphoses over space and time. Similarly, the women involved in the "Boston" marriages described by Lillian Faderman and Carroll Smith Rosenberg contrast with the butch/femme couples depicted by Sue-Ellen Case or the Blues singers analyzed by Hazel Carby, just as the mannish lesbians cannot be conflated with the postfeminists discussed by Esther Newton.[6] Neither crushes nor friendships nor chaste religious communities nor prostitution rings should be discounted. Because Hacker begins with explicitly gay and bisexual "ladies," because she cleverly couples women together (like Big Sweet and Zora Neale Hurston, Ida B. [Wells] and Susan B. [Anthony], Angelina Grimké Weld and Angelina Weld Grimké, Amy [Lowell] and Ada [Russell]), because she mentions "bulldaggers" and Sappho, even the purportedly heterosexual women begin to seem like candidates for the lesbian hall of fame. The line between straight and gay blurs as the ballad progresses.

Adrienne Rich famously called "the lesbian continuum" that graduated spectrum of women loving women that makes it exceptionally difficult to demarcate where passionate friendship, intimacy, bonding end and where homosexuality begins.[7] Proximity turns even Jane Austen into potential material in Hacker's poem: Did she sleep in her sister Cassandra's bed only during the cold, damp English winters, some readers have wondered. Or "the grandmother of Frankenstein": Didn't Mary Wollstonecraft adore Fanny Blood before she fell for any man, as several biographers have surmised? Using Rich's article as a lens as well as Hacker's cataloging, Madame de Sevigné's passionate relationship with her daughter Madame de Grignan can be located on a lesbian continuum of feminine tenderness. Maybe, in thrall to a woman-centered eroticism, Jane Austen, Mary Wollstonecraft, and Madame de Sevigné were only passing as straight. Or perhaps, regardless of their purported sexuality, they created texts that critique heterosexuality or express a lesbian vision evident to those readers equipped with what Barbara Johnson calls "an inner lesbometer" (159).[8] It all depends on how we define the term "lesbian author," as Bonnie Zimmerman has explained most cogently.[9] Rejecting the reigning binary between hetero- and homosexuality allows Hacker to uncover exactly the work it does, its blanketing of the differences among women with various erotic proclivities.[10]

"'Diversity' is a salutary reminder that not all questions can be answered" ("TW" 433), according to Martha Vicinus, and Hacker underscores the same point by posing many riddles that have not and perhaps cannot be solved:

> Who snuffed Clara's *mestiza* flamboyance
> and bled Frida onto her canvases?
> . . . .
> Who was Sappho's protegée and when did
> we lose Hrotsvitha, dramaturge and nun?
> What did bibulous Suzanne Valadon
> think about Artemisia . . .?

The gaps in a fragmentary past may never be filled in to form a continuous account since so many factors have conspired to create them: the eradication of documents by church and state agencies; the lies, secrets, and silences women imposed on themselves for self-protection; the absence of an adequate language when discourse has been heterosexualized, medicalized, or legalized for surveillance purposes. About the lives and loves of many of the women in the poem, Hacker and her readers will remain ignorant.

Although at mid-point in the poem Hacker declares "There's no such tense as Past Conditional" (contrasting her native English with her adopted French), in a curious way "Ballad of Ladies Lost and Found" strives toward a consciousness of the past as conditional—contingent on our suppositions, speculations, conjectures. Past conditional: if I had been . . ., I would have had . . . . "Not an unusual tense," Nancy K. Miller instructs me over e-mail, "but a good one for longing." If we had been able to answer questions about the whereabouts of "Anabella, Augusta-Goose,/Fanny, Maude, Lidian, Freda and Caitlin" (Byron's sister and wife, Keats's beloved, Yeats's passion, Emerson's second wife, D. H. Lawrence's and Dylan Thomas's partners), we would have had not simply a different knowledge of our past but a more multifaceted, richer past altogether. If we knew more about these women than what the men felt about them, if we had documents about the women's relationship with other women, couldn't they too be nominated to the lesbian pantheon?[11] Despite the poet's evident yearning for information, the "lesser lives" of these women were not thought worthy of recording either by themselves or by their acquaintances.[12]

That so many of Hacker's subjects were poets, singers, painters, activists, novelists, scientists, rhetoricians, hostesses, educators, muses, or pioneers also makes women's aesthetic and intellectual history seem conditional—dependent on (sometimes undisclosed) erotic experimentation or (more broadly) on female-centered intimacy. If all the notable "ladies lost and found" might have been lesbians, then our aesthetic matrilineage would have been too. Terry Castle uses the trope of "the apparitional lesbian" to stand for all those women misrepresented by sanitized biographies, encouraged or forced to camouflage their own eroticism, denied or disembodied by contemporaries. Undoubtedly the lesbian was repressed because she personified a clear-cut challenge to male authority over women and their desire; however, as Castle reminds us, "Lesbian creativity has been responsible . . . for much that we take for granted in modern culture, especially (though not solely) in the world of the arts" (18). Hardly an anomaly in cultural history, the lesbian emerges from the "Ballad of Ladies Lost and Found" as the prototype of the creative woman. Like "quinquagenarian and portly" Amy Lowell, who wrote a poem about her aesthetic matrilineage entitled "The Sisters" (1925), Hacker composes a literary critical retrospective of her female precursors; but unlike Lowell, Hacker displays no animosity or anxiety about the tradition she inherits, perhaps because of a levity born of the archival work being done by her scholarly contemporaries.

Whereas Lowell finds her "older" sisters "rather terrifying," Hacker judges the oddity, isolation, social ostracism, and even the deaths of her predecessors exhilarating; her ballad thus exemplifies Castle's belief that "the feeble, elegiac waving off—the gesture of would-be exorcism—[can become] instead a new and passionate beckoning" (47).[13] Moving beyond puzzlement ("Where" is this one? "Who" was that one?) about her apparitional precursors, Hacker's own identification finds confirmation when her daughter is described as a version of Madame de Sevigné's ("my Madame de Grignan's only nine") in the next to the last stanza about literal as well as literary mothers. Finally, the last stanza's power depends on the poet coming out from behind her earlier anonymity:

> Tomorrow night the harvest moon will wane
> that's floodlighting the silhouetted wood.
> Make your own footnotes; it will do you good.
> Emeritae have nothing to explain.
> She wasn't very old, or really plain—
> my age exactly, volumes incomplete.
> "The life, the life, will it never be sweet?"
> She wrote it once; I quote it once again
> midlife at midnight when the moon is full
> and I can almost hear the warning bell
> offshore, sounding through starlight like a stain
> on waves that heaved over what she began
> and truncated a woman's chronicle,
> and plain old Margaret Fuller died as well.

With its extra quatrain, this longer stanzaic conclusion comprises a sonnet bringing out the "I" of the poet in a wonderfully balanced line, its parallelism heightened by a deft caesura: "She wrote it once; I quote it once again." These phrases take on heightened resonance through a witchy mix of allusions: what Emily Dickinson called the "Lunacy of Light" (*Poems* 593) flooding a shadowy wood reminiscent of Djuna Barnes's mysterious novel about expatriate homosexuals, *Nightwood*, during a midlife/midnight harvesting.

By the end of "Ballad of Ladies Lost and Found," Hacker has harvested the lost literary ladies to find and found her own historical lineage by reanimating the shades exorcised in the past. Indeed, the romance of history replaces the heterosexual plot, much as Julie Abraham claims it did for lesbian novelists writing at the beginning of the twentieth century. When we read the line "She wrote it once; I quote it once again," it becomes oddly performative, for Hacker's "She" (Margaret Fuller et. al) metamorphoses into our Hacker, who wrote it once for us and whom we quote once again. At the same time, the line echoes the other beautifully balanced directive: "Make your own footnotes; it will do you good." Addressing her readers, Hacker urges them to dispense with annotations or explanations (such as this one), to engage instead as amateur historians in decoding the puzzles of the past. The poet provides a justification for her pedagogic assignment by explaining that Margaret Fuller "wasn't very old, or really plain." Her own refrain, "plain old Margaret Fuller died as well," must be taken with a grain of salt; perhaps it represents an instance of the very projection that propels the romance with history: Hacker's dread that unforeseen circumstances might truncate the work or the sweet life she hopes to achieve. Composing this piece at forty-three, just a few years older than Fuller at her drowning, Hacker heeds her haunting muse to record the warning bells and tumultuous waves Fuller must have heard as her boat began to wreck itself off the New York shore.

Lesbian Aesthetics

If Hacker finds the lesbian as woman-identified-woman most propitious for the projects of lesbian historians, Jeannette Winterson ratchets up the sexiness of the lesbian as feminist-separatist, aligning erotic and aesthetic experimentation in "The Poetics of Sex." From Monique Wittig and Luce Irigaray to Diana Fuss, contemporary thinkers have examined the linguistic and generic choices homosexual writers face, linking lesbianism to stylistic issues. Postmodernist in style, "The Poetics of Sex," with its title portentous of a poetics of lesbian sexuality, can in no way be said to epitomize Winterson's astonishingly diverse productions; however, it does typify a host of texts that posit the lesbian as a vanguard being uniquely able to eradicate or evade hegemonic definitions of gender and the heterosexual scripts upon which they hinge. As Wittig indicated by using the phrase as the title of her essay collection on lesbianism, "the straight mind" necessarily plays a major (though sabotaged) role in literature created by those deemed crooked, deviant, queer, abnormal, sick, or simply evil.

In "The Poetics of Sex," the voice of the straight mind—a disembodied faculty in an ideological straitjacket—punctuates the narrative. Each section

of the tale is prefaced by an italicized question posed by a heterosexual inter-
locutor and appearing in this order:

> *Why Do You Sleep with Girls?*
> *Which One of You is the Man?*
> *What Do Lesbians Do in Bed?*
> *Were You Born a Lesbian?*
> *Were You Born a Lesbian?*
> *Why Do You Hate Men?*
> *Don't You Find There's Something Missing?*
> *Why Do You Sleep with Girls?*

Assuming heterosexuality as the normative position, each query implies that
lesbianism is questionable, that it cannot be taken as a given, natural, or satisfy-
ing phenomenon. The absence of man stands at the heart of the matter: illogic
notwithstanding, either the lesbian wants to be a man or she hates men. That
the question about origins (*"Were You Born?"*) appears twice suggests heterosexual incredulity, homosexual monstrosity. That the questions circle back to
the beginning means, of course, that they will be repeated ad nauseam. That
they are italicized marks a kind of insistence, leading one to suspect that their
author will not simply fade away into silence. The series of queries in "The
Poetics of Sex" constitutes an interrogation in which the lesbian subject is
deemed guilty, not ever to be proved or assumed innocent.

   Representing legal, religious, and scientific rulings against homosexuality, the question sequence smacks of the juridical deposition of a court of law,
the canonical interdiction of a clerical authority, the medical investigation of
a diagnosing board of physicians. At the same time, the cycle displays the
absorption of heterosexuals with homosexuality, their consuming need to
organize society around this central axis of hetero- vs. homo-, a phenomenon
Eve Kosofsky Sedgwick has extensively explored in *Epistemology of the Closet*. In addition, the prurient voyeurism of *"What Do You Do in Bed?"* exhibits
the fascination with which heterosexuals approach their need to define themselves against a fetishized Other. The lesbian text, Winterson shows, must
acknowledge the hegemony of the straight, homophobic mindset that polices
legal, ethical, and medical definitions of homosexuality. Like Judith Roof,
who postulates "narrative's heteroideology" to emphasize the link between
conventional plots and heterosexual development, Winterson seeks to open
up a defiant counternarrative to express what has been labeled perverse (*C*

xxvii). She does this by outing heterosexuality, making it visible as a parochial set of culturally buttressed assumptions. In the process of denaturalizing heterosexuality, she also attempts to naturalize homosexuality.

Each segment of Winterson's narrative of two young women meeting, falling in love, withstanding the difficulties of maintaining their relationship, and living together happily ever after implicitly talks back to the heterosexual inquirer. Without deigning to answer the cross-examiner directly, the initially unnamed narrator of the story tells her tale to the reader, who can then juxtapose it against the straight mind's question. So, for example, the portion of the story prefaced by "*What Do Lesbians Do in Bed?*" contains a paragraph about the narrator meeting her lover, Picasso, at art school, making a pass, and finding herself back in Picasso's studio:

> We were in our igloo and it couldn't have been snugger. White on white on white on white. Sheet Picasso me sheet. Who was on top depends on where you're standing but as we were lying down it didn't matter.
>
> What an Eskimo I am, breaking her seductive ice and putting in my hand for fish. How she wriggles, slithers, twists to resist me but I can bait her and I do.
>
> (415)

In cadences quite distinct from that of the straight mind, the exultant narrator playfully relishes a multitude of figurative descriptions of love-making. Not transparency but a generous opacity of style presents the sameness of the two partners ("White on white on white on white") as well as their difference ("I" am "an Eskimo," "she" is a "fish"). Jokes (as in "Who was on top depends on where you're standing") mock not only the solemnity of the straight mind but also its inflexible ignorance. Of course, part of Winterson's rhetorical pleasure resides in refuting the straight mind's central premise, namely that heterosexuality universally and necessarily constitutes the foundation of desire, cultural productivity, and sexual reproduction.

When Monique Wittig concluded "The Straight Mind" with the startling aphorism "lesbians are not women," she meant that the lesbian's refusal to play women's economic, political, and ideological roles removes her from traditional gender categories altogether (20). Winterson uses a plethora of conceits to agree, even as her metaphors insist on the naturalness of lesbian love. A writer, the narrator of "The Poetics of Sex" often describes her love-making with Picasso in animal terms. When she is not reaching her hand through the ice for a fish, she "flick[s] her hind-quarters and skip[s] away"

(412) or her "bull-lover makes a matador out of [her]" (413). These analogies jostle against other registers in which the lover is food ("loins of pork, beefy upper cuts and breasts of lamb" [412]), or flower ("I will cover you with my petals" [412]), or sea ("She was salty, well preserved, well made and curved like a wave" [414–5]). The mutability of the identities or roles bequeathed by such analogies is part of the point, the indeterminacy of their excessive successiveness: "Pin her down? She's not a butterfly. I'm not a wrestler. She's not a target. I'm not a gun" (414). Like the contributors to a critical anthology entitled *The Lesbian Postmodern*, Winterson ponders lesbians' and postmodernists' common investment in eluding any governing master-metaphor or metanarrative.[14]

The playful plethora of Winterson's closure-resistant metaphors is matched by the mutuality of her lesbian couple. Chameleon "quick-change artists we girls" (413), the painterly Picasso and the writerly narrator direct their artistry onto their relationship, promoting self-fashioning through their interchangeable role-playing. The chutzpah of naming her female artist Picasso—not only a crucially innovative painter but also a famous sexual athlete-as-minotaur—emphasizes the important part imaginative work has always played in shaping ideas about sexuality. After Picasso is informed by a "fairy in a pink tutu" that she "will give birth to a sex toy who has a way with words" (416), the lovers also become mother and child, "bound by cords too robust for those healthy hospital scissors." Through this language, Winterson gestures at the decisive role a preoedipal bond between mother and baby has performed in theoretical language about lesbianism.

"From Sigmund Freud to Julia Kristeva," Diana Fuss explains about the drawbacks of this discourse, "preoedipality defines the fundamental psychical organization of the homosexual subject who never, it seems, fully accedes to the position of subject but who remains in the ambiguous space of the precultural" (*IP* 59). Psychoanalytic terms that ally the lesbian couple with nostalgia for the mother-infant relation tend to taint lesbianism with regression to a pregenital nonsexuality or narcissistic mirroring. Yet, given the absurdity of giving "birth to *a sex toy*" (italics mine), it is hardly surprising that the reciprocity of the mother-baby dyad never arrests the propulsion of the erotic in definitively genital subjects like Picasso and her offspring: "Flesh of her flesh she fucked her" (417). No blurred "lesbian continuum" here, but instead the "commitment of skin, blood, breast, and bone," the "carnality [that] distinguishes [lesbianism] from gestures of political sympathy with homosexuals and from affectionate friendships," to quote the words

Catharine Stimpson used to critique the image of the woman-identified-woman ("ZDD" 364).

Does Winterson's linguistic exuberance at the multiple ways of figuring female desire elaborate on Luce Irigaray's idea about a woman's language *"always in the process of weaving itself, of embracing itself with words, but also of getting rid of words in order not to become fixed, congeal in them"* (*TS* 29)? Certainly the profusion and instability of metaphors for the lovers and their love-making hint at an inventiveness quite distinct from the stagnant reign of what Irigaray calls "a ho(m)mo-sexual monopoly," by which she means the law of heterosexuality that exclusively valorizes men's organs, needs, desires, or exchanges of women (171).[15] After Picasso gives birth to a "sex toy" with "two greedy hands and an open mouth" (417), she baptizes the narrator "Sappho" (416) and watches her embracing and getting rid of words so as not to become congealed in them:

> Here comes Sappho, scorching the history books with tongues of flame. Never mind the poetry feel the erection. Oh yes, women get erect, today my body is stiff with sex. When I see a word held hostage to manhood I have to rescue it. Sweet sweet trembling word, locked in a tower, tired of your Prince coming and coming. I will scale you and discover that size is no object especially when we're talking inches.
>
> I like to be a hero, like to come back to my island full of girls carrying a net of words forbidden them. Poor girls, they are locked outside their words just as the words are locked into meaning. Such a lot of locking up goes on the Mainland but here on Lesbos our doors are always open. (417–8)

Winterson seems to be meditating directly on Irigaray's statement that outside a patriarchal economy, "women's desire would not be expected to speak the same language as man's" (*TS* 25). Without the patronymic, Sappho and Picasso exist beyond patriarchal kinship, the exchange of women, and the law based on what Lacan called the Name of the Father.[16] Wrested from familial ties, marriage, and property lines, their identities as lovers plant them on a Lesbos that hints at the possibility of lesbianism as a separate place outside the confines of patriarchal history. Indeed, the only ferryman they encounter—Phaeon runs a "Lesbian Tours" business—has been satirically miniaturized into a pathetic voyeur of this libertarian Herland. At her most outrageous as a deliverer of a *parler femme* or mother tongue, Sappho transcends the condemnatory sentences of the straight mind by declaring, "the real trouble is that we have rescued a word not allowed to our kind"; this, of course, is the word "Happy" (419).[17]

Discrediting homophobic portraits of doomed lesbians through the blissful complementarity of "equal . . . twin souls" (420) unregulated by the ownership or hierarchy dynamics of the heterosexual paradigm, "The Poetics of Sex" also exuberantly deploys Sapphic allusions. Like Michael Fields, Edna St. Vincent Millay, Isadora Duncan, Renée Vivien, H.D., Virginia Woolf, Marguerite Yourcenar, and Olga Broumas, authors who write "for" and "as" Sappho to invent a classical inheritance of their own,[18] Winterson links the lesbian tradition with an empowering classical precursor. Throughout the tale the natural landscapes of wind and water merge with cultural imagery of Greek artistry, but nature has been intersecting with culture from the beginning sentence, where Picasso's "Blue Period" alludes to her menstrual cycle but also to one of her namesake's painting phases. While Monique Wittig and Sande Zeig produced a provocative blank page under the entry for Sappho in their *Lesbian Peoples: Material for a Dictionary* (1979), Winterson audaciously invents a Sappho reunited with her lover on Lesbos, where—art and nature thus allied—they paint and write and live together, feeling "fresh and plentiful": "She is my harvest and I am hers. She seeds me and reaps me, we fall into one another's laps" (422).

As in the conclusion of the Marilyn Hacker poem, the language of harvesting accrues to the recurrent production of art and of love, though Winterson also puns on the season of fall, the sexual swoon of falling, and the first fall from innocence as well as on the homonym of "laps" and "lapse." The last lines of "The Poetics of Sex"—"She is painting today. The room is orange with effort. She is painting today and I have written this"—draw upon Winterson's recurrent obsession with fruit from her first novel, *Oranges Are Not the Only Fruit* (1985), to her later *Sexing the Cherry* (1989). Throughout these texts, Winterson envisions erotic desire and reproductive mechanisms outside heterosexual models.[19] Whether such alternative imaginings involve hybridity (cross-dressing, drag, a third sex) or new technologies (cloning, grafting, artificial insemination, parthenogenesis, cyber personae), they constitute the lesbian artist's commitment to thinking experimentally about how two might lovingly produce three or four or more without the subordination of one.

In its representation of lesbian desire, Winterson's tale issues a resounding "yes" to Elizabeth Grosz's query: "Can feminist theory move beyond the constraints imposed by psychoanalysis, by theories of representation and signification, and by notions of the functioning of power relations—all of which implicitly presume the notion of a masculine or sexually neutral (which also means masculine) subject and the ontology of lack and depth?" ("RFD" 69). Empowered by the visionary ability to leap over historical facticity in a way scholars cannot, Winterson imagines an escape from the cul-de-sac Grosz poses. But the question is answered quite differently by those less sanguine about separatist female communities and about the lesbian as a vanguard feminist.

Psychoanalyzing Lesbians

Lesbian writers rejecting the conventional love plot may be drawn to the implausibility of nonrealistic forms not in the utopian mode mined by Winterson but in the dystopic, surreal manner of Rebecca Brown, whose answer to Grosz's query engages the same issues that Grosz herself, Judith Butler, and Teresa de Lauretis examine in theoretical speculations based on Gayle Rubin's early assessment of Freud's applicability to lesbian sexuality. "Forgiveness," which examines the inadequacy of psychoanalysis's definitions of gender and sexuality, explains why gay critics have recently swerved away from images of the lesbian as woman-identified or as feminist-separatist and toward her queering. At the core of desire and the start of this weirdly evocative, short tale stands the Freudian concept of castration—the amputation of a body part:

> When I said I'd give my right arm for you, I didn't think you'd ask me for it, but you did.
>
> You said, Give it to me.
> And I said OK.

Though the cut-off right arm of the speaker cannot be defined as a penis, the mobility of the Lacanian phallus (connected neither to the penis nor to men) allows this wound to stand for the paradigmatic injury or lack that so haunts psychoanalytic approaches to gender differences and sexual preferences.

Like a number of texts in the lesbian tradition, "Forgiveness" eschews gendered characters—the unnamed narrator and her partner are "I" and "you" and thus indeterminately gendered—so the story functions something like a Rorschach test, promulgating a multitude of narratives about the tensions between feminist, lesbian, and psychoanalytic speculations. Whereas the absence of the patronymic endows Winterson's lovers with the freedom of liminality, the dearth of any names or gendered pronouns in Brown's "Forgiveness" brings to mind Judith Butler's point that "For Lacan, names . . . *sustain* the integrity of the body" (*BTM* 72). Literalizing the threat of castration by taking the love vow "I'd give my right arm for you" verbatim, Brown examines precisely the subjects that trouble the theorists, namely the centrality in Freud's and Lacan's ideas of the castration complex, penis envy, and the status of the phallus.

Though this resonantly Kafkaesque parable eludes any single interpretation, it reverberates in fascinating ways with a crux in Freud's essay on "Female Sexuality" (1931). "Very different is the effect of the castration complex on the girl," Freud explains:

> She acknowledges the fact of her castration, the consequent superiority of the male and her own inferiority, but she also rebels against these unpleasant facts. So divided in her mind, she may follow one of three lines of development. The first leads to her turning her back on sexuality altogether. . . . If she pursues the second line, she clings in obstinate self-assertion to her threatened masculinity. . . . Only if her development follows the third, very circuitous path does she arrive at the ultimate normal feminine attitude in which she take her father as love-object, and thus arrives at the Oedipus complex in its feminine form.   (198–9)[20]

As severe as many explicators of this passage, Rebecca Brown turns it on its head, for her heroine begins in the normal (feminine) attitude, here presented as a totally debilitating masochism; next moves through a rebellious form of lesbianism, which Freud called "the masculinity complex"; then arrives at the frigidity of a complete renunciation of desire. How readers are led to assign gender to Brown's anatomically indeterminate characters—the central couple of "Forgiveness" could be heterosexual or homosexual—dramatizes her insights not only into the problematic language of psychoanalysis but also and shockingly into the unnerving commonalities of heterosexual and homosexual desire, straight and gay psychologies. Just as startling is the potential disjunction Brown confronts between feminist agendas and lesbian intimacy.

The first section of "Forgiveness" traces the narrator's emotional reactions to the physical event of voluntarily having an arm amputated, the psychic shock of a wounding renunciation that might very well transform this character into a decidedly female figure for readers who identify the feminine within a pervasive Victorian ideology that allotted abnegation, renunciation, service, and capitulation to the female of the species. Her wish to be true to her word, to prove she meant what she said, her feeling that her lover was testing her, her belief that the lover "really wanted [the arm], and needed it": all these sincere efforts to display devotion through self-sacrifice infuse the persona with conventional femininity. Bleeding through her bandages, looking at the limb floating in a bathtub of maroon water, the feminized narrator watches her partner wrap the appendage in saran wrap to get it bronzed. So evocative of the surrealists' fracturing of the female form in sculpture and painting, this making of the arm a trophy to mount above the mantle might cause some readers to assume the partner male, an idea plausibly confirmed by his reaction to the uncontrollable bleeding that occurs at night when the scab cracks open: "I don't like it when your bleeding wakes me up," the lover declares; "I think you're sick. I think it's sick to cut off your own arm." This conversation, followed by another night of bloody sheets, leads to the lover's abrupt departure.

In a reflection on the link between gender and body image, Elizabeth Grosz addresses the problem women experience preserving a narcissistic sense of bodily wholeness since "women are considered and consider themselves to have suffered an amputation more debilitating than most—the amputation implied by castration" (*VB* 71). "Forgiveness" eerily glosses Grosz's inquiry, "Do women experience the castration complex as a bodily amputation as well as a psychosocial constraint?" (*VB* 73). As in Freud's essays, where the dissimilarity between girls and boys is "the difference between a castration that has been carried out and one that has merely been threatened" (192), the female has been robbed of a body part and thus plunged into a chronic state of self-insufficiency or incompleteness. Bleeding on the bedsheets, reminiscent of menstrual blood, stands for the narcissistic "wound" or "scar" or "sense of inferiority" (188) Freud's girl discovers in the "fact" of her "organic inferiority" (200). While acceptance constitutes Freud's normal femininity, the typical masculine reaction consists of "horror of the mutilated creature or triumphant contempt for her" (187), as in Brown's fable. In its effort to dramatize the grotesque masochism defined as femininity and the sadism attached to masculinity, the first part of "Forgiveness" parallels the poem "Bleeding" by May Swensen in which a cunt/cut apologizes for the messy blood produced by a penetrating, phallic knife:

> I can't stand   bleeding said the knife and sank in farther.
> I hate it too   said the cut I know it isn't you it's me[21]

Certain aspects of the narrator's efforts to deal with the castration underscore the self-destructiveness of normative femininity by dramatizing her pathetic thralldom to the assumed superiority of a lover taken to be an omniscient god. Perhaps, Brown's persona muses after her abandonment, the lover has inflicted this amputation "as a test" or "to teach me something" and so is "watching" her from afar. Acting "like I couldn't care less about my old arm," she disavows the loss. As in so many of Freud's case histories of hysterics, disavowal becomes repression, repression devolves into forgetting the trauma altogether: "I convinced myself, in trying to convince you, that I had never had an arm I'd lost." But not thinking about the arm entails subjective vacuity, thinking "of nothing almost happily," as well as the emergence of corporeal signs of unspoken trauma. The site of absence becomes the locus of feeling, the shameful scar tissue fetishized as the most sensitive body part—an erogenous zone of touchy desire: the smoothness at her shoulder appears "Round and slightly puffed, pink and shiny and slick. As soft as pimento, as cool as a spoon, the tenderest flesh of my body."

The disjunction between Freud's view of castration and that of Rebecca Brown constitutes the substance of lesbian-feminist attacks on psychoanalysis, for what Freud took to be the biological "fact" of castration Brown has dramatized as an act of dismemberment performed on the female body. From the point of view of those lesbian-feminist theorists who came to view Freud's discourse itself as a performative act of dismemberment, the lover of "Forgiveness" stands for the father of psychoanalysis who first talks the woman into granting her castration and then blames her for it. Rebecca Brown's concern with psychoanalysis is exactly that of Elizabeth Grosz: "At stake here is . . . the question of whether feminists should or should not abandon a discourse that paints so bleak a picture of women's containment within the psychical norms of masculinity" ("LL" 275). In the context of the lesbian tradition that *The Terrible Girls* evokes, the first section of the story "Forgiveness" satirizes normative heterosexuality as a sickening fetishization of female lack and self-hatred. Without agency or desires of her own, the female narrator effects her own castration as well as her partner's cruel phallic authority. At the same time, male abhorrence of dismemberment and fear of punishment for sexual transgression breed an identification of women with castration and thus fuel misogyny.

However, what if we decide the indeterminate couple is not heterosexual, but homosexual? As the title of the volume in which the tale appears suggests and as its cunning form intimates, what if both characters are "terrible girls"? Later in the narrative, when the partner reappears, the reader is given immediate confirmation through a series of feminine metaphors that he might be a she and the relationship a same-sex one. After returning with "big sweet pretty brown eyes" and "lips quivering," the lover weeps, apologizes, begs forgiveness, swears she has changed for the better. The words "pretty," "sweet," "sweeter," "tears," and "baby" recur with some frequency, as the partner asks to be rocked by the narrator and cries herself to sleep. Even before this occurs, the narrator herself displays symptoms of a less compliant response to castration that recalls not normative feminine submissiveness but the rebelliousness Freud termed the "masculinity complex" and identified with homosexuality.

If, in confronting biological deficiency, a process of "denial" sets in, Freud believed, "a girl may refuse to accept the fact of being castrated, may harden herself in the conviction that she *does* possess a penis and may subsequently be compelled to behave as though she were a man" (188). As Judith Roof astutely points out, "[s]eeing the lesbian as masculine solves the problem of lesbian sexuality by rendering it as essentially heterosexual—as a relation between a woman who thinks she's a man and another woman" (*LK* 211). Is Brown's narrator a lesbian in the grip of a "masculinity complex" after the departure of her female lover? Certainly, the one-handed heroine rebels against the amputation when she finds the novelty of learning "to eat a quarter pounder with one fist" wearing thin and understands "What I wanted was my arm." Freud's analysis of the girl's horror of her own mutilation pertains to the narrator's wish for the return of her member: "She has seen it and knows that she is without it and wants to have it" (188). However, to the extent that the narrator wants not a penis but her own arm back, Rebecca Brown is pulling Freud's leg, for while the male of the species may have a monopoly on penises, he has none on arms.

In an essay examining exactly the issue that fascinates Rebecca Brown, Judith Butler claims that the detachability of the Lacanian phallus from the penis means that other body parts may provide a signifier of investiture, a phallus for the lesbian. If the phallus as transcendental signifier is a compensatory fantasy men deploy to ease anxiety about "the body [that] is in pieces before the mirror and before the law," then "an arm, a tongue, a hand (or two), a knee, a thigh, a pelvic bone" could symbolize having or being the phallus (*BTM* 81, 88). Butler's term "the lesbian phallus" means that the lesbian need not counter castration with penis envy. Similarly, Rebecca Brown's narrator rebels by refusing to give up her phallic desire. Hardly a male wannabe, the lesbian narrator seeks not a penis but an arm whose loss has robbed her of a sense of completeness, the totality of her body image. Given the importance of fingers and hands in lesbian lovemaking, moreover, the arm as lesbian phallus symbolizes the presence of power in the absence of the penis.[22]

Or perhaps, as Teresa de Lauretis has speculated about other characters in fiction, Brown's heroine wants not a lesbian phallus but a fetish.[23] Clinging to the expectation of acquiring what she has lost, in the middle of the tale Brown's persona decides to go searching for her arm in pawnshops where the proprietors advise her about a prosthesis for the missing limb. According to de Lauretis, lesbian desire is perversely driven by castration's disavowal, but lack has less to do with a penis or a phallus, more to do with narcissistic loss: lesbian desire is "constituted against a fantasy of castration, a narcissistic wound to the subject's body-image that redoubles the loss of the mother's body by the threatened loss of the female body itself" (*PL* 262). In an analogous way, Brown's narrator in "Forgiveness" eschews artificial limbs or reconstructive surgery when she wonders "if I wasn't looking more for something else besides my severed arm. I wondered was I really searching for you?" What De Lauretis's and Brown's lesbians share is a wish not for the penis or the phallus but for access to another female body through symbols that are clearly not substitutes of either.

In the last section of "Forgiveness," Brown's narrator moves beyond her refusal to accept the fact of castration to what Freud would call the frigidity of "turning her back on sexuality altogether," but which Brown presents as a perfectly comprehensible form of rage at an inability to get out of the destructive psychosexual system that has her heroine in its grip. "Why did you do it?" the narrator wonders about her lover's sadistic appropriation of the arm, only to be answered by the lover's need to be comforted, as she asks to be welcomed back, promising that she has become "good and . . . truly different." Once again the maternal bond frames the lesbian couple:

> You made me rock you and I did and then you cried yourself to sleep as innocent as a baby. When you were asleep I walked you to the bedroom and put you to bed.

Or has the transformation of the lover into an apologetic, sweet, brown-eyed young woman caused readers to view the narrator as a man? Should the partner's femaleness produce the masculinity of the narrator, the heterosexual plot instantly turns figurative: the amputation of a male narrator makes the wound a metaphor of an exceptional psychic loss. From this vantage, Brown's allegorical tale analyzes how men and women hurt each other, soliciting impossible sacrifices that breed recrimination and anger between the sexes. A boyfriend or husband, for example, has been asked to relinquish a job, a blood relative, or his autonomy by a girlfriend or wife who then blames him for his degeneration into servility and leaves until she discovers the error of her ways.[24]

Whether male or female, the narrator's thoughts revolve around her/his inability "to replace what you had hacked away from me" and then his/her belief that "given time, you'd do something else again, some new and novel variant to what you'd done to me, again." Lovingly giving what was asked has meant being hurt, maimed, disabled, and abandoned. Being hurt, maimed, disabled, and abandoned generates compensatory fantasies, resentment, withdrawal, rancor, and a retaliatory refusal to forgive, forget, and communicate, an obstinate negation of any continuance of the relationship. To the extent that this painful dynamic plays itself out in same-sex as well as in different-sex relationships, the malevolent rebukes of an ambiguously gendered narrator debunk the celebratory depiction of lesbianism that Winterson's "The Poetics of Sex" produces:

> even if you had changed, no *really* changed, truly and at last, and even if you knew me better than I know myself, and even if I'm better off than I've ever been, and even if this was the only way we could have gotten to this special place where we are now, . . . I would never believe you again, nor forget what I know of you, never forget what you've done to me, what you will do. I'll never believe the myth of forgiveness between us.

Troping on Alice B. Toklas's mirthfully malicious remark that she could forget but not forgive wrongs done to her in the past, Brown's furious speaker makes a mockery of any mythologizing of lesbian loving.[25] What Judith Butler declares about Monique Wittig constitutes the substance of what Brown's story insinuates about Winterson's: Wittig's radical separation of "straight and gay replicates the kind of disjunctive binarism that she herself characterizes as the divisive philosophical gestures of the straight mind" (*GT* 121).

What possible difference do gender identification or gender of love choice or feminist politics make on the psychosexual dynamics of relationships, Rebecca Brown seems to ask in her vision of a possibly homosexual couple, here isolated from any homophobic framework and paradoxically just as cruel as some heterosexuals can be. Intimacy and its discontents may be less regulated by ideologies of gender sameness, more governed by the agonistic duelling of giver and getter, dutiful attendant and magisterial director, servant and master. The self-proclaimed "sex radical" Pat Califia, who identifies "more strongly as a sadomasochist than as a lesbian" (158), points out that because "sexual orientation is defined solely in terms of the sex of one's partner," its labels "tell you nothing about [an individual's] sex life" (187). Did gay women like Califia rush to endorse sadomasochism (S/M) in order to restore the glamour of taboo, which had been eliminated by the sanitized respectability of the woman-identified or feminist-separatist lesbian, as Cheshire Calhoun has speculated (218)?

S/M as a consensual activity ("I said OK") allows Califia and Rebecca Brown to dramatize the fervent power struggle generated by what Califia calls "the dual-sex system" in which the "top" metes out punishments, the "bottom" suffers feelings of unworthiness, and the issue remains one of who forgives whom.[26] A moralistic women's movement, vanilla lesbians, antipornography activists, and separatists constitute the problem for Califia, whose work calls into question any stable classification called homosexuality:

> There are lots of "heterosexual" men who have plenty of anonymous sex with other men. There are celibate faggots and dykes. There are lesbians who've been married for thirty years and have six children. There are heterosexual women who frequently have sex with other women at swing parties. For many people, if a partner or a sexual situation has other desirable qualities it is possible to overlook the partner's sex. Some examples: a preference for group sex, for a particular socioeconomic background, for paid sex, for S/M, for a specific age group, for a physical type or race, for anal or oral sex. (187)

When interpreted through Califia's lens, "Forgiveness"—detaching lesbianism from the women's movement—focuses on a "bottom'"s conversion from abjection to rage in a queer performance that denaturalizes heterosexuality even as it calls attention to the impossibility of splitting homosexuality from heterosexuality.[27] Governed less by a gender-polarized feminism, more by a transgressive resistance rooted in an alliance with homosexual men, queer theory—as expresssed by Brown's story—hints that earlier definitions of the lesbian as woman-identified and as feminist-separatist blocked the honest articulation of desires not always in accord with politically correct ideologies. Sex is sex, be it hetero- or homosexual, and any effort to dichotomize the two replicates historically homophobic structures of thinking.

Maybe, in other words, the embodiment of Brown's speakers, their genitalia, their names, the sex acts in which they engage, their gender identities remain indeterminate because they are irrelevant. "Forgiveness"'s *folie à deux* demythologizes the idea that any erotic connection exists beyond the dynamics of dual-termed power ploys, for "I" and "you" operate in painfully diametrical ways and what "I" desire and "you" want simply do not mesh or mesh all too well. Like the Annie Leclerc described by Jane Gallop, Rebecca Brown emphasizes "an acute sense of the otherness of the other woman" (*TTB* 167): sexual sameness does not mean the eradication of other differences (physical, racial, religious, class-based). Indeed, sexual sameness might highlight other dissimilarities—for example in the nature and degree of desire, in the locus of pleasure, in what each wants for herself and the other.[28] Elizabeth Grosz's question—"Can feminist theory move beyond the constraints imposed by . . . notions of the functioning of power relations"— assumes that power relations must involve a masculine subject, but Brown insists on their inexorable sway over any two human subjects. Just as feminists ask, "What difference does gender make?" lesbian thinkers inquire, "What difference does the gender of love-object choice make?" and audaciously answer: at times, none at all.

The lesbian in contemporary representations may emerge as a paradigmatic female, a prototypical feminist, or a queer, but she frequently signals possibilities about women's humanity beyond the impoverished probabilities established by many heterosexual scripts. What the metalesbian literary texts I have discussed illustrate about the intellectual history of the lesbian is the trajectory of her metamorphoses: the woman-identified-woman and feminist-separatist so prominent in the seventies and eighties continue to play roles, but recent skepticism about the viability of the concept "homosexuality"—saturated by the homophobia that historically put it into place[29]—has led to a diversification of lesbian communities. Instead of positing "a fundamental identity of lesbians," Sonya Andermahr explains, "by the 1990s lesbians were increasingly represented in cultural analyses as a heterogeneous group whose cultural practices continually cross over into the mainstream" (15).

Off our backs, one of the first feminist newspapers to address lesbian issues, took an antipornography slant divergent in tone and in editorial persuasion from the prosex, pornographic lesbian magazine it spawned, *On Our Backs*. Similarly, gay critics now analyze lipstick lesbians, retro-butch and femme couples, nuclear families of donor-inseminated lesbian mothers, the radical sex advocates Pat Califia calls "sluts in utopia" (151), the brash bisexual "sexperts" Susie Bright counsels, and popular icons of lesbian chic (such as Madonna, Martina Navratolova, Jodie Foster, Sandra Bernhard, kd lang, and Ellen DeGeneres.).[30] But creative writers will continue to play a major role as well, bringing the ramifications of the theories to life, fleshing them out through the sometimes bizarre calculus of the imagination. News of the demise of the aesthetic in feminist speculation has been greatly exaggerated.[31] For poems and stories can bridge the gap between women outside the academy and theorists inside universities seeking to illuminate lesbian lives and loves. And because creative writers must heed the logic of their own inventions, they are apt—as Hacker, Winterson, and Brown demonstrate—to literalize explanatory postulates, translating them into concrete maxims that convey their emotional consequences. Not simply elaborating upon theoretical hypotheses, the fictional "I"s of Hacker, Winterson, and Brown—like the personal "I"s of recent autobiographical critics—invent scenarios so ingeniously nuanced that they, in turn, will call forth new conceptualizations from theorists.

Perhaps because of the potential invisibility of erotic investments, the woman who loves women often becomes eclipsed in contemporary academic contexts whose very rubrics—Women's Studies, Gay Studies, queer theory—marginalize her; however, the fields of history, aesthetics, and psychology have witnessed such remarkable dialogues between creative writers and critical thinkers that for the first time the lesbian has taken center stage in cultural prominence. Yet in the "high" art realm upon which I have concentrated, what it is the lesbian does with her partner still remains largely unarticulated, so perhaps in decades to come the gay linguistic matrix will heed Marilyn Frye's call for "a finer-tuned descriptive vocabulary that maps and expresses the differences and distinctions among the things we do, the kinds of pleasures we get, the stages and styles of our acts and activities, the parts of our bodies centrally engaged in the different kinds of 'doing it' " (117–8). Still, through the efforts of creative and critical writers, the lesbian has taken on the body and, thus emboldened, she is nobody's apparition now.

4

Eating the Bread of Affliction:
Judaism and Feminism

At most Passover celebrations, participants make a
Hillel sandwich: *matzoh*, the unleavened bread taken in
haste by the ancient Jews on their flight from slavery,
is eaten with *maror*, a bitter herb, usually horseradish.
Sometimes, to set teeth further on edge and to dramatize the paradox of a feast commemorating the misery
of slavery as well as the joy of liberation, the *matzoh* is
topped with *maror* and *charoset*, a mixture of apples,
honey, and cinnamon that represents work (the mortar
and bricks made for the pharaohs) but also the exhilarating relief of release: deliverance from bondage in
Egypt. While the sharpness of the horseradish brings
stinging tears to the eyes, the tongue tastes intense
sweetness.

Eating the bread of affliction had nothing to do
with nutrition, appetite, or taste—not health, not
need, not desire—or so I thought, as if I could
detach all three from my Jewish identity. If anything, my scholarly commitment to feminism only
further convinced me that my health, my needs, my
desires depended on being a Jewish non-Jew, a secular Jew. It took some time for me to feel anything
but bitterness about Judaism as a religion. Yet I have
come to believe that Jewish experience has profoundly shaped the evolution of feminist thinking in
our times. Still, even now the vexed relationship
between Judaism and feminism seems to mean that

the pleasure I and many of my contemporaries can receive from our heritage will always be mixed with sorrow, the pride with grief, the joy with anger, sweetness with bitterness, honey on the tongue with tears in the eyes.

The First Seder

The first time I put together a seder of my own must have been in the late seventies or early eighties, because the girls were quite young. Figuring time the way parents do, say 1980 and that would mean Simone was three, Molly seven. Why would an assimilated nonbeliever attempt this kind of event? Perhaps it was related to the fact that as Jews we were such a tiny minority in our midwestern college town that I had to explain Chanukah at all the daycare centers and elementary schools my children attended, getting *dreidels* through the mail from my mother in New York and handing around jelly beans for the bets. Maybe it was because the little one, Simone, wanted to grow up and become not Christian but, in her own language, "Christmas." Or that the older, Molly, had insisted on enrolling in Sunday school at the only synagogue in town, a conservative *shul* where she learned all about customs never practiced at home. Could the motivation have come from a rebellious determination to resist conforming to an overwhelmingly *goyische* society, to affirm family roots? If so, the nostalgia was a fictive one for what had never been. Neither my husband nor I came from religiously observant families.

Yet there we sat, a jar of Manischevitz gefilte fish in the refrigerator, matzoh-ball soup simmering on the stove, chicken roasting in the oven, red wine and grape juice on the table, and a copy of the Maxwell House *Passover Haggadah*, deluxe edition, at each place setting.[1] Of course, I had participated in other seders: in my Brooklyn childhood, just a particularly good meal with *matzoh* passed around the table along with rye bread; during City College days, with Israelis who smoked, drank, and argued politics throughout the prayers; in graduate school, with Orthodox friends whose rigorous adherence to Hebrew made the whole event incomprehensible to me. But at this seder, I was reading with skills related to my new-found involvement in feminist criticism. Sandra Gilbert and I had just published *The Madwoman in the Attic*; we were beginning to think about the possibility of a sequel, examining the achievements of women writers in the twentieth century; and, because we had collaborated successfully on selecting the essays for another book, *Shakespeare's Sisters*, we were also deciding to continue working together as editors, though the idea of compiling a *Norton Anthology of Literature by Women* would not arrive till the next year. What did it mean to interpret the *Haggadah* by taking on the role Judith Fetterley had just called that of "the resisting reader"? Not merely a confirmation of my earlier estrangement from Judaism, this experience actually fueled more anger than I had thought possible, given my noninvolvement, my life as a Jewish non-Jew.[2] Sandra and I had begun *The Madwoman* with a discussion of the interrelatedness of ideas about authority and masculinity in the history of Western culture, and the *Haggadah* seemed to dramatize the spiritual, social, ethical, and political repercussions of that connection. The God of Maxwell House was a "King of the Universe," "our Father" (34), "the Ruler in His kingdom" (52), blessed be "He," who witnesses and then punishes the pharaoh's cruel decree. The Egyptian tyrant had commanded that "Every son that is born ye shall cast into the river, and every daughter ye shall save alive" (17). Was the God of the Jews enraged by the death sentence against the boy babies or the survival rate of the girls? The text leaves itself open to such a scandalous question not only because its God is presented in terms of male domination but also because His followers in the Bible, His interpreters in the past, and His celebrants in the present function together as an exclusive men's club.

Thus, the Maxwell House God's anger causes him to "smite every firstborn in the land of Egypt, both man and beast," as he vindictively demonstrates his superiority to all other gods: "on all the gods of Egypt I will execute judgment I, the Eternal" (17). With "a strong hand" and "an outstretched arm," this God takes revenge out of regard for his covenant with Abraham, Isaac, and Jacob, for he is "our God, and the God of our fathers" (45). His ancient interpreters include only the male of the species: the wise Rabbis Eliezer, Joshua, Elazar, Akeebah, and Tarphon. And His newly inducted followers—whose four questions the seder leader must answer—consist of the "wise son," the "wicked son," and the "simple son," along with "him who hath no capacity to inquire." Male god language, the preservation of an exclusively male genealogy both in the Bible and in its interpretive community, and the assumption that normative Jewish presence in the present time is masculine: How could these surprise me? Yet they took on new meaning unfolding before the eyes and ears of my girls because this *Haggadah* metaphorically casts every daughter into the river, even as it saves alive the sons and their lineage as the only liturgical and historical Jewish reality.

The authority of that reality seemed grounded not only in assumptions of male superiority but also of Jewish—and only Jewish—righteousness. I was dismayed watching Molly and Simone dip their fingers in their cups to sprinkle grape juice on their plates as they lustily shouted out the ten plagues visited on the Egyptians: "blood, vermin, murrain, hail, darkness, frogs, flies, boils, locusts, and the slaying of the first-born." We had an Egyptian friend; the plagues, followed by the drowning of the Egyptians in the Red Sea, seemed a bit grisly or ghoulish, sort of like overkill. What if the idea of the Jews as a chosen people was as vexed as the idea of masculinity as a chosen gender? Was chosenness a form of self-righteousness? of sanctimoniousness? an ideology of racial or ethnic superiority? If the Maxwell House *Haggadah* was right, more-over, God "brought us forth from" bondage "that He might give us the land which He swore unto our ancestors" (25). We were supposed to exclaim, "The following Year Grant Us To Be In Jerusalem" (53). "Grant Us to Be In"—not felicitous phrasing. In any case, though, did teaching the kids about Jewish ceremonies necessarily induct them into a Zionism I had always questioned? The same year as our seder, some thirteen years after Israel's occupation of the Sinai Peninsula, the Golan Heights, the West Bank, East Jerusalem, and the Gaza Strip, the Copenhagen International Women's Conference served as the setting for a diatribe delivered by the PLO representative, Leila Khaled. To the consternation of many Jews on all sides of the Zionist issue, Khaled highlighted the injustices suffered by Arab refugees, heralding the idea—tragically illuminated two years later during the invasion of Lebanon and the massacres at Sabra and Shatila—that the Palestinians were the Jews of the Middle East.[3]

MA NISH-TA-NAW HA-LAI-LAW HAZEH MEEKAWL HA-LAY-LOS? (Why is this night different from all other nights?) Indeed, why is this God, this religion, this version of the past different from all other patriarchal cultural constructs? After the gefilte fish, the matzoh-ball soup, and the roast chicken, with some snickering the adults sitting around the table agreed not to read aloud the line "Gentlemen, let us say Grace." After opening the door for Elijah, we refused to ask God to "Pour out thy wrath upon the heathen who will not acknowledge thee. . . . Pursue them in wrath and destroy them" (38). Enough is enough, I thought, so we all sang *"Dayenu"* while the kids found the hidden piece of *matzoh*, the *afikomen*, using it to mop up the remaining *charoset*.

Although at the time I did not know it, my personal anger at this particular seder resembled the responses of a generation of women writing during the seventies, eighties, and now in the nineties, feminists reacting to gender asymmetries in the legal, liturgical, and spiritual traditions of Judaism. From Rachel Adler and Cynthia Ozick to Judith Plaskow, Jewish women have explored their bitterness about their secondariness in their own heritage. In "The Jew Who Wasn't There: *Halakhah* and the Jewish Woman" (1973), Adler documented the ways in which women are categorized with children and slaves in Jewish law—excluded from the *minyan* (the community of prayer) and exempt from the commandments that shape the Jewish man's life (praying, hearing the *shofar* [horn] at the New Year, wearing such sacred symbols as *tallitot* and *tefillin*)—leading her readers to wonder, "Are women Jews?" In "Notes toward Finding the Right Question" (1979), Ozick admitted with some pain that "My own synagogue is the only place in the world where I am not named Jew" (125), attributing the problem to the Torah itself:

> The relation of Torah to women calls Torah itself into question. Where is the missing Commandment that sits in judgment on the world? Where is the Commandment that will say, from the beginning of history until now, *Thou shalt not lessen the humanity of women?* (150)

More recently and most extensively, in *Standing Again At Sinai* (1990) Judith Plaskow has confronted the ways in which "The central Jewish categories of Torah, Israel, and God all are constructed from male perspectives," only to find herself wondering "What can we claim that has not also wounded us?" (3, 1).

Countless other scholars have analyzed particularly vexed areas of Judaism for women, but I did not read them.[4] By an accident of birth, I was a Jewish feminist, but by virtue of that very fact I could not conceive of becoming a feminist Jew, a label that would have struck me as a contradiction in terms. In the catalogue of quintessentially misogynist sayings listed under "Know Your Enemy" in Robin Morgan's *Sisterhood Is Powerful*, I underlined the daily orthodox prayer: "I thank thee, O Lord, that thou hast not created me a woman" (31). As a literary critic supplied with at least a cursory biblical background, I understood how difficult it is to reclaim what has wounded the imagination. The linking of the covenant between God and Abraham with circumcision (Gen. 17:10); the maxim that a woman who bears a male child is unclean for seven days, while she who bears a female baby remains contaminated for two weeks (Lev. 12:2–5); the law "Do not lie with a male as one lies with a woman; it is an abhorrence" (Lev. 18:22)—how hilarious this sounds if we suppose it to be meant for a female reader; the punishment allotted a man raping a virgin, which consists of a fine paid to her father and the rapist having to marry the woman without the right to divorce her (Deut. 22:28–29): How could the Torah seem like anything but an anachronistic, wounding *patrius sermo?*

In these same years, the essayists and scholars I did read—Adrienne Rich and Carolyn Heilbrun, Florence Howe and Annette Kolodny, Alicia Ostriker and Nancy K. Miller—wrote about androgyny, marginality, and maternity; about women's experience and metaphors of the feminine in the works of American colonists, British poets, and French psychoanalysts. Like me, they examined many different aspects of what we were beginning to call the cultural construction of femininity, a virtual cornucopia of femininities except, oddly enough, the one manifest in the quite startling fact that so many of our peers in this undertaking were Jewish.[5] Why did the enormous energies of feminist critics derive so frequently from Jewish women who sometimes explicitly, sometimes implicitly denied their Jewishness or its impact on their feminism? Did my own sense of alienation and anger reflect the feelings of the others, feelings that might explain these silences-even-in-the-midst-of-speech? Throughout this period of time, my collaborator was composing a series of eloquent, evocative poems and essays about being an Italian-American, but even that didn't inspire any comparable undertaking by me or my cohorts.[6]

Indeed, some time ago, on setting out to draft this essay I felt so unnerved that I decided not only to engage in the usual background reading, in this case looking for recent meditations by feminist critics on the relationship between their Jewishness and their feminism, but also to raise the subject directly by surveying a number of my contemporaries, knowing full well how very different—in degrees of Orthodoxy, geographical origins, attitudes toward assimilation and native languages, as well as economically—our backgrounds were bound to be.[7] Curiously, both publicly in print and privately in correspondence, many expressed a sense of estrangement not unlike my own.

Writing retrospectively about her sense of herself amid a tumultuous feminist movement that throughout its beginnings "claimed universality," Adrienne Rich explained in her essay "Split at the Root" that she "saw Judaism, simply, as yet another strand of patriarchy; if asked to choose I might have said (as my father had said in other language): *I am a woman, not a Jew*" (89). Carolyn Heilbrun, also invoking her parents' severing of their roots, found that "being Jewish was for me altogether unreal" (*RW* 23).[8] Like Rich and Heilbrun, many feminist critics came from assimilationist and highly secular Jewish backgrounds: Elizabeth Abel describes her family's household as "vehemently atheistic," while Rachel Blau DuPlessis remembers being brought up as "an explicit secular humanist (in the Ethical Culture Movement)." Indeed, Judith Gardiner and Nina Auerbach depict the religion of their girlhoods not as traditional Judaism but, in Auerbach's phrase, "its New York offshoot, Freudianism."[9]

Rich's title "Split at the Root," then, may refer explicitly to her sense of herself as "neither Gentile nor Jew" because born of an interfaith marriage, but implicitly it describes many other women's sense of estrangement, ignorance, and indignation about a Jewishness in early life shared but often denied, derided, or diluted by parents or at a later time split off in antagonism from feminist aspirations. Thus, one anonymous respondent to my queries confides that, though her identity and ideals are "very specifically those of a firmly secular, highly assimilated person of Jewish-diaspora descent," these same identity and ideals depend "on an intimate loathing of Judaism as a religion." For her, the "unthinkability" of this "too unstructurable and ungroundable set of issues . . . feels like the very Abject." In a fascinating analysis of the ways in which her Jewishness has also "always been defined through contradictions," Annette Kolodny recalls her grandfather taking her to an Orthodox synagogue on High Holy Days, at the same time teaching her that "religion was the opiate of the masses": "It wasn't until I was in my teens," Kolodny wryly admits, "that I realized the statement . . . wasn't an original insight of my grandfather's."

Significantly, Kolodny and her beloved grandfather stopped going to temple when she reached puberty and would have been segregated from the men in an upstairs women's section of the synagogue: "We rejected my rejection, together," she writes. Less fortunate in this respect, Florence Howe—recalling her childhood education in Hebrew and Yiddish from a "*Zaida*" who feared he was "wasting" his time on a girl—summarized "the lesson that orthodox Jewry had taught me": "there are rewards for good women students, but to get them they must keep their place. Education prepares women well for submission or stupidity" (255–56). Just as ambivalent about Judaism as Kolodny and Howe, Alicia Ostriker, who terms her grandparents, her parents, and herself "socialist Jews" and "atheists," begins a meditation entitled "Entering the Tents" with the sentence "I am and am not a Jew" and later in it elaborates:

> to Judaism I am marginal. Am woman, unclean. Am Eve. Or worse, am Lilith. Am illiterate. Not mine the arguments of Talmud, not mine the centuries of ecstatic study, the questions and answers twining minutely like vines around the living Word, not mine the Kabala, the letters of the Hebrew alphabet dancing as if they were attributes of God. These texts, like the Law and the Prophets, are not-me. (542)

Published in 1989, this piece would have been inconceivable earlier when she was working on *Writing Like a Woman* and *Stealing the Language: The Emergence of Women's Poetry in America*, paradoxically at least in part because the problem it addresses (women's marginality in Judaism) had made Judaism seem marginal to Ostriker's feminism.

Similarly, when Sandra Gilbert and I found in Lilith the prototypical madwoman in the attic, I remained almost willfully ignorant of any connection that might have existed between our ideas and those that began appearing in *Lilith: The Jewish Women's Magazine*. Like the rebel Lilith, defiantly inhabiting a liminal zone outside the Jewish community, and like the disobedient, stiff-necked Jews who had escaped Egyptian pursuit only to find themselves in the wilderness unable to drink the bitter waters, many scholars in the so-called second wave of feminism felt themselves embittered, hopeless about receiving spiritual sustenance suited to our desires. In our revulsion toward "the terrible past" and "in the bitterness of youth," we could only forget, deny, distance ourselves from our Jewish backgrounds; yet, as Adrienne Rich intimated in one of her poems about being split at the root, for some there may have been an awareness even then that such denial was an aspect of "the task of being ourselves," a responsibility that would eventually require or enable us to heed her prayer: "May the taste of honey linger / Under the bitterest tongue" (*FD* 190).

The Second Seder

By the mid-eighties, my family and friends sat down to the seder with a mimeographed, revised *Haggadah* at each place setting and with *kepot* (no longer called *yarmulkes*) available for female as well as male heads. Actually, I was far too dispirited to create such a liturgy. We owed it to our Catholic friend, Mary Jo Weaver, who was wrestling with her own recalcitrant tradition and who had adopted the girls as her honorary nieces, thereby rather bizarrely taking responsibility for their further induction into their own heritage. Say it was 1986: Molly, getting ready for her *bat mitzvah*, had searched through the Torah for a nonsexist portion and was learning to read her passage in Hebrew, although the visiting student Rabbi had refused to change gender-specific pronouns in the translation, prohibited Mary Jo from participating in the service, and discouraged Simone from performing a cello solo at the service; *Shabbat* was a day of rest, and no amount of argument would persuade him that music was played, not worked. The youngest child and therefore the one who was supposed to ask the four questions, Simone had found some time earlier that her most disturbing questions—whether people could be counted on to die in their birth order, whether they could find each other after death—remained unanswered at temple, so she overslept most Sundays and now scornfully let her older sister recite her part.

Many photocopied *Haggaddot* like ours exist, and quite a few have been privately circulated or published.[10] They celebrate the *Kiddish* and the Washing of the Hands by calling on *Shekhinah*—the female aspect of divinity—as a "Presence, Source of Life." The four questions are asked by daughters now, not sons. The story of the liberation from Egypt includes legends about the prophecies of Miriam, the savior of Moses, as well as accounts of the heroism of the two midwives, Shiphrah and Puah, both of whom refused to obey Pharaoh's command to kill male babies, and of the Pharaoh's daughter, who circumvented her father's law by adopting Moses. We named the plagues in sorrow over the pain that exists in the world, sprinkling wine on our plates to diminish Egyptian suffering, and consecrated sips from our cups to those strangers in many lands who suffer the grief of oppression. "This year we are slaves," all at the table proclaimed at the blessing of the *matzoh*, "But next year we shall be free women and men." We opened the door for Miriam and filled a cup of wine in her name to commemorate the joyous dance with tambourines she performed in the desert with other women. When we made the bittersweet Hillel sandwich with *maror* and *charoset*, we recalled that Hillel had asked, "If I am not for myself, who will be for me? And if I am only for myself, what am I? And if not now, when?"

What did it mean to read the Passover story in relation to the injunction "In every generation it is the duty of each woman to consider herself as if she had come forth from Egypt"? My Sabbath *goy*, my *schiksa* friend, had reproduced from a feminist *Haggadah* a passage entitled "Remembering" about *Pesach* in 5703 (1943 C.E.) when the uprising of the Warsaw Ghetto began. "Blessed is the heart with strength to stop its beating for honor's sake": a poem by Hannah Senesh, a resistance fighter, was accompanied by an account of her tragic dilemma. Her mother would be killed by the Nazis if Hannah did not reveal the names of other members in the movement, but Hannah knew she could not betray the resistance. Her mother replied that by not informing, Hannah proved her love. Though seated at the head of the table (I was supposed to be in charge), I found my eyes filling with tears, unable to read the words on the page. "If I am not for myself, who will be for me? But if I am for myself only, what am I? And if not now, when?"

My husband's family was from Russia and Poland, mine from Germany. We are both first-generation Americans, but his parents had arrived right after World War I, while mine had miraculously come forth on the brink of the second, only some five decades ago, just a few years before my birth. In fact, my mother's father was drafted as a doctor in the Great War on the German side—I had a photo of him in uniform and on horseback to prove it— and during the Depression my father had recited the poetry of Heine to himself when he was sent with bushels of money to buy an apple at the market in Hamburg. Only later did those who were able to leave disperse: to Israel, to England, to Central and South America, to New York. "*Das einzige amerikanische Kind*," the only American-born child, I was not to dwell on these uncertainties. Instead, I was supposed to be happy, have fun, live the normal life the others had abandoned, remain mystified by the German spoken only when the kids were not meant to understand. Along with German culture and their history and their property and most of all the community of each other, the immigrants in my family relinquished what little faith they had. "*Quatsch*," my father would call Judaism. Rot. Nonsense. Yet my mother had seen to it that her German- and her American-born children received at least a minimal education in a Reform congregation so we would "know what it means to be Jewish."

They were not exactly "survivors" because they had not been incarcerated in the concentration camps. Yet like many survivors, my parents and the tiny circle of relatives in our vicinity would never again be the people they had been.[11] First hiring herself out as a maid and then keeping house and sewing gloves until midnight to sell to visiting customers and neighborhood stores, my mother mourned her youthful ambitions for college in Nuremberg. Hammering out dents in the fenders of cars, my father never worked less then nine hours a day, six days a week, haunted by the deaths of the parents he had left behind, his abrupt descent into the working class, his inability to attain in English the fluency he had enjoyed in *Hochdeutsch*.

The atmosphere of dread and humiliation, of grueling work and social isolation, made itself palpable on their hands—in the dark, dead callus from a crochet hook in my mother's palm; in the tenacious dirt beneath my father's scrubbed fingernails. "*Alt und arm und krank und Jude, ein vierfach Elend!*"— a variant of Heine's line, the source of the inscription on the Jewish hospital in Hamburg where my brother had been born, became their self-mocking motto: "old and poor and sick and Jewish, a four-fold misery."[12] During the McCarthy hearings, my parents intently watched the television screen to see if "it" would happen again, but the fragmentary, allusive stories they rarely recounted to my brother and me left us mystified about what had actually happened to grandparents, aunts, uncles, and cousins. We were our parents' hope, just as they had been their family's and Molly and Simone were mine. Yet, as Emil Fackenheim, a scholar of the Holocaust, has put it, "a resurrected hope is not like a hope that never died" (69).

When the murder of Jews became national policy in the homeland of Bach, Beethoven, and Brahms, when the "Aryan"/"non-Aryan" polarity organized a great divide into which all Jews were to be thrown and, dead or alive, buried, many people besides my father believed themselves to be witnessing what Martin Buber called the "eclipse of the light of heaven, eclipse of God" (23). But for my parents, as for many other highly assimilated European Jews, a shattered faith in a religion that had never really shaped their imaginative or practical lives was itself eclipsed by a shattered faith in virtually any social group or political party or economic coalition or geographic assembly or national identity. What trust they had left they placed in relatives and close friends, personal ties that had provided the tenuous, fragile umbilical cord to a new world which they inhabited warily. Reading from the feminist *Haggadah* about the egg, hard-boiled to signify how an oppressed people harden (their resolve? their hands? their hearts?) under slavery, I began to decipher in my own commitment to feminism a response if not to Judaism then to Jewish experience that turned out also to inform the feminist criticism of many contemporaries. While we had documented the influence of Civil Rights on the women's liberation movement, we never understood the impact of our own past. Despite the antagonisms between Judaism and the women's movement, Jewish history furnished a leavening for the second wave of American feminism, especially in the academy.

Clearly, those of us who grew up Jewish during the postwar years inherited a distrust of public authority and a reliance on private bonds that anticipate the feminist imperative to interrogate (male) institutions of authority and to valorize (feminine) networks of reciprocity. Just as important, we had been served up a monitory lesson about conformity and acquiescence: living through debates over the immorality of "blaming the victim," some of us nevertheless harbored suspicions about a generation of adults blind to the writing on the wall because of their belief that they had integrated successfully into mainstream European culture. These were suspicions that I, for one, was discouraged from expressing, but they nevertheless persisted. Why hadn't our parents left earlier, organized more effectively, saved their families? Or if they had to remain in Europe, why did their survival depend on risky evasions, tenuous lies, grievous sacrifices?

Typical of the children hidden from the Nazis, Susan Suleiman, provided with false papers, a false name, and a false faith during her escape from occupied Budapest, attributes to her wartime "adventure" a lapse in memory and a reconceptualization of history: after the time spent hiding out in the countryside, "I could not remember my name," she explains, and she began to think "of history as a form of luck."[13] Typical of the children brought up by parents who fled Europe, Naomi Schor finds her Jewishness "bound up with the Holocaust": "when I was a teenager I thought I was Anne Frank," she explains; "Her diary probably had a more profound impact on me and my sense as a subject of writing (as well as history) than any other book I read during adolescence." Typical of the children brought up by American-born parents, Andrea Dworkin recalls "the first time" the "earth moved" for her when, at ten years of age, she visited a "shaking, crying, screaming, vomiting" cousin caught in the vise of a terrible anniversary, the month "her youngest sister had been killed in front of her, another sister's infant had died a terrible death, their heads had been shaved . . ." (*OB* 5). In multiple ways, what our Jewish backgrounds foregrounded was the problematics of hyphenated identities—German-Jewish, Polish-Jewish, Hungarian-Jewish—or, to put it another way, the dangers of difference. Repositories of Otherness, Jews in European history had been forced to dramatize for the entire world the deathly double bind of integration and separatism when played out within a hostile dominant culture, the stranglehold of anti-Semitic stereotyping that could not fail to produce hatred as well as self-hatred.

Of course, precisely the category of alterity and the consequences of its attendant stereotypes form the basis for feminist investigations of women's situations in male-dominated societies. Beginning with an analysis of woman as Other, two stages in feminist literary criticism developed to examine, first, the ways in which misogyny generates disabling engendered images that operate to silence, marginalize, or demean women and, second, the strategies by which female aesthetic traditions provide unique tropes to empower women's efforts to escape a secondary, subordinated, or self-subverting position. More recently, in a logically inevitable phase inaugurated by postmodernist theorists as well as by scholars of African-American and Gay Studies, both the "ghettoization" of women's worlds or works and the "universalizing" of generalizations about them have become suspect, for such critical moves could re-state debilitating stereotypes or might naively discount differences among women or could underplay the significance of the interactions of men and women in a particular historical, aesthetic, or ethnic context. Even in this third stage, however, the project has continued to depend on refuting what Elaine Showalter has defined as the prefeminist "assimilationist" position taken by women writers, namely the view that their achievements—being "as good" as those produced by men—should be judged as qualitatively no different from those created by men (*FLT* 350, 359).

Both the category of "Other" and the repudiation of "assimilation" depended on insights not only achieved directly after the Second World War but also framed in the context of the history of anti-Semitism. Simone de Beauvoir's *The Second Sex* (1949), which introduced the crucial notion of female alterity, negotiated between, on the one hand, her assertion that "The biological and social sciences no longer admit the existence of unchangeably fixed entities that determine given characteristics, such as those ascribed to woman, the Jew, or the Negro" and, on the other, her belief that "To decline to accept such notions as the eternal feminine, the black soul, the Jewish character, is not to deny that Jews, Negroes, women exist today—this denial does not represent a liberation for those concerned, but rather a flight from reality" (xiv).[14] Even more pointedly, Betty Friedan's *The Feminine Mystique* (1963) relied on a comparison between the housewife in the home and the prisoner in a concentration camp: in a chapter that alludes to Bruno Bettelheim's work on the "zombies" who inhabited Nazi camps, Friedan argued that "The comfortable concentration camp that American women have walked into, or have been talked into by others, is . . . a frame of reference that denies woman's adult human identity" (308).

Similarly, exploring Hitler's assertion in his 1934 Nuremberg speech that "woman's emancipation is a message discovered solely by the Jewish intellect," in *Sexual Politics* (1969) Kate Millett argued that "As in the case of the Jews (why persecute your finest talents?) the Nazi method with [gentile] women was hardly practical"; she therefore interpreted sexual politics as an ideology that shapes all psychological and emotional facets of existence, rather than an isolatable political or economic phenomenon (223, 221). No wonder, then, that Naomi Weisstein's 1969 touchstone essay elaborating the ways in which "psychology constructs the female" was originally titled "'Kinder, Kueche, Kirche' As Scientific Law" (207). As disturbing as the metaphorical conflation of woman and Jew has become for Holocaust historians, it continued to play a crucial role in the influential poetry of Sylvia Plath, whose ferocious curses against "Herr God, Herr Lucifer" and the man

with "a Meinkampf look" were articulated by means of her adoption of a
Jewish mask that bespoke a sense of herself as a displaced, doomed victim
(246, 224).

Behind the project of many feminist critics, propelling or motivating it,
resides a distrust in official authority that can sometimes be traced back bio-
graphically to Jewish roots. Explaining her personal suspicions inside and
outside the academy, Annette Kolodny remarks, "Somewhere lurking in my
responses to everyone I meet is the unarticulated question, 'Would you hide
me?' " According to Nina Auerbach, "the Holocaust and the blacklist were
twin specters" of a youth in which she "grew up mistrusting society in general. . . . Official authority has always looked stupid and menacing. . . . I associate this sense of exile, mistrust, and damn-the-consequences pride in
integrity with Judaism." Jane Gallop believes that Jewishness bequeathed "a
'negative' identity" of being "set apart from a larger culture." Her sense of
herself as "an internal alien within American (Christian) culture"—"being
proudly not-Christian"—has "analogies in my theoretical positions and in
my implicit definition of woman as proudly not a man." Naming this sense of
being set apart "productive alienation," Judith Frank explains that her own
estrangement from Judaism does not stop her from feeling in certain spaces
like Woody Allen in *Annie Hall* when he imagines himself as a hasid at the
dinner table of Annie's aggressively Gentile family.[15]

None of the critics I have mentioned presents herself professionally as
representing a Jewish community, and not a few would (and have) disclaimed
the association entirely.[16] Lillian Robinson, for example, came from a "free-
thinking" family whose "lexicon in the matter of the Jewish religion ran the
gamut from 'fanatic' . . . to 'hypocrite.' " Yet this "free-thinking tradition"
trained her "to treat the very idea of a sacred text skeptically, which is a pretty
good beginning for someone seeking to expand and enrich the literary canon."
Similarly, Nancy K. Miller admits that she does "not always want to speak 'as a
Jew' "; however, she concedes that "being both Jewish and a feminist is a crucial, even constitutive piece of my self-consciousness as a writer" (*GP* 97). Privately, she has explained that in her New York childhood "Most everyone I
knew was Jewish and yet the world seemed divided into who was and wasn't.
(Perhaps this crucial division of the world into two was what predisposed me
both to feminism and to structuralism)."

Miller's reference to structuralism, as well as her sense that "Most everyone I knew was Jewish," should remind us of the general influx of Jews into
American, English, and Comparative Literature during the postwar years. Like

Leslie Fiedler and George Steiner, Jacques Derrida and Geoffrey Hartman, some of these contemporary scholars are religiously observant or flauntingly ethnic, while others are self-confessed "terminal Jews," to use Fiedler's phrase for those with whom Jewish tradition dead-ends (179). Clearly sharing a devotion to the book, which may have been fostered by a religion based on reading, interpreting, blessing, kissing, and parading classical Jewish texts, as well as an absorption with what Steiner calls "the unhousing" of language (3–11), many have extrapolated a career in letters from their own complex relationship to, say, German or Hebrew or Yiddish or Ladino or, for that matter, English. Obviously, too, the orientation toward education in Jewish culture also brought many Jews into the academy.

For Jewish daughters during the postwar years, teaching in the humanities became a viable means of advancement into the American middle class since training in medicine, science, and law was generally assumed to be the prerogative of their brothers. For Jewish daughters of Eastern European background, a division of labor that defined men's spiritual role as intellectual and women's secular job as providing the material conditions to make men's holy work possible helps contextualize a paradox that may have shaped the evolution of a generation of feminist scholars: on the one hand, the strength and success of Jewish female immigrants—mothers and grandmothers— and, on the other, their exclusion from the intellectual fruits of their labor.

For many feminist critics, moreover, Jewish devotion to the text and to education has been supplemented by the equally long history in Judaism of a strong commitment to each individual's social responsibility. Indeed, precisely what Judith Kegan Gardiner considers the "habit" of "fighting for social justice," what Rachel Brownstein refers to as being "by definition and by blood on the side of the oppressed," reflects the ethical teachings of Judaism that insist upon personal responsibility for acting justly in this world. Annette Kolodny therefore attributes her own "powerful sense of wanting to live in a just universe," as well as her "passionate moral outrage at *in*justice," to Judaism. Similarly, Elizabeth Abel, considering a Jewish inheritance "deeply intertwined with the labor movement," sees her own feminism as "in part the extension of a political perspective that had to do less with thinking of myself as Jew than with thinking of myself as positioned by my (Jewish) heritage already on the left." Yet exactly such concern about political and social justice would underscore the exclusion of women from, in Ostriker's words, the "questions and answers twining minutely like vines around the living Word."

The jarring contradiction between women's liminality in Judaism and the lesson of, say, Passover—"You shall not oppress a stranger, for you know the feelings of the stranger, having yourselves been strangers in the land of Egypt" (Exodus 23:9)—may have spawned not only the feminist movement in Judaism but also feminism itself as well as feminist scholarship: not only the work of Adler, Ozick, and Plaskow, but also that of Bella Abzug, Shulamith Firestone, and Gloria Steinem as well as Blanche Wiesen Cook, Natalie Zemon Davis, Estelle Friedman, Linda Gordon, Linda Kerber, Ruth Rosen, etc.[17] Thus, according to Naomi Schor, though the "rush" to establish "ethnic credentials" after "years of assimilation" seems "spurious and opportunistic," a pattern of "working on the underdog (aesthetically), the victim," is "connect[ed] to being Jewish."

At the same time, these jostling terms—"credentials" and "assimilation," "victim" and "Jewish"—raise issues related to what Nancy K. Miller calls "the shifting line between the poignancy of self-representation and the didactics of representivity" (*GP* 95). Her insight reminds us that the tensions between Judaism and feminism result in an acute awareness of the interlocutionary setting within which language reverberates, the atmospheric change that accompanies the shift from "I am" to "You are" syntax. In the mid-eighties, two incidents jolted me into the realization that, regardless of any personal disavowals, others would embed me in the history I was only just beginning to comprehend. First, at a retreat for American and Continental feminists in upstate New York, a participant from Amsterdam turned to me and cheerfully, even benevolently, remarked, "Your type doesn't exist any more in Europe." Then, several years later, at a speaking engagement in London, an audience member waiting behind me in line at the drinking fountain commented with some astonishment, "I didn't know you weren't Caucasian." Despite Sandra Gilbert's subsequent and hilarious etymological riffs on the terms "type" and "Caucasian," we were both struck by how "You are" sentences inundate "I am" sentiments.

"Why did he call me a Keek?" Simone asked about a hostile paper boy. "He meant Kike," I explained, wondering again about what Miller calls "the didactics of representation." Or "How could she say that in front of me? 'Jew him down . . . I'll just Jew him down?' "—a phrase that clearly outraged Molly, used by a respected, devoted music teacher. In the absence of Jewish efforts at self-definition, would Jewish identity be shaped by prejudiced, non-Jewish stereotypes? Had I too quickly rejected as indulgently poignant a self-representation that might have seemed credentializing or indulgently poignant? If my earlier feminist reaction to the *Haggadah* involved me in worries about reclaiming what has wounded the imagination, now I wondered about the effects of disclaiming such traditions altogether.

Couldn't the idea of chosenness be interpreted as a safeguard, a warrant—complete with rights and responsibilities—for survival under hostile circumstances? Given the history of the Holocaust, how can one deny the need for a safe place for Jews, a refuge from the wilderness? What does it mean to suggest that Judaism is so constituted as to silence or marginalize women, when Jewish mothers and their children were criminalized and murdered as non-Aryans? And if Jewish feminists had been in the vanguard of deconstructing patriarchal authority, couldn't it be said that they did so precisely because they saw—stamped on the bodies and minds and spirits of their fathers—the disabling effect of marginalization, dislocation, and emasculation on men?

In her verse-sequence *Sources*, Adrienne Rich writes, "I saw the power and arrogance of the male as your true watermark; I did not see beneath it the suffering of the Jew" (9). But it may have been precisely the unnerving mixture of arrogance and suffering in Jewish history that enabled a generation of us to see a shadow of ourselves in the figure Sandra Gilbert and I have called the "no man." In our three-volume *No Man's Land: The Place of the Woman Writer in the Twentieth Century*, we focused on maimed, unmanned, victimized male characters created by modernist men of letters haunted by a dream of aesthetic potency. Perhaps I had seen in the Jewish "no-men" of the twentieth century the root of my bitterness but also, paradoxically abiding in a memory straining against the impulse to forget, the sweet anticipation of a hope resurrected.

The Third Seder

The third seder is always in the future, or so it seems to me. Yet, marking solidarity with the dead, it brings the past into the present. How odd that this time—the late eighties, the early nineties—has been transformed by the courageous tenacity of Jewish women more religious and, in some sense of the word, more conservative than anyone sitting around the dining room table.[18] A microcosm of sorts, Bloomington's congregation *Beth Shalom* (House of Peace) has a resident rabbi now, a feminist named Joan Friedman whose cantor, Deborah Gordon, serves as Simone's tutor for a *bat mitzvah* preceded by a Mozart trio and centered on her chanting of the Torah portion. Although Simone may harbor private doubts about death-order and death-loneliness, she has been attracted back to Judaism by the neat rankings of the degrees of *tzedakah* (charity) enumerated by Maimonides, a fitting conversion for a daughter of the commandments (a *bat mitzvah*). When Molly is called up after my mother to recite the blessings, to receive an *allyah*, and when Mary Jo appears on the *bema* to hold the scroll, we are looking at a community of women who have passed over the resentments of contradictions and tensions not so much through resolution or transcendence but by dwelling within them in a postmodernist collage that resembles nothing so much as the Jewish heritage itself. No doubt Passover, too, will become such a collection of competing, checkered, even incongruous rituals dedicated to loss in the past, renewal in the future.

Pointless to ask if we have adulterated the tradition to such an extent that we have lost touch with Jewish roots, for both the Passover meal and the *bat mitzvah* are paradoxically more conventional than the Reform equivalents with which I had grown up. Nevertheless, our participation—as well as this sort of writing about it—does pose problems related, at worst, to political correctness and, at best, to ethical insensitivity. Does a return to even a modified form of Judaism involve substituting the metaphysics of identity for the materiality of history and thereby capitulating to a faddish, retrograde identity politics, as Jenny Bourne has recently charged?: Has "What is to be done?" been replaced by "Who am I?" (1). In our efforts to examine the dynamics of anti-Semitism, have Jewish women been guilty of eliding the differences between our history of oppression and that of other peoples and in the process eclipsing the struggles of those others? Or, worse yet from some points of view, in our appreciation of the need for Israel as a Jewish refuge from anti-Semitism, have we ignored, again in Bourne's terms, "the exclusionist basis of Zionism and the racist practices of Israel"? (7). Both American and Israeli racism have been used recently to qualify the trajectory traced here, a progress admittedly eccentric and consciously meant as non-teleological, for many have traveled between its two poles in an opposite direction from mine and still others continue to oscillate between them.

To take the charge of American racism first, clearly all claims about parallel oppression threaten to involve Jews and women of color in a "competition of victimization" that can only trivialize the complexities posed by two quite distinct histories.[19] Indeed, any equation of anti-Semitism and the persecution of African Americans could be said to backfire against Jewish and African-American proponents, with the former committed to resisting analogies to the Holocaust that rob the event of its catastrophic singularity as a rupturing of civilization and the latter dedicated to redressing a grievous inheritance of slavery and colonialism that continues to deny black people economic, political, educational, and social equality. Yet such analogies have always haunted women's imaginations, dating back to the writings of Margaret Fuller and Olive Schreiner in the nineteenth century and forward to the crucial scholarly work on African-American culture done by such historians and literary critics as Gerda Lerner, Florence Howe, and Elizabeth Abel, many of whom resemble Lillian Robinson in her attributing a commitment to multiculturalism to an "awareness of the existence of anti-Semitism as a form of racism."[20] Elizabeth Abel, confronting the "problematic displacement of [her] Jewishness," describes a preference for dealing with other, more unambiguously virulent forms of racism than with . . . anti-Semitism." Rather than allowing our attempts to deal with our various backgrounds and allegiances to splinter the feminist movement, she tries to keep in focus the problems and ambiguities of cross-racial, cross-cultural identifications.

Has so-called "Holocaust blackmail"—the justification of Israeli actions on the basis of a history of genocide—led us to defend the indefensible sexism, homophobia, and imperialism of the Israeli government? Here one can only point to a chorus of voices—including those of Grace Paley, Evelyn Torton Beck, Elly Bulkin, Melanie Kaye/Kantrowitz, Irena Klepfisz, Letty Cottin Pogrebin, and many others publishing in the new *Bridges: A Journal for Jewish Feminists and Our Friends*—that addresses the necessity of distinguishing between the various populations of Israel and a government that too often speaks in the cadences of the Maxwell House God as well as the need of supporting Palestinian and Israeli peace activists whose efforts are dedicated to the proposition that military occupation cannot be countenanced as a safeguard against past or present anti-Semitism.[21] Although we Americans have been taught that only the Jews in Israel will suffer the consequences of a rash trust in Arab coalitions proven capable of terrorism or dedicated to the elimination of Jewry, we have also been admonished to accept our responsibilities to a homeland there for those of us in need. Since we are deeply implicated in Israeli policy, in the eyes of others and in our own eyes, what is to be done except to translate our personal efforts to negotiate between rivalrous commitments into an admittedly controversial politics of cooperation that respects differences, for anything else constitutes a diminishment or, as our own history shows us, a tragic loss. Yet, as Judith Gardiner points out, such a stance will "involve us in difficult controversies . . . with members of our own families and communities as well as with segments of Israeli opinion."

Writing about the loss of Jewish lives in her own time, Muriel Rukeyser mourned the double bind posed by European history:

> To be a Jew in the twentieth century
> Is to be offered a gift. If you refuse,
> Wishing to be invisible, you choose
> Death of the spirit, the stone insanity.
> Accepting, take full life. Full agonies:
> Your evening deep in labyrinthine blood
> Of those who resist, fail, and resist; and God
> Reduced to a hostage among hostages.   (239)

Poised between "death of the spirit, the stone insanity" and the "Full agonies" of "labyrinthine blood," throughout her life Rukeyser herself chose to associate with resistance, failure, and resistance again. Today, at least in part because of the existence of Israel, we Jews need not choose "the stone insanity," for like Moses wandering in the wilderness, we can find nourishment in the desert, suckling "honey from the rock."[22] Yet, unless we too align ourselves with those who resist, fail, and resist again, the gift will be poisoned by an "evening deep in labyrinthine blood" and by the bitterness of those to whom we deny full humanity, thereby dehumanizing ourselves.

Blood on the lintel, a signpost to stay destruction, the blood of a sacrificed lamb to save the blood of a child. Will the ceremonies of innocence at *Pesach* be drowned each year in a doomed sense of bad faith, inauthenticity, ignorance, and anger? Or will we continue to eat the bread of distress, hoping that—bitter with *maror*, sweet with *charoset*—it will speak to the bittersweet experience of those who have come to hunger for coexistence between feminism and Judaism, between women and men, between Jew and Gentile, between Palestinian and Israeli? When the hidden piece of *matzoh* is found by the child, and should the broken *afikomen* fit like a jigsaw puzzle piece into the other half of *matzoh* on the seder plate, could we almost taste a spring in which kindness endures forever? Or is the concealed *afikomen* called *tzafoon* (that which is hidden) because it always eludes us?

A Postscript

Although I have left this essay in the form it was originally published in 1994, it seemed appropriate to append a postscript after I was invited to attend a panel at Princeton University in the fall of 1998. Cosponsored by Women's Studies and Jewish Studies, chaired by Deborah Nord and Froma Zeitlin respectively, the event brought together speakers—Rachel Brownstein, Natalie Zemon Davis, Marianne Hirsch, Susan Suleiman, and me—who were asked to deliberate on our return to ethnic "sources" after careers built on scholarship that for the most part focused on non-Jewish subjects.

From Rachel Brownstein's discussion of the contemporary fiction of Allegra Goodman to Natalie Zemon Davis's confession that she always enjoyed setting out to "*épater les goyim,*" from Marianne Hirsch's analysis of family photographs and the Holocaust to Susan Suleiman's reading from her memoir about a childhood in wartorn Hungary, the presentations confirmed a growing dialectic between questions previously raised either in feminist or in Jewish Studies contexts. In my presentation, for instance, I mentioned my new interest in Holocaust poetry written in the English language, explaining that much of it was composed by women writers. Lively questions issued from the audience: Should Jewish feminists define themselves as white? Did Jewish feminists participate in the reinvention of *midrash?* Had we come to feminism as daughters, to Judaism as mothers, or vice versa? But for me, the most fascinating revolved around the issue of delay: Why had we waited so long to attend to our backgrounds? Had we been ashamed of being Jewish? Were we afraid of exposing ourselves as Jews?

The answers to these questions helped illuminate what the interplay between gender and Jewishness means in contemporary research. Somehow, it did not seem professionally appropriate (to many of us) to write about Judaism during the sixties and seventies. The humanities, as organized by its departments within higher education, appeared to require us to disentangle ourselves from our ethnic roots, to credentialize ourselves through national literatures and histories (French, English, American) often evolving in non-Jewish contexts. Perhaps some of us were drawn to history or literature precisely as a way of distancing ourselves from our immigrant ancestry, as part of an assimilation process. (Curiously, training in French seems to have allowed some scholars to negotiate between their Jewish but highly secular European families and their participation in American establishments of higher education.) In any case, gender analysis broke that rigid bifurcation between the professional and the personal first. Given Jewish paranoia (a perfectly realistic fear of anti-Semitism), perhaps we needed the security of tenure to venture work on ethnicity? Weren't we all afraid of dogs? Didn't the organizers worry that posters for Jewish programs would be desecrated? Wasn't it weird that our event was staged at Princeton—so recently all male, all WASP?!

For my part, I believe that the work done in African-American Studies set the ground for our return to Jewish Studies, just as James Baldwin's essays established the parameters for reconceptualizing the categories of black, white, and Jew.[23] After black scholars convinced feminist thinkers about the importance of race, identity politics provided a vocabulary for Jewish women to take seriously their own hyphenated identities, to speak "as" Jewish-American women. Yet because Jewishness is such a disputed term—a diverse spectrum of experiences, beliefs, and customs—such an identity remained quite porous. Faith in God; orthodox or reform, conservative or reconstructionist liturgical approaches to spiritual matters; a mystical tradition; Zionist history; venues of social activism; the languages of Yiddish or Hebrew; types of cooking practiced in the Catskills or in Tel Aviv; just jokes: what Judaism signified varied greatly from individual to individual. For the most secular of us, ignorance of our Jewish heritage impeded our ability to reflect on the interaction between feminism and religion. At the same time, since many Jewish-American feminists had been viewed as whites by African-American critics, we experienced a curious jostling of sometimes chosen, sometimes conferred subject positions. In addition, as feminists we could not be unaware of the hostility that greeted gender investigations in Jewish Studies programs established and populated almost overwhelmingly by unsupportive or just uninterested men. No wonder that many of us continue to find it a challenge to make gender and Jewishness work together as balanced or alternating methodological lenses.

5

The Graying of Professor Erma Bombeck

*The female complaint serves in particular to mediate and
manage the social contradictions that arise from women's . . .
allegiance to a phallocentric ideology that has, in practice,
denied women power, privilege, and presence in the public
and private spheres. To the extent that women employ the
complaint as a mode of self-expression, it is an admission and
a recognition both of privilege and powerlessness[.]*
—Lauren Berlant, *"The Female Complaint"*

Quite a bit has changed at Indiana University's English department since the moment in 1973 when I first
arrived at the office to get my teaching assignment,
only to be hailed by a senior professor who asked me
to type his syllabus on a stencil. That I was promptly
invited to teas held by and for the wives, where we
discussed their husbands and my colleagues, added
proof positive to the professoriate's masculine gender. Any wonder that the women's bathroom had a
urinal in one of its two stalls? Now on the brink of
the year 2000 the department's twenty female professors constitute a sizeable proportion of the population. Appointed in the fall of 1983, our first female
chair made her earliest action a renovation of the
restroom facilities.[1]

A phenomenon related to the "dramatic gains"
women made at the Ph.D. and the assistant-professor
levels during the seventies and eighties (Huber 59–60),

one that may have surfaced in your department as well, involves the emergence in the nineties of a band of new faculty affectionately called "The Young People," a very disparate, sometimes desperate amalgam of individuals with little in common except the quite startling fact that they—in the infinite variety of their sexualities, ethnicities, costumes, dietary restrictions, tattoos, piercings, and spiritualities—came more recently to the profession than I did. OK, all right, they are *younger*. And if *they* are "The Young People," what is left for me except to become (please pardon the expression) an "Old Boy"? Since the man who mistook me for a secretary is dead, am I destined to replace him? Being in the middle—not being one of "The Young People" but not wanting to become "An Old Boy"—plummets me and many women of my generation not only into depression but also into the dilemma of escalating demands on our time. For while "The Young People" need to be freed up to do research so as to insure their ability to get tenure, "The Old Boys" resist investing in a future not their own. Meanwhile, in institutions unlike Indiana (where we capitalize on grotesquely underpaid graduate assistants), members of a third, growing group composed of exploited adjuncts—paid a measly pittance for each course taught, sometimes at several institutions—confront such frazzling work conditions that they cannot possibly be asked to do more by way of helping to keep the institution running (Uchmanowicz).[2]

Although all mid-career, tenure-track faculty are supposed to assist in the management of the institution, what happens when every departmental, college, or university committee wants and needs a representative woman, especially a woman of color or a white woman with tenure—though for the most part such people remain scarce in comparison to their male peers (De Palma 11, McKay "NP" 363)?[3] Since all lecture platforms, regional conferences, and fellowship advisory boards should display their commitment to cultural diversity and the democratization of higher education, a senior African-, Asian-, Chicano-, Native-, or Euro-American woman active in feminism may become a target of opportunity, sought out precisely for her consciousness about the importance of her visibility in such venues. So, if chairs and deans tend to "overutilize" those of us who "continue to be disproportionately underrepresented in the senior ranks across all fields and disciplines," as Annette Kolodny demonstrates (86, 84), how can *we* manage to slough off *our* responsibilities? Because, in order for us to survive and fashion a niche distinct from that framed by the Old Boys, who rarely claimed us as their own, we will need to discard some of the conflicting demands made on our time. In particular, those of us trying to juggle professional and personal commitments may find it especially difficult to seize the day and make it work for (rather than against) the mainte-nance of some modicum of serenity in our lives.

"Is man's time more valuable than woman's?" Florence Nightingale asked in 1859, by which she meant "Is man's time [considered] more valuable than woman's?" Nightingale pointed out that "Women are never supposed to have any occupation of sufficient importance *not* to be interrupted" (839), and in 1929 Virginia Woolf concurred that "women's books should be short-er, more concentrated, than those of men, and framed so that they do not need long hours of study and uninterrupted work. *For interruptions there will always be*" (*RO* 78, emphasis mine). Tenured female professors today are expected to be able to interrupt research for teaching, teaching for service activities, and all those for various domestic exertions—cleaning, cooking, shopping, banking, nursing, rearing, aerobicizing, and (the most tiring of them all) bolstering—presumably with no cost to our health or welfare. Any wonder that responses to a 1986 questionnaire mailed out to almost three thousand women in the American Studies Association and the Organization of American Historians sounded like "outpourings of anxiety, frustration, and despair" (Coiner 203)? A decade later, those of us embroiled in relation-ships with aging parents, importunate partners, sick friends, and/or needy children may continue to find ourselves so frazzled as to be unable to tell whether the personal interrupts the professional or vice versa.

These work and family conflicts induce doubts about what professional-ization itself means—not only for us as individuals but also as collective partic-ipants in the feminist venture. For the large-scale entrance of female faculty into the humanities departments of colleges and universities since the seventies has brought exhilarating opportunities but also daunting contradictions gener-ated by the complex circumstances of our institutionalization: in particular, the unnerving paradox that women entered the professoriate in substantial num-bers at exactly the moment when the profession itself came under intense pres-sure to downsize.[4] I want to use my local grievances—about exorbitant tempo-ral demands issuing in later-career stress—to address what (in my epigraph) Lauren Berlant calls "the social contradictions that arise" from women's recent participation in organizations that have, for centuries, "denied women power, privilege, and presence" (243). Like the complaints Berlant studies, mine is meant not as a personal whine (OK, maybe just a bit) but more as an acknowl-edgment of both the entitlement and the vulnerability senior women experi-ence within historically male-dominated institutions. I suspect that the strain this paradoxical combination of privilege and powerlessness has placed on us as individuals will test, stretch, and in the process transform the temper of our feminism in academe, for we have to contend with educational structures still sometimes masculinist in their practices, while simultaneously coping with tensions within an increasingly diversified, even conflicted female community.

Advice for the Work-Worn

If the maddened housewife Erma Bombeck were morphed into a harried associate or full professor, she would throw up her hands in despair of finding large-scale solutions and offer instead stopgap survival strategies culled from colleagues working in a new program called "Psychological Offenses against Obligations that Proliferate"—or POOPed. Haplessly learning to live with proliferating perplexities may be all that housekeepers in academe can expect to achieve.

Heaven forfend that I might seem to be urging women to shrug off their commitment to school-sustaining services! No, I proffer the POOPed project precisely because women "are the most conscientious members of the campus community" in matters of governance (Carnegie 39) and women's propensity to take on such caretaking responsibilities threatens their well-being. Of course, nothing can be done to alleviate your teaching loads or scholarly projects: about the dozens of student papers you have to grade every month, for example, or the multichapter manuscript you are trying to complete on "The Time of Her Life: Florence Nightingale's Crimean Caper." But all the rest of your duties—the ones about which non-academicians like state legislators and (for that matter) your aunt seem blissfully unaware—need to be curtailed. For the sake of brevity, I offer a list to help those suffering from later-career stress, those of you (in other words) about to be inducted into POOPed.

Deploy Your Calendar

Go nowhere without your calendar unless being without it helps diminish obligations that proliferate (as in "Oh, I'm so sorry, I'd love to attend the Parents' Weekend Tailgate Buffet—but I forgot my calendar"). And convert your calendar from an enemy into a friend. How? Let me suggest Innovative Scheduling. Been asked to follow your stint on the College's tenure committee, which meets from 1 P.M. to 4 P.M. every Tuesday afternoon, with attendance at the Dormitory Regulations Board, from 4 to 6 P.M.? How can you, if you have canceled out all late Tuesday afternoons for high-priority sessions with a "physical therapist" (your long-haired terrier or short-haired Siamese)?

Undoubtedly, you have noticed that when you block off four days for an out-of-town lecture at, say, New England's Ivy University, not only does your Chair accept the legitimacy of your absence from both the Hiring and the Graduate Admissions committees but your Dean understands why you cannot attend his Task Force on Bringing the Liberal Arts into the Business Community. Take this as a clue: when you find yourself on the brink of exhaustion (around midterm), set aside four days for an out-of-town vacation with your partner at Ivy. (Or better yet, do so and don't go.)

"Just Say No"

This is exceptionally difficult for many women, so begin by role-playing with a friend, using what one of my acquaintances calls the " 'No' Buddy system" whereby anyone tempted to say yes too often phones a buddy who reinforces the necessity of saying no. Or turn these words into a mantra that you speak into a tape-recorder and play them repeatedly while you are asleep (if you *do* sleep): "I am very proud that you asked me to attend the bimonthly meetings of the Board of your prestigious Institute on Theorizing Post-Transspecies Sexuality at Dry Gulch State College, Professor Oink; however, I find myself so swamped that I simply cannot . . ." etc.

Sometimes, it is easier to "Just say no" in a note composed in the past tense and mailed after the event—as in "I wish I could have given my 'Disciplining Nightingale: Transspecies Sexuality Lashed to the Post' in your lecture series Professor Cockadoodledoo. Unfortunately, though, my time was unexpectedly taken up by . . ." (You have to be careful here not to implicate yourself in elaborate narratives you might forget.)

If just saying no is too difficult for you, but you still like the idea of buying boxes of notecards at the Chicago Art Institute's gift shop, try another strategy, the "I'm anticipating saying yes" tactic. Say Assistant Professor Heehaw-Croak, whom you met while waiting at a limo stand at Ivy, sends you her 932-page manuscript "Can the Post-Transspecies Cyborg Guffaw?" for your reactions, suggestions, and/or a blurb. An attractive card (Magritte? Cassatt?) is the answer, with the following message (thought up by Iris Murdoch or so the legend goes): "Thank you for sending me what looks like a fascinating manuscript on a new and different subject. I *very much* look forward to reading it."

Double Time

Let's say that you have to commute every other weekend from Southern Mississippi State to Alaska University, where your partner has just obtained a part-time job (albeit one without benefits). Or perhaps you must spend two afternoons chauffeuring your kids every half an hour for three continuous hours from and to Suzuki violin lessons, swim meets, and/or 4-H small reptile workshops. Think of this as an opportunity, not a liability. Use a laptop, a mobile phone, a dictaphone, a tape recorder, and/or a pad and pencil to tackle the 342 letters of reference you need to write in which you will "recommend with the greatest enthusiasm" a whole bunch of people you also met at the Ivy limo stand (before you became proficient at "Just Say No").

Implored to pick up the Women's Studies guest speaker at an airport an hour and a half from campus? Asked to dine with the English department's prospective hire? Tell the Women's Studies people about the English hire and the English people about the Women's Studies guest speaker and slink away to the local YMCA—not the university gym where you will be immediately accosted by an importunate senior who needs help with her honors thesis, a performance piece entitled "Beast Citizenship after Humanism: Guerilla Girls Woolf Down a Presidential Shtick." (Perhaps this hint belongs under the next rubric, though.)

Hide Out

You have probably instructed your undergraduates to use office hours, the office mailbox or phone number, and e-mail to reach you, but they still call you at home during dinner time. Evade such interruptions by never answering your home telephone, using screening devices instead. Either pay for Caller ID or make your personal phone machine proactive by putting an inhibiting message on it. My favorite sinister recording: "You know what to do," a robotic voice on the machine intones, followed by the jab: "just do it." A chirpier one comes from an upbeat friend in Religious Studies: "This is triple o-three and quadruple o-two. If I'd wanted to talk, I would've called *you*." Force students to find you at school to explain about the ailing grandmother whose affliction makes impossible their attendance at your final exam. At home you are then able to concentrate on refereeing the journal submission on "AlieNation: Crimean Perspectives on Nightingale; or, Why They Called Her '*Florence*.' "

Nightingale's example brings to mind another surefire way of hiding out. Murmured in a mildly sedated manner, the phrase "Due to doctor's orders" remains a nice locution to explain why you cannot attend "Excellence Through Education," a fund-raising retreat with the trustees and alumni of your institution to be held at a nearby rustic (read: no flushing toilets, no separate bedrooms) campground.

Impersonate a Young Person

Since the first obligation of the Young Person is to do her research, you may be tempted to "pass," to deny your identity as a mid-career person. To turn your monograph "Transspecies Sex *IS* Pedagogy (When You Get Your Students' Goat)" into a theoretically savvy book, you first need to bone up on the *au courant* vocabulary of your field. This will not be easy because you may not have had the time to browse in the library for a decade or two.

In the past, for example, I might have certified myself with some talk of hermeneutics, taxonomies, semiotics, and phallogocentrism, all of which would make me a figure of fun with today's Young People in English. Now, instead, I'd let fall from my lips mellifluous murmurs about the scandalous archive of heteronormativity and the imbrication of juridical interventions in global marketizing. In any case, use the Double Time approach and teach the wonderful game of *Buzz Word Bingo* to your precocious fifth-grader or ailing Mom, thereby giving quality time to those in your care while simultaneously training yourself to masquerade as a Young Person.

Impersonate an Old Boy

This may come easier as time goes by. For now, I'd advise you to begin by trying something my male colleagues have been doing for some time. I'm referring to lunch, and by this I do not mean a brown bag meeting with your teaching assistants. At a leisurely mid-day meal off-campus with a glass of Chardonnay and any colleague who is not a Young Person, you can practice certain sentences to prepare for your retirement from the later-career track. Try this sort of thing: "Let's delegate that"; "The Young People should organize it"; "Those Young People certainly talk funny"; "Those Mid-Career types complain a heck-of-a-lot more than we did"; and (my personal favorite) "I don't come in on Tuesdays, Thursdays, and Fridays."

Could Good Girls Grow Up To Become Old Boys (If They Wanted To)?

Overextended in just about every direction, senior women may not judge Professor Bombeck's appraisal of their situation an exaggeration, for the ivory tower failed to serve them as a refuge or club (as it served some men in the past). But unemployed readers or those with less secure positions might find reprehensible a protracted gripe issued from a clearly advantaged situation of job security. After all, tenured professorships do remain astonishingly well rewarded by almost any standard. Yet material conditions within the academy are now rapidly degenerating: budget cuts, greater teaching loads, larger classes, more teaching of requirements and less of upper-division or graduate electives, the diminishment of travel funds, restricted Xeroxing, increasing red tape related to assessment, lack of raises, and a failure to hire replacements for those who relocate or retire—all these discourage everyone. Considering not simply personal perks but the privileges of teaching and writing with some degree of authority about subjects we have freely chosen, Marilyn Frye captures the tone I'm after:

> My point is not "poor me"; I understand that I am still very well set in this world. My point is that the privileges of which I . . . avail myself (or not) are demonstrably mutable, contingent, dissolvable. (36–37)

To rephrase this in the context of my concerns about the institutionalization of feminists within humanities departments in higher education: my point is not "poor us," but the privileges of which we have just begun to avail ourselves (for the first time in history) are especially mutable, contingent, dissolvable if they induce burnout. Since these privileges are not simply a matter of private luxury but relate to our being able to make a difference in the realm of ideas, under-funding in higher education endangers our enterprise. It is ironic that women have entered higher education during an extended period of retrenchment. Although substantial portions of the economy at large continue to thrive, public funding of education does not. Is the term "Old Boy"—hinting that a cloistered life arrested the male of the species at an adolescent stage of boyhood—gendered because most women simply have not arrived at the end of cushy academic careers? Are social organizations structured so that few will?[5]

As female professors, many of us feel expected to spend exorbitant amounts of time nurturing students and colleagues (in short, playing Mommy) and to organize more than our share of the socializing activities—teas, cocktail parties, dinners, reading groups—that soothe and salve insecure intellectuals (in short, playing the Misses) (George 229). Often, women in the academy face the same problems wives in dual-career relationships confront, where both partners work days at the corporation, bank, or legal firm but the woman does more at home than her husband. Worse still, those feminists housed in traditional departments and also involved in setting up pioneering programs in Gender or Lesbian Studies find themselves overextended and underappreciated in two arenas. According to Dale M. Bauer, "That [sort of commitment] means a double share of committee appointments, often a double load of meetings and assignments . . . to be fulfilled on top of the 'regular' hours of one's home department" ("R-E" 19).

"Hyperproductivity," a term Robyn Wiegman links to the academy's exhausting "ability to absorb so much of [our] labor," affects junior as well as senior professors:

> What was once considered the quantity of a life's intellectual work is now required for tenure; what was once a tenure dossier is now an assistant professor application. ("QA" 15)

A sign of the economic times in higher education, hyperproductivity means that junior women are judged by "standards to which the senior members of their promotion and tenure committees were never held" (Kolodny 89). Because "Women entered the academic profession in significant numbers in the 1970s and 1980s," according to Constance Coiner, the "glutted market" allowed "the profession [to] dictate terms to us" (216), with the result that many of us became "insanely overworked" (218). What Wiegman's, Kolodny's, and Coiner's assessment of escalating demands means for the women who find themselves hired in this atmosphere is more pressure at earlier stages of the career as well as pressure that can divide them from their senior female colleagues. At the same time, for those women who have made it into the mixed privileges of senior standing, hyperproductivity can whittle away our number while our small number can cause the taxes on our time to spiral.

Although my local situation may not be paradigmatic, I often regret the high casualty rate among the women with whom I interacted throughout the seventies, eighties, and nineties in Bloomington. Right after I arrived, I was met with the most intense scrutiny from a group of brilliant wives with advanced graduate degrees in English but without paid positions in the department. Understandably frustrated, a fair share displayed grievous manifestations of depression. Those who managed to survive eventually found some peace, though only by taking jobs markedly below their qualifications. Victims of the enforced domesticity Betty Friedan had diagnosed in *The Feminine Mystique*, this group might be predictable. More surprising was the fact that the female assistant professors subsequently hired rarely prospered.

From 1974 on, a large proportion of the young women hired suffered from stress-related illnesses that issued in disability leaves, hospitalization, even early death. In addition, two who could not accept the loneliness of being single women in a very coupled small town simply up and left—not only Indiana University but the profession. One untenured, single woman who made peace with the town nevertheless decided to abandon higher education because she detested the intense pressure to publish that inhibited her ability to write. Four others—did it matter that two were divorced, the other two lesbian?—failed to receive tenure. One exceptionally talented mid-level teacher burnt out as a token and moved to a department where there were other African-American women. No comparable casualty rate appears in the case of the male peers of this group. (If traumas abound in a field relatively welcoming to women, I wonder what happens to female faculty in mathematics, philosophy, and chemistry?)

Even now, when I look around the room at a 4 P.M. department meeting, I see male colleagues who will go home to stable domestic situations, female colleagues whose existences seem more convoluted. True, some enjoy the solitude of a single life, some the pleasures of nonmonogamy; however, others feel isolated because "the family formation is nearly the only visible and sanctioned alternative to work identity in the academy" (Wiegman 16). For this reason, heterosexual or lesbian women without partners or children can be deeply alienated indeed. Commuting relationships, divorces, widowhood, the burden of children or of childlessness, enforced celibacy, ailing parents, and unhappy partners play a large role, requiring sacrifices and necessitating strains. The men (I imagine) are comfortable enough to ponder the issues at hand, while the women (I fear) find their worries about their lives and loves taking up too much of their attention. That the preponderance of women in most humanities departments occurs among the untenured adds other burdens and anxieties.

But can a call for solidarity provide a solution, given the hierarchical structures and shrinking resources facing academicians today? How can senior faculty make this particular public sphere safe for women when professionalization impedes the formation of a cohesive female community that could insulate us from the demands of the research institution? The fissures within what used to be a small, embattled, and therefore relatively unified female community have widened with each passing year: between women of different ranks; between older and younger women; between women within traditional departments and those in multidisciplinary programs. Some may disagree with Evelyn Fox Keller and Helene Moglen's claim that women in higher education "experience different, deeper, and more painful forms of competition with one another than they do with their male peers" (22). However, Rosi Braidotti reminds us that "No one—in these postmodern days— can be so naive as to avoid the issue that institutional power brings out unexpected, if not unsuspected, levels of rivalry and competition among women, as well as between women and men" (207).

To take the divisiveness of status first: once upon a time, a Junior Person could rail against the Old Boys' passing judgment on her tenure case, but now senior women hold positions of authority over junior women. Inevitably, a conflict arises between feminist ideology (stand by your sister, especially if she is vulnerable) and professional ethics (judge intellectual output as dispassionately as possible). Both the older and the younger scholar may be plunged into perplexing double binds. In order to promote the cause of women, in order literally to promote women, the senior scholar may find herself disconsolate over her temptation to lie about the inadequate achievements of a younger colleague. Or she may find herself distressed about allowing herself to be used as an instrument to certify the fairness of firing her younger colleague. Antithetically, the dependent younger scholar whose feminist expectations lead her to assume she will find supportive female colleagues may think it upsetting that senior women passing judgment on her work view it either as a challenge to ideas they helped to put into place or as so different from these orthodoxies that it can be dismissed as inferior. As Valerie Miner, Jane Gallop, and Diane Elam have pointed out, the incongruity between feminist goals of sisterhood and conflicts among women can escalate confusion and anger.[6]

In addition to the power asymmetry between tenured and untenured teachers, generational friction among feminists in the humanities abounds.[7] Older women resent younger women lucky enough *not* to have to be the first to break the gender barriers; however, young women envy older women lucky enough to *be* the first. Older women may believe that they do nothing but mentor young women, while young women may think that they never get sufficient mentoring. Older women feeling bored with projects that seem routinized as academic feminism loses its activist heritage might seem callous to young women still trying to make their own uses of these practices and fearful that there will be no academic positions in which they will be able to do so. Yet young women hustling to attend conferences or to churn out sufficient amounts of scholarship might seem careerist to older women with anxieties about their own ability or desire to keep up in the field. If this sounds like a case of what Madelon Sprengnether calls "academic matrophobia" (205) or like the daughter-blaming Darlene M. Hantzis and Devoney Looser diagnose (238–41), Professor Bombeck would not be foolish enough to fall into the trap of saying so and then being castigated for replicating a "heterorepro" paradigm!

At this point, let's factor in the tension between feminists within traditional departments and those within multidisciplinary programs. Although there have always been disagreements among feminist and nonfeminist or antifeminist women in higher education, now distinct specializations within feminism as well as diverse engagements with it divide the faculty. A feminist who has worked to strengthen feminism within a traditional department may see herself situated within the institution quite differently from the feminist who has labored to foster feminism within a Women's Studies, Gender Studies, or Lesbian Studies program.[8] To those intellectuals who defend the conventional departments of the humanities in which they trained, Women's Studies degrees fail to induct students into sufficiently field-specific methodologies and thus encourage dilettantism. But to intellectuals aware of the rigidities of traditional departments, only multidisciplinary approaches that break with conventional academic paradigms are adequate to the complexities of gender issues.[9]

When Women's Studies programs become departments themselves, directors—no longer having to rely on the charity of other department heads—can appoint their own faculty, offer their own courses, and administer their curricula with some autonomy and integrity. Yet departmentalization may effectively dismiss the very originators of the academic study of feminism by excluding their courses from the curriculum, removing them from governance roles, or demoting them from faculty in the program to adjuncts in the department who are somehow insufficiently professional now and thus marginalized. When bureaucratic alterations involve changing the name of

Women's Studies to Gender Studies, the new nomenclature broadens the base of study, indicating that masculinity is as socially constructed as femininity. But to early activists, it may suggest that institutionalization is purchased at the price of eclipsing women and their specific political issues.[10] Whether schools go the route of mainstreaming within the traditional disciplines, Women's Studies programs, or departments of Gender Studies, "interdepartmental cooperation and a broader institutional vision are called for" during "the first time in history" that "women represent the majority of the college population"; however, retrenchment has "put many faculty members on the defensive, making them more protective of their own special interests" (Schuster and Van Dyne 3, 89).

How discouraging this must seem to our graduate students, given the traumatic effects of downsizing on their professional aspirations. On the lecture circuit, a bemused Henry Louis Gates Jr. used to lament the fact that just as white women and African Americans entered academic discourse, all of a sudden "the subject" disappeared. At the risk of sounding paranoid, I would amend his point to speculate on the irony that when we feminist and minority newcomers started producing a good number of Ph.D.s in our various fields, the jobs vanished.[11] Although we continue to establish new majors and minors, certificates and degrees, our graduate students find it increasingly difficult to get any teaching jobs at all, much less positions in institutions comparable to the ones at which they have trained. To be sure, people in all disciplines feel distressed about the depressed job market in the humanities, but the situation seems particularly poignant for a field that has just gotten established. As departments shrink—losing "lines" and thus making it impossible to retain positions vacated through relocations or retirements—as it becomes increasingly difficult to persuade publishers to print scholarly books that will not generate profits, as the National Endowment for the Humanities and the National Endowment for the Arts as well as affirmative action programs come under attack, the economy of the humanities discourages us from assuming that we will have successors and what successors mean—a future.

Though for the most part in my department the men are balding and the women graying, Professor Bombeck appears to be graying *and* balding, suffering from alopecia triggered by impotent rage causing her to pull out her hair. What should a senior scholar do about the ominous fate of her feminist dissertators? All of the graduate students whose doctoral training I have guided found their progress hampered by the scarcity of jobs.[12]

Demoralized about their future, why should they complete the requirements with dispatch? Even if they do finish their courses and theses, a number of those who manage to get positions are isolated in inhospitable communities, temporarily employed on terminal one- or two-year contracts, teaching too many sections of freshmen composition for too little money, removed from the library facilities necessary for their research, or on the market again with a major publication but unable to obtain a better position. Many senior women believe that even if it means teaching fewer graduates and more undergraduates, we must reduce the size of our doctoral programs and gain better financial support for the smaller number of students we accept; however, feminist critics looking for trustworthy ways to mentor the next generation still feel stymied.

From the Old Boys to the Graying People

Before Professor Bombeck turns into a completely bald madwoman due to the paroxysms of anger that all these material conditions instill in her, she needs to circumscribe the ever widening circles of her guilt—or else guilt (the gift that keeps on giving) will inundate her. Indignant about the exploitation of graduate students, the overvaluation of research in tenure procedures, our failure to pay sufficient attention to the teaching of undergraduates, and our dereliction in explaining the worth of what we do to the society we seek to benefit, she can nevertheless share this shame with all her colleagues because, of course, these are failures of the profession at large.[13] As a feminist, though, Professor Bombeck's guilt seems directly attributable to her ambivalence about assimilation.

Have we feminists changed higher education or has it changed us?[14] Do we retain our visionary hopefulness about the mission of feminism in colleges and universities, its capacity to transform traditional ways of knowing? Or have we begun to feel integrated into an academic system with its own ossified, frequently painful or pointless procedures? Has our incorporation into the professoriate required us to exhibit the selfishness and factionalism inculcated by careerist jockeying? Despite Professor Bombeck's fear that institutionalization might involve an assimilation process contaminated by such forms of cooptation, she remains firm in her belief that women's advancement into the public sphere cannot be inhibited by the distressing complications to be found in it, for there can be no going back to the private house. As this last phrase hints, Professor Bombeck's vertiginous position is one she inherited from Virginia Woolf, who also dithered on this complicated subject.

Dithered?—Virginia Woolf?! In the astonishing series of turnabouts that constitute the first chapter of *Three Guineas*, Woolf's most extended meditation on higher education, feminism's most quixotic thinker tried to decide whether she could help the pacifist cause by contributing money to a women's college. After all, she reasoned, women might be considered logical allies in the struggle against war since their status as outsiders (banned not only from the universities but also from the army, the navy, the stock exchange, the church, and the bar) altered their stature as citizens, qualified their identification with nation, and problematized patriotism for them. Precisely that outsider-station, however, had produced ignorance, poverty, and dependency in women, and so Woolf exults over the 1919 Act that unbarred the professions, for "to depend upon a profession is a less odious form of slavery than to depend upon a father" (16). Yet Woolf knows that the exclusionary education professional men received at Oxbridge "does not teach people to hate force, but to use it" (29). Worse still, the professions "make the people who practice them possessive, jealous of any infringement of their rights, and highly combative, if anyone dares dispute them" (66).

To remain outside higher education and the professions spells feminine subservience; to be taken in entails indoctrination in masculinist pugnacity. Earlier, in *A Room of One's Own*, Woolf concluded that, while it was "unpleasant . . . to be locked out," it was "worse perhaps to be locked in" (24). By *Three Guineas*, however, she reversed this judgment, for—after countless decisions and revisions that include the fantasy of burning down the women's school—she ends up contributing her guinea to its endowment fund. Although feminists should continue to "pour mild scorn upon chapels, upon degrees, and upon the value of examinations" (37), women's welfare nevertheless depends on their advancement within the certifying structures that will enable them to enter into the public life via the professions, where they can then work to prevent war.

To Professor Bombeck, Woolf's conflicted but smart solution captures exactly our current need to support educational structures that empower women to succeed in the professions, although those structures and the professions themselves may be based on slippery ethical values that complicate alliances among women. Perhaps one way to perform what Catharine Stimpson calls "this balancing act" ("WA" 65) of attaining power while maintaining an outsider's perspective on power structures is to keep in mind the two challenges all women aspiring to enter the academy face: in the words of Nancy Zumwalt, "the first is to cultivate excellence in our professional fields. The second is to recognize that we are engaged in a struggle to gain power in the world of work and achievement, power that has by long tradition been denied us" (132). Women's headway in history, anthropology, philosophy, English, fine art, film, Religious Studies, and comparative literature may or may not change the way business is done in those departments, but in any case it will undoubtedly transform the women doing that business.

For perhaps, Professor Bombeck thinks guiltily, guilt itself is part of the quandary of some senior women's burn-out, namely our continued fear that we do not deserve the positions within the public intellectual sphere that we have finally begun to attain. Or, in the grip of nostalgia for earlier definitions of the feminine, do we suffer from what Diana Hume George calls "a pervasive sense of guilt for our individualism, our toughness, the ways in which we have failed to be good women in the traditional sense" (239)? Unlike our mothers and our mothers' mothers, we have an unprecedented opportunity outside the home, outside the banal marketplace of getting and spending—in the wonderful world of the academy! Do we therefore believe that we should demonstrate our eternal gratitude (through selfless service) or preserve anachronistic feminine virtues (of selfless service)? Have a larger number of women than men entering the workforce internalized the idea that a profession is not a right or a responsibility so much as a serendipitous gift—one they did not earn? Fearing failure, given the ever higher standards of hyperproductivity, do women ensure it by overloading themselves? In other words, are the herculean labors of forty- or fifty-something women who "go the second mile as campus citizens" (Carnegie 43) a destructive form of penitence for the irrational dread that we are impostors undeserving of our station? Is the term "Old Boy" gendered not only because of historical but also because of psychological factors? To put this more clearly, can Good Girls grow up or are they destined to remain trapped in the later-career stress syndrome, ailing Angels in the House of Academe?

While some of her scrupulously ethical friends suffer from the Angel in the House of Academe syndrome, the fractious Professor Bombeck fusses about two quite different but related problems: first, about wanting her female contemporaries to gain the niche once monopolized by the Old Boys, but without turning into Old Boys since those guys rarely used their institutional power with pedagogic fairness or intellectual generosity; second, about her own and many of her colleagues general cynicism vis-à-vis the power of feminism within academic systems that have proven to be exceptionally recalcitrant to change. Nor are these two issues unrelated, for they pertain to the curious liminality of academic women neither ensconced as insiders nor ostracized as outsiders, people dealing in myriad ways with new privileges and old privations. According to the authors of *Women of Academe: Outsiders in the Sacred Grove*, the "tension" between a historically based "mistrust of authority" and "the need to exercise it in their own interests—and the larger interests of the academy—runs through the experience of professional women generally" (Aisenberg and Harrington 63). If Professor Bombeck periodically worries that women granted the confidence and security accorded the Old Boys might become as exclusionary as these precursors had been, this is because women—for the most part quite marginal within the upper reaches of academe—have not yet had a chance to prove what they would do with academic positions of power.

Professor Bombeck asks you to consider whether you can name one senior feminist teacher/writer in the humanities who has acquired the honorific trappings accorded the most magisterial of the Old Boys in your field.[15] Few of us have attained the highest accolades and positions in our various areas. Despite the rise of feminist methodologies within the academy during the past twenty or so years, the "'erotics' of discipleship" continue to surround those charismatic "masters" who epitomize elite theory for an analyst of the humanities like John Guillory, men adored for their "discourse of mastery" (182, 203). In addition, many senior women remain isolated as tokens in humanities departments, the only female tenured or full professor among a host of men. Even the most successful female teachers tend not to be situated in the most prestigious institutions (DePalma 23) and tend not to publish as much as their male peers ("Footnotes" A12). Accorded "second-hand citizenship status," women faculty remain "a small minority among administrators in higher education"; earn substantially lower salaries at all academic ranks; and have less job security (Carnegie 40–1). That women "enter their tenure probationary period" during the same time in which they have to decide to postpone, forego, or begin a family has been used by some researchers to "explain why women do not achieve tenure at the same rates as men" or to speculate that "childbearing is not compatible with tenure" (Finkel and Olswang 125, 130).

Laying to rest her precipitous dread that Good Girls might grow up to become Old Boys, Professor Bombeck nevertheless feels skeptical about feminism's ability to solve the problems at hand because the quite varied connections of women to the academy make inoperative any feminism founded on all women having the same degree of estrangement from or investment in it. Were a larger number of senior women finally allowed to grow into their maturity, however, were they to survive the perils of midcareer stress, who knows what they might be able to achieve or what alliances they might build? Maybe, one such being—remembering the misuses of institutional power with which she had to contend in order to receive her own education—will dedicate herself to bringing more disadvantaged people into college and university classrooms, fostering their success by helping to improve blatantly ineffectual, underfunded primary and secondary school systems. Perhaps, attempting to broaden the bases and uses of knowledge, another will commit herself to creating newly inventive roles for humanities graduate students and professors that will empower them to deal with continued inequities (such as inadequate child care and health benefits for working-class families, sexual violence, gender disparities on all levels of the workforce, rising rates of anorexia and bulimia among adolescent girls, and the abrogation of civil rights among certain sectors of the population).

Seeking to hold onto Carolyn Heilbrun's faith in "feminism's wonderful capacity for change and for expansion and inclusion" (271), hoping with Akasha (Gloria) Hull "that just yearning to impact beyond the academy probably adds something fine to what we do" (62), Professor Bombeck looks forward to that time when the Young People encounter in the Graying People not a gendered monolith but a mirror of their own diversity, a process already well underway, for the categories I have employed to spotlight women's unprecedented situation conceal a mixed group of men dedicated to the proposition that they have never been and never need become Old Boys. Because some matured in the profession during the nineties, a time "certain to be the last decade in which tenured white males over fifty control what gets published and who gets tenured," many of these men do not find the massive gender "changes [that] have taken hold within a single generation" threatening (Kolodny 100). Others, older men who have all along mentored female graduate students and colleagues, support feminist goals in their local communities. What sorts of coalitions should feminist women and men build with whom and how? That even an Erma Bombeck transplanted from the home to the academy and tenured cannot propose large-scale solutions ought to come as no surprise to readers accustomed to her panicky babblings at moments of crisis, muddled procrastinations fueled not only by a profound conviction of her personal ineptitude but also by "a social system . . . that makes women solely responsible . . . and sets impossibly high standards for their performance" (Walker, N. 6).

Though women share a historical past of exclusion from higher education, what we face is a future in which our different roles mean diverse relationships to it. In this confusing period, feminism has to respond to a chorus of quite distinct, specific voices addressing very particular issues and contexts. As Berlant puts it, "feminists must embrace a policy of female disidentification at the level of female essence. . . . We must align ourselves, in our differences from each other, to perform, theorize, constantly intensify the rupture of the private, and inhabit, as much as we can, the constantly expanding negative terrain that will transform the patriarchal public sphere" (253–4). Disidentification: the term means we will not always be in agreement, not always respect each others' institutional choices, not always find ourselves on the same side of disagreements, but we should not let these differences obscure our commonalities of history and purpose because, after all, our gains are so recently won and so very fragile that we need time to see what their fruition might mean.

Nor have those gains redressed our initial exclusion from academia.[16] Nor do they portend future triumphs, since women's entrance into other professions in the past has signaled a decline of those occupations—are women only allowed to come into a particular vocation when it is in the process of economic devolution or does it devolve in status because of their participation?—in a phenomenon sociologists term "feminization." Brenda Silver, a critic who has written extensively about Virginia Woolf's protests against the tyrannies and servilities of the public professions and the private sphere, considers her own frustration at ongoing "battles about critical authority and institutional change" in light of other "women who differ from me in significance ways":

> If I get angry when the anger born of these differences threatens to subsume my own anger and my voice, I can also acknowledge that all these angers, all these voices, are necessary to feminist critique today. . . . [T]he angers that continue to animate feminist consciousnesses and critiques may well be the most compelling source of our strength. (370)

Despite the discontent it induces, institutionalization has transformed women from singular anomalies in higher education to a substantial and diverse group of players who share a stake in tapping feminist angers to fight a feminization of the profession that would diminish all of us and endanger the society at large.

PART II
Contending Forces

6

What Ails Feminist Criticism?

Originally, when this essay was a talk entitled "Who Killed Feminist Criticism?," I relished the idea of a rousing arraignment in which I dramatically pinned the blame for the problems currently facing feminist criticism on a host of nefarious culprits—some of them the most prestigious people in the field. Hinting that the grave, rather than the bed, might furnish the final setting in this turn-of-the-century melodrama, I used a murder mystery title to fuel suspicion that feminist criticism's evolution would circumvent the happily-ever-after of the love plot to land at the demise demanded by its major narrative competitor. Yet clearly feminist criticism has not been mortally wounded or robbed of its stamina: prominent feminist scholars serve as the presidents of major professional organizations; feminist journals and books proliferate; and feminist methodologies routinely shape most literature programs. Besides, wouldn't my original scenario play into reactionary efforts to dismantle the gains Women's Studies advocates have made in higher education? And why would I be so ungenerous as to castigate individuals whose extraordinary intellectual achievements have profoundly enriched my own thinking?[1]

An equally serious drawback to my initial charge depended on the ways in which the story I was telling could be misunderstood as a self-serving generational account,[2] in which early feminist critics (prominent in the seventies) felt beleaguered by the attacks of their successors (in the eighties and nineties), a group that just happened to be comprised of theorists of color and of lesbianism. Oh dear! The rank smell of racism and homophobia reeked from a script that might lead to insinuations that either menopausal rage or maternal rivalry had plunged me into a femicidal fury at the critical daughters supplanting their predecessors. The fact that most of my middle-class, white contemporaries had established quite comfortable niches within the academy made my complaint seem only more self-indulgently whiny. But, despite my anxieties about the misconstruction to which my argument may still be liable, despite my decision to lower the metaphorical decibels from death to disease, the revised title continues to express my apprehension about the state of feminist literary criticism.

Indeed, there are reasons to consider a number of developments in the eighties and nineties a hazard to the vitality of feminist literary studies. In stating my case against "what" (not "who") has enervated our undertaking, I do not wish to mount a generational argument because generations remain hazy phenomena, their chronologies varying greatly, depending on how they are defined. More to the point, the problems that trouble me cross generational lines, no matter where they are drawn. Nor do I want my essay to play into the racism and homophobia of a culture all too willing to exploit disagreements among women in a backlash against all or some of us. In the hope of making my comments constructive, I switched the metaphor from murder to illness in order to argue that—appearances of vigor to the contrary—feminist criticism suffers from internal ailments about which one can postulate possibilities of recovery. As important, when I point to individual thinkers whose stylistic strategies have made the practice of feminist criticism perplexing, I want not to berate the writers but rather to diagnose the disorders their idioms inculcate. At the risk of protesting too much, I need to add that the scholars on whom I focus were chosen precisely because their innovative work has played such an influential role in our discipline. The rhetorical complaints their prose exhibits concern me because they have proven to be catching (among some populations in epidemic proportions).

In particular, I hope to show that a number of prominent advocates of racialized identity politics and of poststructuralist theories have framed their arguments in such a way as to divide feminists, casting suspicion upon a common undertaking that remains damaged at the turn of the twentieth century. What does it mean that otherwise sagacious proponents of these two at times antagonistic camps—African-American as well as postcolonial materialists, on the one hand, and Foucauldian as well as Derridean theorists, on the other—have produced discourses that in various ways hinder the tolerance and understanding needed for open dialogue? About the language crisis at which feminist theory has arrived, Nancy K. Miller notes the predicament related to pronouns of subjectivity:

> between the indictment of the feminist universal as a white fiction brought by women of color and the poststructuralist suspicion of a grounded subject, what are the conditions under which as feminists one (not to say "I") can say "we"?
>
> (*GP* 74–5)

In its most recent phase of "metacritical dissension," rhetorical indictments of the "feminist universal" and the "grounded subject" constitute my major consideration because the maladies I treat—what I will call "critical election" (with its analogue "critical abjection") and "obscurantism"—threaten the relationship feminists within the academy have sought to maintain with one another and with women outside it. This will be the rather depressing substance of speculations about the development of feminist criticism that will conclude by historicizing its current contentiousness in order to hold out the hope that we might be emerging out of it. To return to the metaphor of my revised title: we may be in the process of clambering out of the sickbed to surmise the possibilities of hopping into more exciting berths.

Critique, Recovery, and the Engendering of Differences

Many Western narratives begin with Edenic scenes, so let me start the story of feminist criticism in the paradise of a roused, indeed "raised" consciousness "when we dead awakened," to recycle Adrienne Rich's famous phrasing.[3] Since this part of the tale has been told so often and since happiness tends to be brief, if not boring (at least in the provenance of narrative time), I will keep this section to a minimum. During a series of moments in the nineteen-seventies, as I tell my undergraduates (who were kept busy getting born during this same decade), female academics brought the women's movement into such departments as English and history, anthropology and psychology, fine arts, film, religion, and education. Outside the field of English literature, one thinks of the now classic works of Gerda Lerner, Gayle Rubin, Sherry Ortner, Juliet

Mitchell, and Nancy Chodorow; of Linda Nochlin, Laura Mulvey, Mary Daly, Angela Davis, and Carol Gilligan. Imbued with the exuberance of pioneers, this group of scholars revised disciplinary-bound models generated to explain masculine ways of being. They examined how such paradigms excluded or marginalized female experiences and then reinvented them so as to account for the uniqueness of women's cultural situation.

The first stage of feminist criticism, which Elaine Showalter has called "critique," undercut the universality of male-devised scripts in philosophy as well as science, in intellectual as well as social history ("TFP" 129). Within the specifically literary context that is my subject, critique meant the proliferation of books about the uses to which male authors had put images of female characters and feminine imagery. From Kate Millett's *Sexual Politics* to countless interpretations of the engendered narratives at work in canonical texts by Shakespeare, Milton, Faulkner, and Mailer, feminists produced fresh readings that stressed the manner in which the work of art participated in the construction of debilitating or liberating sexual ideologies influencing or influenced by authors, publishers, and readers. Important volumes produced by such thinkers as Toni Cade Bambara (*The Black Woman: An Anthology*), Vivian Gornick and Barbara K. Moran (*Woman in Sexist Society*), Mary Helen Washington (*Black-Eyed Susans: Class Stories by and About Black Women*), Lillian Robinson (*Sex, Class, and Culture*), and Tillie Olsen (*Silences*) were based on Simone de Beauvoir's insight into women's alterity and spawned numerous analyses of the images and stereotypes of "the second sex" in male-authored literature. This work continues, as does the related task of approaching noncanonical texts that are used to lay bare the relationship between gender and genre (in, say, the Western or science fiction, film noir and hip-hop or rap, fashion photography and television journalism).

Although critique remains a vital aspect of feminist analysis, it was quickly followed by the second stage that Showalter dubbed "gynocriticism." The recovery of female literary traditions began in the late seventies with books whose bold, inclusive categories appear evident in their titles. *Literary Women* (by Ellen Moers) and *Women Writers and Poetic Identity* (by Margaret Homans), *Black Women Writers* (by Barbara Christian) and *Reinventing Womanhood* (by Carolyn Heilbrun) sound upbeat, monumental in their generalizings about the previously neglected subject of female literary achievement.[4] The images or themes or lexicons to which women writers appeared especially drawn, their uses of a recurrent cast of characters, their attraction to certain authorial strategies, gender-related standards at work in the publication or reception of their books, the distinctive reading patterns of female readers: all sustained the attention of feminist scholars. From early on, feminist criticism included lesbian, African-American, and postcolonial voices proposing multiple versions of womanhood; however, the centrality of gender as a conceptual lens was what black and white, heterosexual and lesbian feminist critics agreed to privilege in their critical conversations.[5]

Concern about individual authors previously neglected or out of print invariably drew scholarly attention to the narrative of literary history with its interest in aesthetic evaluation and periodization. Therefore, books began appearing about the specificities of women's cultural situation within, say, the Renaissance or the modernist period. In East Asian and Middle Eastern Studies, Spanish and German literature departments, as well as in English and American Studies, the methodologies of recovery continue to produce major publications.[6] The heady influx of French feminist thinking may have appeared more epistemologically glamorous, less dowdy than some Anglo-American empirical studies; however, two of its major proponents relied on comparable strategies of critique and recovery. Hélène Cixous and Luce Irigaray decried Western culture's valuation of a masculinity identified with rationality and vision over and against a femininity associated with emotionalism and embodiment. To such speculations they appended meditations on a recoverable and empowering *écriture féminine* or *parler femme*.[7]

By the eighties changes were taking place that laid the groundwork for the third phase of feminist criticism, which I will call the engendering of differences. Among people occupied in critique, more attention began to be paid to images not only of femininity but also of masculinity, not only of heterosexuality but also of homosexuality in historically specified sites in the past and in popular media of the present, including the electronic forms that saturate contemporary culture. Among people absorbed by recovery, the evolution of a series of distinctive subtraditions generated research and classes on Native-American, Chicana, Asian-American, and especially African-American literary legacies. I use the verb "engendering" for the third stage because it engaged feminists in the activity of bringing gender to bear upon other differences: sexual and racial differences primarily, but also economic, religious, and regional distinctions. Antithetically, it also included thinkers bringing sexual and racial identifications (as well as economic, religious, and regional affiliations) to bear upon gender, thereby accentuating dissimilarities among women, divergences among men.

Notable in the emergence of scholarship on lesbian and gay topics, critics such as Teresa de Lauretis and Terry Castle, Diana Fuss and Eve Kosofsky Sedgwick explored such subjects as the social construction of heterosexuality, psychoanalytic models of lesbian desire, and the representational repercussions of homophobia. Prominent in the rise of ethnic studies, African-American feminists such as Nellie McKay and Hortense Spillers, Deborah McDowell and Akasha (Gloria) Hull analyzed such issues as the links between racial and sexual stereotyping, the distinct inflections of African-American women's literary history, the impact of a racist past on depictions of maternity or the relationship between the sexes. Under the influence of thriving postcolonial research, the historically unprecedented number of self-defined lesbian and black intellectuals publishing from within higher education investigated the interaction between heterosexual and homosexual, white and black cultural phenomena in manifold national arenas.

In the face of this vigorous growth, why do I even consider the dire possibility that feminist critics suffered a series of debilitating bouts of disease? One answer is encapsulated in Barbara Johnson's witty point that "Nothing fails like success."[8] Maybe critique and recovery have become so much a part of the interpretive way we behave in the literature classroom that their ubiquity leads us to take both approaches for granted. Just as important, while many scholars pursue work in all three phases, the methodological moves they make might now seem somewhat predictable.[9] Another reason, as powerful as that of ennui, relates to a sense of vulnerability experienced by some early practitioners of feminist criticism in higher education, produced by the intense attacks they received from their successors or by the perceived fragility of their enterprise.[10] While critique, recovery, and the engendering of differences continue to play significant pedagogical roles, I believe all three became eclipsed by interventions performed within areas of scholarship ratified as theoretical.

Perhaps inevitably, since the engendering of differences foregrounded disparities among women, it set the stage for a questioning of the categories that the concept of gender itself proposed. Self-reflexive theorizing about criticism undermined the term "women" upon which feminist literary practice previously depended.[11] Because I am distressed about the debilitating effects of this fourth phrase of "metacritical dissension," I will examine its dismantling of the category "women" in two arenas populated by scholars not always allied. On the one hand, feminist criticism was disparaged by some African-American and postcolonial thinkers as universalizing a privileged, white womanhood; on the other, it was maligned by several poststructuralists as naively essentialist about the identity of women.

Given the inevitable doubling that occurs when one contends the contentiousness of others, several caveats are in order here. Needless to say, the powerfully subtle methodologies provided by African-American, Postcolonial, and Poststructural Studies have greatly enhanced the ways in which we think about culture and society, race and sexuality. I hope the first section of this book authenticates this claim. Needless to say, too, one cannot conflate African-American with Postcolonial Studies because they have had quite different histories, just as one should not consolidate the poststructuralism generated by one philosophical approach with that produced by another. The fact that I have earlier deployed the ideas of many of the brilliant scholars I am about to critique proves, I trust, that I do not intend to ghettoize their writing as instances of some sort of separate or "bad" version of feminist criticism. Indeed, the brilliance of their conceptualizations paradoxically contributed to their regrettable stylistic influence over numerous practitioners in the field of feminist studies. Taking these particular points for granted, my analysis deals with one bewildering consequence that qualifies the linguistic practices these approaches have occasionally sponsored. Although feminists of racial identity politics and of poststructuralism did not always agree with one another, together their words combined to make "women" an invalid word.

What Do You Mean "*We*," White Woman?

In 1981 the landmark volume *This Bridge Called My Back: Writings by Radical Women of Color*, edited by Cherrié Moraga and Gloria Anzaldúa, heralded a barrage of diatribes directed against white feminists throughout the decade. Attentive to what the editors term "a class and color war that is still escalating in the feminist movement" (61), the collection includes many thoughtful instances of writing; however, one rather eccentric piece curiously dramatizes the escalation of that war, namely doris davenport's comments on "black wimmin's" aversion not only to the bigotry and naïveté of "white wimmin" but also to their very being:

> Aesthetically (& physically) we frequently find white wimmin repulsive. That is, their skin colors are unaesthetic (ugly, to some people). Their hair, stringy and straight, is unattractive. Their bodies: rather like misshapen lumps of whitish clay or dough, that somebody forgot to mold in-certain-areas. Furthermore, they have a strange body odor. (87)

Given a slave past that had set in place black women's subjection to white women and given the unconscious racism permeating the women's movement from its inception in the nineteenth century, davenport's acrimony founds itself on comprehensible grounds. Yet though such a passage may be attempting to redirect racist formulae against those who historically have done the stereotyping, much of the writing in *This Bridge* about racism in the movement—originally meant "to make a *connection* with white women"— actually functions "more like a separation," as Cherríe Moraga and Gloria Anzaldúa conclude in their editorial speculations (61).[12]

If black women had served as a bridge upon which black men (in the Civil Rights movement) and white women (in the feminist movement) walked, a refusal to fulfill this role meant standing up to be made visible, a laudable step in establishing the rights and perspectives of women of color most powerfully urged by Audre Lorde.[13] But when bell hooks published *Ain't I a Woman: Black Women and Feminism* (also in 1981), she couched its excellent point about the propensity of feminists to use the word "women" to mean "white women" in a curiously condemnatory vocabulary directed against all other efforts of black and white feminists to expand the word "woman" to encompass women of different colors. Held culpable, for instance, were black separatist activists such as the members of The Combahee River Collective, whom hooks dubbed "reactionary" in their endorsement of the racism they supposedly attacked (150). And Michele Wallace, hooks's most famous contemporary in the African-American feminist scene, was dismissed as the author of a book judged to be "neither an important feminist work nor an important work about black women" (11).[14] Censorious about white thinkers engaged in purportedly antiracist and feminist meditations—Catharine Stimpson, for example, and Adrienne Rich—hooks argued that "white women were not sincerely committed to bonding with black women and other groups of women to fight sexism" (142), for they remained unwilling to admit that "the women's movement was consciously and deliberately structured to exclude black and other non-white women" (147). Harmful and hurtful as white exclusions have been, hooks universalized them as intentionally so.

Two smart articles—one published by Hazel V. Carby in 1982 and the other by Chandra Talpade Mohanty in 1984 (and revised in 1991)—extended hooks's insight into the implicit whiteness of the word "women" by questioning reductive images of "the" third-world woman, but the way in which they did so explains why white feminists began to feel beleaguered by blatantly imperative efforts to right the wrong of black female instrumentality. Employ-

ing the approaches of African-American and Postcolonial Studies, Carby and
Mohanty set out to show that all generalizings about "women's experience"
perpetuated the negation of black womanhood. Hazel Carby's "White Woman
Listen!"—a title revising Richard Wright's *White Man, Listen!*—makes explicit through its subtitle ("Black Feminism and the Boundaries of Sisterhood")
this scholar's argument with mainstream feminists who are accused of providing racially prejudicial analytical frameworks. Yet Carby's claim that white
feminists stereotype Asia and Africa as, for example, barbaric in the practice of
genital mutilation ignored numerous feminist attacks on the mutilations carried
out by gynecologists on nineteenth- and twentieth-century white women in
England and America. Carby was primed to overlook such critiques; she was
impelled to disparage any feminist theory founded on female commonality by
her conviction that "white women stand in a power relation as oppressors of
black women" (214).

Like Carby, Mohanty attempted to undo the homogeneity of standard
conceptualizations of black women, but in the process she contributed to the
essentializing of white women. According to Mohanty, Western feminism
works hand in hand with imperialism because of the "ethnocentric universalism" informing contemporary scholarship. Carby's hostility—as in her
final query, "of white feminists we must ask, what exactly do you mean
when you say 'WE'??" (233)—finds expression in Mohanty's argument that
Western feminists "discursively colonize the material and historical hetero-
geneities of the lives of women in the third world" (174). A "homogeneous
notion of the oppression of women as a group" buttresses stereotypes about
the "average third-world woman" as ignorant and poor, the object of scrutiny, the first-world woman as educated and modern, the subject of history
(176). Part of the problem, not the solution, the white feminists pictured by
Mohanty pursue projects that "tie into" economic and ideological modes of
exploitation (192). Thus Mohanty's title—"Under Western Eyes: Feminist
Scholarship and Colonial Discourses"—hints that the scopophilic gaze or
imperial eyes of first-world feminists scrutinize to wage war on third-world
women.[15]

If we consider the rhetorical impact of hooks's, Carby's, and Mohanty's
arguments, we can see why, though they sought to serve the interests of
women of color, they promoted consternation among white women. Any
number of examples could drive home this point.[16] In her self-deprecating
White Woman Speaks with Forked Tongue, one quintessentially guilt-ridden
author confesses that even though she was born a privileged, middle-class,

West-European sinner, she has witnessed the evil of her colonizing ways. "Writing is never innocent," Nicole Ward Jouve concedes, and "White writing is less innocent than any other." Then she goes on to cite the requisite anti-authoritarian authority: "As Gayatri Spivak has said, every First World Woman's book is typed out on a word processor made cheaply by the low-paid labor of a Third World Woman" (viii). In keeping with Jouve's stance, not only some faculty but many students these days make obeisance to the necessity of considering (without subordinating) race, class, gender, sexuality, and nation in routinized litanies that often translate into depressingly knee-jerk essays that reject out-of-hand the speculations of a given literary or theoretical work simply because it neglects to discuss X (fill-in-the-blank—bisexual Anglo-Pakistani mothers; the heterosexual, working-class, Jews-for-Jesus community of Nashville, etc.). Too often, each text becomes grist for a mill that proves the same intellectually vapid—though politically appalling—point that racism, classism, sexism, and homophobia reign supreme.

Albeit a crucial goal, the raising of feminism's racial consciousness has instilled an impossible, inhibiting dream of innocent rectitude in numerous white scholars keenly aware of America's and England's long intellectual history of prejudicial thinking about people of African origins. White feminists' fear of saying the wrong thing, of sounding racist, means that they often silence themselves on racial matters altogether or—in thrall to a fantasy of finding the correct antiracist stance—they become ventriloquists, echoing the words of a handful of "specialists" whose color somehow certifies them as experts on race (as if whiteness itself were not a racial category). Yet, Sara Suleri quite reasonably wonders, how effective can it possibly be to require all critics to be matched to their subjects through a string of hyphenated adjectival qualifiers:

> The claim to authenticity—only a black can speak for a black; only a postcolonial subcontinental feminist can adequately represent the lived experience of that culture—points to the great difficulty posited by the "authenticity" of female racial voices in the great game that claims to be the first narrative of what the ethnically constructed woman is deemed to want.   (137)[17]

To the extent that white critics deprived of their assumption of white privilege take refuge in "critical abjection" (the silence or ventriloquism of white deference and deferral), the politics of racial authenticity may be experienced as an attack on feminism's endorsement of all women's right to self-expression. As Janet Todd has observed, since anti-racism commands more general assent than feminism ever did, it is often used in a curious way to discredit women and women's endeavors. Or, to be more specific, the language of accepted anti-racism is frequently used to denigrate the feminist enterprise. ("AAD" 243)[18]

That Gayatri Chakravorty Spivak became the most often cited authority on the matter of white feminists' racism may be related to the ways in which she combines an attention toward racial identity politics with the poststructuralist methodologies to which I am about to turn.[19] According to Spivak, the "disenfranchised" woman who cannot recognize herself as the subject of feminist theory teaches us "that the name of 'woman,' however political, is, like any other name, a catachresis" (*OTM* 137) and therefore she asks that we "name (as) 'woman' that disenfranchised woman whom we strictly, historically, geopolitically *cannot imagine*, as literal referent" (*OTM* 139). Engaged in a project as ambitious as it is complex, Spivak valiantly seeks to make deconstruction and feminism answerable to the colonized; however, at times the process leads her to set herself up as a righteous representative of subordinated peoples (the honorable third-world spokesperson) who remains quite distinct from empowered and therefore degenerate readers (perverted first-world citizens).[20] For example, Spivak castigates "highly privileged women [who] see their face in the mirror and define 'Woman'—a capital *w*—in terms of the reflection that they see there: sometimes they look at their face, sometimes they look at their genitals, and in terms of that, they adjudicate about woman as such. I have very little patience with that" (*PC* 119). Yet about herself she claims, "the word 'woman' is not after all something for which one can find a literal referent without looking into the looking glass. And . . . what I see in the looking glass is not particularly the constituency of feminism" (*PC* 70).

In other words, unlike narcissistic, affluent feminists who gaze at themselves in the mirror and then project their image onto others, Spivak looks simply because she seeks a referent, all the while understanding not only the disparity between her self-image and the constituencies of feminism but also the necessity of postponing indefinitely an identification that effaces subalterns, proletariats, and peasants. The aggression Jacques Lacan locates at the mirror stage in the rivalry between which image is deemed "self" and which "Other" surfaces in Spivak's competing for perceptual supremacy over first-world feminist critics. What undermines these deliberations—like those of hooks, Carby, and Mohanty—is a posture of "critical election," the counterpart of "critical abjection." An assumption of moral superiority on the part of scholars convinced of their ability to speak for those despised and rejected by everybody else, critical election holds sway, I suspect, to conceal the uncomfortable contradiction between claims to a radical politics genuinely opposed to hierarchal power structures and venues of writing inevitably configured by such structures (as, for example, they brace career advancement in the academy or the intellectual scaffolding of first-world philosophizing). What else can explain why—while defining the colonized woman we "should name (as) 'woman' . . . whom we strictly, historically, geopolitically *cannot imagine*"—Spivak inserts the remark, "I know the kind of woman I am thinking about. And I also know that this person is not imaginable by most friends reading these words" (*OTM* 137)?

What Do You *Mean*, Woman?

To certify the Derridean assumptions upon which thinkers such as Spivak draw, many poststructuralists sought to use the race-based interrogation of the term "women" undertaken by African-American and postcolonial scholars, even though a number of prominent black intellectuals criticized the elitism of what Barbara Christian called "The Race for Theory" undertaken by the followers of white, male philosophers.[21] For if early feminists exposed "humanism" as a euphemism for masculinism, if some African-American and postcolonial critics went on to exhibit "feminism" as a code word for a privileged white women's movement, then poststructuralists could delegitimate *any* generalizing, abstract appeal to "women" as propagating a phallogocentric metaphysics of presence. However, just as the language of critical election and abjection contaminates feminist prose with self-righteousness, obscurantism undermines the writing of feminist poststructuralists who rely on counterintuitive maxims recycled as fiats, a logic at odds with normative syntactic procedures, and utopian ontological paradigms.

When in 1985 Toril Moi's *Sexual/Textual Politics* pitted Anglo-American empiricists against French theorists (to illustrate the purported naïveté of the former, the supposed sophistication of the latter), Julia Kristeva emerged as an exemplary figure whose anti-essentialist pronouncements challenged any stable definition of selfhood: "To believe that one 'is a woman' is almost as absurd and obscurantist as to believe that one 'is a man,'" Kristeva proclaimed, and, even more famously," ' *woman as such* does not exist' " (Moi 163, 165). In her attempt to denaturalize gender, Kristeva can represent many poststructuralists in the nineties who mapped the ways in which "the subject" (no longer a self or a subjectivity) was constructed through a range of linguistic as well as psychological, social, and political discourses. To the extent that feminism depends upon a stable notion of sexual identity, it degenerates into a form of romanticism, according to Kristeva. For those thinkers employing deconstruction in the service of feminism, therefore, the term "women" transmutes infinitely by virtue of the discursive relations within which it is located.[22]

Yet Moi's recycling of Kristeva's maxims (without their philosophic rationale) turned them into quasireligious pieties at odds with exactly the pliancy that most poststructuralists espouse as an antidote to speciously determinate or naturalized modes of thinking. That is, when the playful indeterminacy of gender becomes axiomatic, it loses its playfulness and its indeterminacy. Also engaging in the totalizing she condemned in her predecessors was Judith Butler, one of the most important poststructuralist thinkers in the nineties. Nor should this surprise us, since—regardless of their impressively acrobatic efforts—Butler and Moi, like the feminist thinkers whose publications preceded them by no more than a decade, remain inevitably fixed in the terms the culture provides. That those terms persist— saturated with misogynist, racist, and homophobic messages—adds to the societal importance of feminists' attempting to achieve the sort of lucidity poststructuralist prose rarely exhibits.

Judith Butler analyzes gender as a performance producing the delusion of an abiding self that is "always already" constructed through discourse and thus neither an originatory given nor a volitional agent. Butler set out to demonstrate that sex—just as culturally constructed as gender—is made to seem natural or real or fixed through regulatory practices that set in place the "heterosexualization of desire" (*GT* 17):[23]

> If gender is drag, and if it is an imitation that regularly produces the ideal it attempts to approximate, then gender is a performance that *produces* the illusion of an inner sex or essence or psychic gender core; it *produces* on the skin, through the gesture, the move, the gait (that array of corporeal theatrics understood as gender presentation), the illusion of an inner depth. ("IGI" 28)

Possibly because of its difficult task of dislodging commonly held assumptions, possibly because of the influence of Foucault and Derrida, recondite abstractions characterize postmodernist feminist theory in general, Butler's books in particular.[24] The consequence for criticism of a linguistic model deriving from philosophy has been to divorce feminist speculations from literary texts or to subordinate those texts to the epistemological, ideological, economic, and political issues that supplanted literary history and aesthetic evaluation as the topics of writing about women. Given poststructuralist assumptions about the undecidability of meaning, the death of the author, the non-referentiality of language contaminated by hegemonic power structures, and the contingency of evaluative judgments, it is not surprising that the aesthetic got marginalized and the first three stages of feminist criticism sidelined.[25]

One especially revealing feature of Butler's style is the preponderance of subject-verb disagreements. I want to speculate that this penchant—by reflecting the difficulty of sustaining a Foucauldian critique of the singular self and the biological body—reveals the tensions continually at play in efforts to combine poststructuralism with feminism. Since my argument depends on a pattern of mistakes in agreement, I will cite four examples here from *Gender Trouble*, its sequel *Bodies That Matter*, and a recent essay entitled "Imitation and Gender Insubordination," placing the location of eighteen others in this footnote[26]:

> The *totality* and *closure* of language is both presumed and contested within structuralism. (*GT* 40)

> The division and exchange between this "being" and "having" the Phallus is established by the Symbolic, the paternal law. (*GT* 45)

> Importantly, the erotic redeployment of prohibitions and the production of new cultural forms for sexuality is not a transient affair within an imaginary domain that will inevitably evaporate under the prohibitive force of the symbolic.
> (*BTM* 110)

> For psychoanalytic theorists Mikkel Borch-Jacobsen and Ruth Leys, however, identification, and, in particular, identificatory mimetism, precedes identity and constitutes identity as that which is fundamentally "other to itself." ("I" 26)

Note how prone Butler's prose is to a compound subject with a singular form of verbs that eschew action and instead denote a condition or stipulate a mode of existence.[27] Her dual subjects often involve not persons but abstractions that are treated as if they have combined in her mind into a single force that therefore requires the singular verb. (This tendency to make conceptual processes the subject of sentences explains the prevalence of "ity" words in current theory: irresolvability, performativity, postcoloniality, generativity, locationality, historicity, citationality, etcetericity.) In a curious way, the reliance on intangible subjects and (often) the verb "to be" replicates Butler's Foucauldian rejection of humanism, her conviction that "regimes of discourse" speak through individuals whose very conceptions of their identity are thereby constituted and regulated. That the result is so often a grammatical lapse, however, hints at a conflict between what Butler seeks to argue and the terms available to her.

When the subject gets multiplied into two and when these two speak together, alas!—they end up sounding just like one. The singular verb keeps putting the lie to grammatical subjects asserting their doubleness, bearing witness paradoxically to Butler's own confession at the end of *Bodies That Matter* that "the temporary totalization performed by identity categories is a necessary error" (*BTM* 230). Telling in this regard, too, is a passage in which she explains, "I use the grammar of an 'I' or a 'we' as if these subjects precede and activate their various identification, but this is a grammatical fiction. . . . For there is no 'I' prior to its assumption of sex" (*BTM* 99).[28] Like Butler's frequent use of lists of unanswered questions, her subject-verb disagreements hint that this Professor of Rhetoric remains haunted by the "necessary error[s]" and "grammatical fiction[s]" that shape "the unstable and continuing condition of the 'one' and the 'we'" that she studies quite brilliantly in the shifting allegiances of feminists, lesbians, and gay men (*BTM* 242).

Even for those to whom Butler's syntactic penchant appears a legitimate extension of the rule that a singular verb may be used when nouns form a compound word or convey a singular notion, the pattern bespeaks a quandary, for it demonstrates how often the most vigilantly antitotalizing theorist of poststructuralism relies on stubborn patterns of totalization (two treated as one). This, in turn, may lead some readers to hypothesize that the concept of "the subject" itself totalizes all subjectivities as passive, isolated products of discursive power-knowledge regimes (often assumed to be essentially malign).[29] When Butler decides to engage in "an application that Nietzsche himself would not have anticipated or condoned" by extending his aphorism "there is no 'being' behind doing" with her own "There is no gender identity behind the expressions of gender" (*GT* 25), the thinker (Nietzsche, Butler) who produces language is only the product of it and thus, as Seyla Benhabib points out, "the responsibility for this discourse cannot be attributed to the author" (*SS* 216). Setting aside Nietzsche's virulent misogyny, another of his famously hyperbolic pronouncements—"I am afraid we are not rid of God because we still have faith in grammar" (483)—might be rephrased, in light of Benhabib's objections: Does the rescinding of grammar, of subject-verb agreement, eradicate the ideals of individual social responsibility and collective political agency?[30]

If nominalism teaches us that "the self" and "women" are illusory categories of nonexistent entities, perhaps only a newly imagined image of "our bodies, our selves" can help human beings out of the "necessary error[s]" and "grammatical fiction[s]" of "the temporary totalization performed by identity categories." As influential in the nineties as Butler, Donna Haraway provided such a figure in the cyborg. Founded on a thoroughgoing rejection of biologism joined with a skeptical foregrounding of the ways in which power pervades and thus implicates the conceptual apparatus used by critics, Haraway's cyborg stands out as the character best exemplifying the valorization of fragmentation, indeterminacy, marginalization. Haraway would repopulate feminism with cyborgs since "Painful fragmentation among feminists (not to mention among women) along every possible fault line has made the concept of woman elusive, an excuse for the matrix of women's dominations of each other" (197). Breaching, confusing, and thereby confounding the boundaries between organism and machine, animal and human, male and female, cyborgian consciousness rejects the need for unity as the totalitarianism of totalizing, calling instead for partial identities, contradictory standpoints, and shifting affinities.

Because biology and in particular women's unique capacity to give birth served historically as a powerful explanation or even an influential justification for debilitating gender roles, Butler and Haraway attempt to debiologize such roles. Yet, according to Rosi Braidotti, who understands that the cyborg "announces a world 'beyond gender,'" Haraway claims "that sexed identity is obsolete without showing the steps and the points of exit from the old, gender-polarized system" (170).[31] In fact, the cyborg dwells in what Haraway herself terms "a postgender world" (192), a domain not yet inhabited by contemporary women who, when they experience its features—the breaching of boundaries between the organic and the inorganic or female bodies as mechanically engineered—know it in the form of interventions such as breast implants, estrogen therapy, mood-altering or birth control or fertility drugs, and anticancer chemo- and radiation therapies whose positive effects have often been matched by equal or greater negative ones. The disjunction between the nowhere of the cyborg's utopian fluidity and the everywhere of ordinary people's embodiment (with all its attendant ills) calls to mind Butler's "necessary error" of "temporary totalization" (which in turn might recall Spivak's "strategic choice of a genitalist essentialism in anti-sexist work today" [*TPC* 11]).[32]

Taken together, poststructuralist publications suggest a fissure between deconstruction of "the subject," on the one hand, and feminism's dependency on the collective word "women," on the other. The terms of the impasse impel Butler and Spivak to resort to formulations that they themselves characterize as inadequate, while Haraway invents a nonce identity that no one will see when she looks in the mirror. Susan Stanford Friedman, after endorsing the problematizing of subjectivity undertaken by poststructuralists, deduces their logical perspective on feminist criticism: "more fluid and flexible critical practices are needed that do not regard sexual or gender differences as an *a priori*, fixed, primal, or primary assumption to be grasped in pristine isolation" (31). Even a "provisional privileging of gender" remains suspect for Friedman since "gender is only one among many axes of identity" and so feminist critics—accused now of "blindness" in their foregrounding of gender—should be terminated so practitioners in the new field of Identity Studies can be hired (14).

Diagnosis/Prognosis

This effort to trace the sources of the language crisis at which feminist criticism has arrived during its fourth and most quarrelsome phase obviously leaves me open to charges that, first, I have demonized debate, ignoring the ways in which new insights challenging received wisdom may have to emerge (or seem to emerge) as a threat and, second, that the contention is contagious since I have myself engaged in antagonistic in-fighting. To the first objection, I can only resort to my view that critical election, abjection, and obscurantism perform a disservice to the libertarian politics and pedagogies endorsed by many of those whose astute ideas play a justly prominent part in feminist thinking. The brouhaha this essay immediately roused as a talk— causing me to be labeled an anti-intellectual and a racist, much to my shock— testifies to the ways in which critical election, abjection, and obscurantism have contributed to an atmosphere of censorship that silences or patrols our feminist debates. About the second objection, I would add that although I have enlisted in the conflict, I do so in order to draw attention to a divisiveness that plays into the hands of conservative elements all too happy to see the women's movement self-destruct. Perhaps because stylistic foibles are easier to catch than originality or subtlety of conceptualizing, much of the prose provoked by the reflections of hooks, Carby, Mohanty, and Spivak as well as Moi, Butler, and Haraway either mimes their critical election and obscurantism or acquiesces with critical abjection—without duplicating their remarkable discernment.

At our conferences and on the pages of our journals, feminist conversations—their integrity, elasticity, inventiveness, pertinence—have been damaged by kneejerk critical maneuvers that turned into default positions: touting one's own virtuous radicalism by labeling all other thinkers in the field reactionary; pitting theory against practice or activism against scholarship; using one category of gender, race, nation, or sexual orientation to find the other terms wanting; exploiting identity politics to legislate who should be certified to produce various types of investigations; a reliance on arcane lexicons accessible only to the initiated; and a tendency simply not to do the research, not to footnote or acknowledge earlier thinkers in the field. Quite simply boring, such routinized postures inhibit what one would ordinarily call thinking, making it hard for people to risk ideas that do not toe what is assumed to be a morally superior or epistemologically more sophisticated line.

Not that feminists stand alone in their use of divisive and obfuscatory languages. Undoubtedly, the economic pressures at work downsizing the academy throughout the eighties and nineties escalated the pressure always exerted on humanities scholars to produce a reputation by engaging in arcane, agonistic maneuvers or by feverishly finding innovative vocabularies. For this reason, the language available to critics in general, to feminist critics more specifically has become less limber than it needs to be. Churlish or cultish, its politically or theoretically correct jargon stifles rather than nurtures thoughtful interchange. Within feminist circles, my dissatisfaction with boring default positions reflects the views of many of my peers, though my earlier caveats about reducing these issues to generational paradigms still hold.

Certainly a good number of the scholars who played pioneering roles in the establishment of feminist criticism during the seventies felt discouraged by the nineties. At the main forum of the MLA convention's 1994 sessions on "Feminist Criticism Revised," Barbara Christian led off with a passionate denunciation of higher education's failure to nurture African-American intellectuals: black feminist criticism may be high on the literary critical stock market, she explained, but very few African Americans number among graduate students and faculty in the humanities. Next, Jane Gallop stood up to explain that she would not deliver the essay she had composed because (and I quote in capital letters to capture her tone) it was "THE MOST BORING PAPER I'D EVER WRITTEN." Nancy K. Miller revealed that she had not published her remarks earlier because she was demoralized by the amount of "trashing" going on in feminist circles. Around 1985, Elaine Showalter added, she stopped producing feminist articles, worn down by hostile reactions produced by people who then turned around to ask her for a letter of recommendation. As if contextualizing their ennui, Florence Howe compared the 1990s to the 1950s, cautioning against cultural amnesia, careerism, and generational competition.

To Judith Newton, sitting in the audience, the most insistent note was "the thematization of wound and loss, as one speaker after another touched on the current lapse of historical memory, the rejection or loss of political heritages and commitment, feminist careerism and competitiveness, and the ingratitude of the young" (328). How could this chorus of plaintive voices not sound discouraging and strange to our graduate students, given the huge audience—some five hundred people? Inexplicable, too, in light of the successful careers feminism had sponsored for these eminent scholars. Yet another smart observer, Barbara Johnson, has viewed the very perplexity of the speakers at "Feminist Criticism Revisited" as well as their common inability to define the feminist project as cause for optimism, for she believes there is "something about contemporary academic feminism that requires ambivalence" (2). According to Johnson, ambivalence remains a necessity that testifies to our commitment to a contradictory process of growth. "Once women begin to speak, we begin to differ with each other," she reminds us (3).

What Biddy Martin says about Queer Studies expresses my feelings about how and why feminists should differ: "I want a queer studies that allows for attachments that are not necessarily politically consistent and acknowledges the incalculability of the subject" (*FPS* 14). Patricia Yaeger, who longs "for writing that is improper, unclean, illogical, politically suspect, full of raunchy anecdotes and abortive logic," also captures my wish for criticism that "avoids the too anxious ablutions of postmodern feminists so busy cleaning up each others' acts that they fail to see the mess and pollution lingering around the kitchen sinks of women still caught in the travails of a pre-postmodern world" ("PP" 7). Recently, we have seen one creative rhetorical response to these "too anxious ablutions." When "we" became as impossible a word as "women" for feminists, the "I" emerged in new modes of critical writing, though ever tentative because so attentive to its lack of sovereignty, given its highly localized point of view.

A pioneer in this autobiographical criticism, Nancy K. Miller relates its rise to an "inevitable waning of enthusiasm for a mode of Theory, whose authority—however variously—depended finally on the theoretical evacuation of the very social subjects producing it" (*GP* 20). If poststructuralism had discredited any notion of an imperial subject engaged in a master or metanarrative, if identity politics thwarted any one sort of person representing other types of people, a host of feminists could circulate multiple versions of particularized subjectivities in their own micronarratives.[33] Although at times faulted as a fall into narcissism, personal forms of criticism reap the benefits of racialized and poststructuralist critiques of a transcendent perspective but without resorting to the divisive and obfuscatory languages in which those claims had been established.[34] For scholars seeking to write outside of autobiographical modes, however, the quandary of language remains a significant one.

Given our historic ties beyond the academy to the women's movement, feminist critics have profited from a privileged access to the public sphere that has recently been obstructed, if not broken, by esoteric methodological disputes that obscure what we have to say to one another and isolate us within sectarian dialects. At times, alas, critical election, abjection, and obscurantism turned academic feminists away from any subject other than their own internecine quarrels. Were I tempted to answer the query of my revised title—"What Ails Feminist Criticism?"—in one diagnostic phrase summing up the net effect of rhetorics of dissension, I could call the problem a bad case of critical anorexia,[35] for racialized identity politics made the word "women" slim down to stand only for a very particularized kind of woman, whereas poststructuralists obliged the term to disappear altogether. How paradoxical that during the time of feminist criticism's successful institutionalization in many academic fields, it seems to be suffering from a sickness that can end in suicide.

But what of my promise to use the disease metaphor as a means of imagining some hope for recovery? Thinking dialectically about stage four, I wonder whether several symptoms of rejuvenation mean that dissension has functioned as a purgative period in a much-needed (though painful) process of growth. Besides producing hybrid forms of autobiographical criticism more supple in its attentiveness to various kinds of difference that are distinctively structured, many practitioners within the third stage of feminist criticism—the engendering of differences—have managed to highlight dissimilarities among women without squelching conversations about them. As the first two chapters of this volume try to demonstrate, African-American and postcolonial scholars as well as lesbian thinkers are currently making such a transformative mark in our field that they have paved the way for a race- and sex-change in feminist literary criticism, whose practitioners no longer labor under any presumptions about the whiteness or heterosexuality of their subjects. Although, to my mind, identity politics represents a dead-end, race- and nation-based approaches to gender have greatly enriched our field; although, to my mind, poststructuralist essentializing betokens an impasse, poststructuralist skepticism about the fixity of gender has proved invaluable. Distressing as the rhetorics of critical abjection, election, and obscurantism have been in our recent past, unproductive as such racialized and poststructural dictions surely will be in our future, their proponents have nevertheless played a major role in transfiguring feminist studies.[36]

At the risk of exhibiting my own thralldom to such ground-breaking writers as Hazel Carby, Gayatri Chakravorty Spivak, and Judith Butler (as well as my ongoing imaginative reliance on the literature produced by men), I will end here with a private admission. Though the title of my essay can be faulted for pathologizing certain tendencies in feminist rhetoric, though I used it to characterize the subversion of the term "women" as a malady, it actually derived from Keats's poem "La Belle Dame sans Merci"—"O what can ail thee, Knight at arms, / Alone and palely loitering?"—in which Keats's knight suffers less from a physical illness, more from a psychological enchantment, his fascination with a woman whose unearthly beauty represents the realm of imagination that can alienate him from the everyday world of actuality. The magical foods furnished by La Belle Dame—"roots of relish sweet, / And honey wild, and manna dew"—threaten to make the nourishing provisions of reality nauseating to those who, falling under her sway, will then be destined to starve to death. Seductively transformative, the languages of identity politics and poststructuralist abstractions have captivated many of us, lending sophistication to our field; however, at this point they should be reinvented to deal with the here and now, in an activist framework that will inspire our students by addressing the societal conditions with which they must contend.

In accord with Susan Bordo's "feminist chauvinism," her efforts "to help restore feminism's rightful parentage of the 'politics of the body' " she studies and of the bodies of literature many others explore ("FFP" 183), I find myself echoing the words of Rosi Braidotti, who understands the word "women" as "a general umbrella term" and who exclaims, "I wish feminism would shed its saddening, dogmatic mode to rediscover the merrymaking of a movement that aims to change life" (167). By contesting the debilitating rhetorics of critical election, abjection, and obscurantism, I would like to think I'm supplying food for thought about how to find more mirthful scholarly lexicons.[37] What should be tried are not only nutritious but also delicious linguistic practices so we can heal feminist discourse of infirmities that have made us cranky with one another. For a robust feminist criticism needs to get into training to assume the vital roles we will undoubtedly want it to play in the twenty-first century.

7

Feminist Misogyny; or, The Paradox of "It Takes One to Know One"

In a self-reflexive essay representative of current feminist thinking, Ann Snitow recalls a memory of the early seventies, a moment when a friend "sympathetic to the [woman's] movement but not active [in it] asked what motivated" Snitow's fervor:

> I tried to explain the excitement I felt at the idea that I didn't have to be a woman. She was shocked, confused. *This* was the motor of my activism? She asked, "How can someone who doesn't like being a woman be a feminist?" To which I could only answer, "Why would anyone who likes being a woman *need* to be a feminist?"
>
> Quite properly my colleague feared woman-hating. . . . Was this, as [she] thought, just a new kind of misogyny? (33)

Though Snitow eventually finds "woman-hating— or loving— . . . beside the point," she admits that she "wouldn't dare say self-hatred played no part in what I wanted from feminism," a remark that takes on added resonance in terms of her first reaction to consciousness raising: "'Woman' is my slave name," she felt back then; "feminism will give me freedom to seek some other identity altogether" (9).

"'Woman' is my slave name; feminism will give me freedom to seek some other identity altogether": Snitow's formulation dramatizes a curious contradiction feminism exhibits from its very inception to present times. The oxymoronic title of this essay—feminist misogyny—risks political incorrectness and implicitly asks us to pause, to consider the efficacy of the appellations "feminism" and "misogyny," not to derail our commitment to social justice but to make it more savvy, more supple. For when put to the test in the "Can you really tell?" game, current conceptualizations may not always help us distinguish feminist from misogynist claims.

On the one hand, can you judge the sexual politics of the thinker who wrote the sentence "There is a pleasure, . . . an enjoyment of the body, which is . . . *beyond the phallus*"? What does it mean that this apparently liberated sentiment comes from Jacques Lacan (the same Lacan who boasted, "[women] don't know what they're saying, that's all the difference between them and me")?[1] On the other hand, can you surmise the ideology of the writer who declared that "woman is body more than man is" (*NBW* 95) or of the theorist who stated that *"woman has sex organs more or less everywhere"* (*TS* 28)? What does it mean that these two quotations, authored by feminist theorists Hélène Cixous and Luce Irigaray, eerily reiterate a proposition made by masculinist writers from Rousseau to Ambrose Bierce so as to deny women equal educational opportunities, specifically the idea that "to men a man is but a mind. . . . But woman's body *is* the woman" (Morgan 34)?[2]

Pursuing the same inquiry, we might ask why Denise Riley chose the allusive title *Am I That Name?* (1988) for a book advocating a poststructural approach to feminism, when the line (originally spoken in the femicidal atmosphere of Shakespeare's *Othello*) conflates the "name" woman with the name-calling that demotes woman to whore?[3] Finally, who would guess that this critique of Adrienne Rich—"The feminist dream of a common language . . . is a totalizing and imperialist one"—issues not from Lacan or some modern-day Iago but from the Women's Studies scholar Donna Haraway (215)? If the histories of feminism and misogyny have been (sometimes shockingly) dialogic, as I will try to suggest, what impact should that have on the ways in which we understand the once and future state of feminist theory?

The first subject of my meditation, Mary Wollstonecraft, may seem just as incongruous as its title because we generally view Wollstonecraft as a pioneer whose feminist efforts were tragically misunderstood by the misogynist society in which she lived. And, of course, as the aesthetic foremother of feminist expository prose, Wollstonecraft established a polemical tradition mined by such literary descendants as Olive Schreiner, Emma Goldman, and Virginia Woolf, as well as by contemporary thinkers from Simone de

Beauvoir to Kate Millett and, yes, Cixous and Riley. Indubitably, all of these theorists profited from and extended Wollstonecraft's insistence on righting the wrongs done to women. Paradoxically, however, they also inherited what I am calling her feminist misogyny. Indeed, the very troubling tenacity of this strain in feminist expository prose calls out for further thought.

That Wollstonecraft did, in fact, function as an effective advocate for women is probably self-evident, especially to anyone familiar with the political and literary culture into which she interjected her views. Though I will be examining a pervasive contradiction in her life and work, in no way do I mean to diminish or disparage her achievements. Quite rightly regarded as the founding feminist text in English, *A Vindication of the Rights of Woman* (1792) links the radical insurrection of the French revolution to the equally radical insubordination of the feminist project. Nor do I think we should judge Wollstonecraft by late twentieth-century definitions of feminism and find her wanting, "as if "—to quote Frances Ferguson—"Wollstonecraft would have turned out better work if she had had a word processor or a microwave oven" (60–61).

Although she has been faulted for adhering to a suspect faith in reason as an innate human characteristic,[4] Wollstonecraft exploited Enlightenment language to claim that—at least theoretically—men and women were alike in being endowed with reason, a divine faculty that only needed to be cultivated so as to perfect the human species. Many of the thinkers of her time emphasized the differences between the sexes, with the influential Rousseau demanding that women's education "should be always relative to the men. To please, to be useful to [men,] . . . to advise, to console us, to render our lives easy and agreeable: these are the duties of women at all times" (Wollstonecraft *VRW* 79). But Wollstonecraft believed that because both sexes shared an equal capacity for reason, women—considered as *human*, not as sexual, beings—should benefit from the educational programs historically only afforded men. In addition, Wollstonecraft's commitment to rationality made her especially sensitive to representations of female irrationality that enslaved women's hearts and minds.

From her meditations on the Bible and Milton's *Paradise Lost* to her interpretations of Pope's, Dr. Gregory's, and Rousseau's treatises, Wollstonecraft's analyses of debilitating female images assume that we are what we read, and therefore these passages in *A Vindication of the Rights of Woman* constitute one of the earliest instances we have of feminist criticism. According to Wollstonecraft, female readers necessarily internalize male-authored and manifestly false impressions of who they are and what they should aspire to be, impressions that weaken rather than strengthen women's self-image. Confronting the socialization process effected by reading as well as by other child-drearing practices, Wollstonecraft used her expository prose and her two novels to theorize about the psychological and cultural engendering of femininity. None of her contemporaries devised as sophisticated a model for understanding the social construction of womanhood, speculations that laid the groundwork for Simone de Beauvoir's famous claim that "one is not born a woman, but rather becomes one."[5] Yet it is in this area—Wollstonecraft's analysis of the feminine—that we will find most striking evidence of the contradiction in her thinking that I am terming "feminist misogyny."

What image of woman emerges from the pages of *A Vindication of the Rights of Woman?* Repeatedly and disconcertingly, Wollstonecraft associates the feminine with weakness, childishness, deceitfulness, cunning, superficiality, an overvaluation of love, frivolity, dilettantism, irrationality, flattery, servility, prostitution, coquetry, sentimentality, ignorance, indolence, intolerance, slavish conformity, fickle passion, despotism, bigotry, and a "spaniel-like affection" (34). The feminine principle, so defined, threatens—like a virus—to contaminate and destroy men and their culture. For, as Wollstonecraft explains, "Weak, artificial beings, raised above the common wants and affections of their race, in a premature unnatural manner, undermine the very foundation of virtue, and spread corruption through the whole mass of society" (9).

Here in *A Vindication*, as in the next sentences I quote, femininity feels like a malady:

> [Women's] senses are *inflamed*, and their understandings neglected, consequently they become the *prey* of their senses, delicately termed sensibility, and are *blown about* by every momentary *gust* of feeling. Civilized women are, therefore, . . . *weakened* by false refinement. . . . Ever *restless* and *anxious*, their *over exercised* sensibility not only renders them *uncomfortable* themselves, but *troublesome* . . . to others. . . . [T]heir conduct is *unstable*, and their opinions are *wavering*. . . . By *fits and starts* they are *warm* in many pursuits; yet this *warmth*, never concentrated into perseverance, soon *exhausts* itself. . . .*Miserable*, indeed, must be that being whose cultivation of mind has only tended to *inflame* its passions!
> (emphases mine, 60–61)

According to this passage, civilized women suffer from an illness, a veritable fever of femininity, that reduces them to "unstable" and "uncomfortable," "miserable," exhausted invalids. Wollstonecraft's description of women's restlessness, of the "warm gusts" of inflammation they suffer, sounds like nothing less than contemporary complaints about hot flashes and menopausal mood swings, as if the long disease of femininity has itself become a disabling "change of life." At the close of the paragraph in which these words appear, Wollstonecraft takes to its logical conclusion the implications of women's "fits and starts": When "passions" are "pampered, whilst the judgement is left unformed," she asks, "what can be expected to ensue?" She promptly answers, "Undoubtedly, a mixture of madness and folly!"

Elsewhere in a related series of metaphors, women operate like "gangrene, which the vices engendered by oppression have produced," and the mortal damage they inflict "is not confined to the morbid part, but pervades society at large" (178). Even if she is not noxious, the female is obnoxious, a diminished thing that has dwindled, dehumanized, into something like a doll, providing merely an aimless leisure pastime for men: "She was created," Wollstonecraft claims, "to be the toy of man, his rattle, and it must jingle in his ears whenever, dismissing reason, he chooses to be amused" (34). Like a virus spreading corruption; like an illness condemning its victim to madness; like gangrene contaminating the healthy; like a jingling toy distracting irrational pleasure-seekers: because femininity figures as, at best, frivolity and, at worst, fatality, the principal character emerging from the pages of *The Vindication of the Rights of Woman* is the femme fatale.

Wollstonecraft's derogations of the feminine, to be sure, are framed in terms of her breakthrough analysis of the social construction of gender. The above quotations, for instance, insist that women's "senses are inflamed" because "their understandings [are] neglected"; that women are artificially "raised" above the race; that the gangrene of their vices is "engendered" by oppression; and that they are "created" to be toys. Thus, her thesis—that a false system of education has "rendered [women] weak and wretched"—emphasizes the powerful impact of culture on subjectivity, the capacity of the psyche to internalize societal norms (7). Indeed, Wollstonecraft stands at an originatory point in feminist thought precisely because she envisioned a time when the female of the species could shed herself of an enfeebling acculturation or feminization. Yet although (or perhaps because) *A Vindication* sets out to liberate society from a hated subject constructed to be subservient and called "woman," it illuminates how such animosity can spill over into antipathy of those human beings most constrained by that construction.

Laying the groundwork for the first and second wave of the women's movement, *A Vindication of the Rights of Woman* implies that " 'Woman' is my slave name; feminism will give me freedom to seek some other identity altogether" (Snitow 9). About the "few women [who] have emancipated themselves from the galling yoke of sovereign man," therefore, Wollstonecraft speculates that they are virtually transsexuals. Just as Newton "was probably a being of superior order accidentally caged in a human body," she imagines that "the few extraordinary women" in history "were *male* spirits, confined by mistake in female frames" (35).[6] No wonder that, as Mary Poovey has pointed out, Wollstonecraft often speaks of herself "as a philosopher," "as a moralist," even "as [a] man with man," concluding her work with a plea to "ye men of understanding" (79–80).[7] Rarely, in other words, does she present herself as a woman speaking to women.

Curiously, then, Wollstonecraft's radical stance nevertheless ends up aligning her with women's most fervent adversaries, as she herself admits: "after surveying the history of woman," she concedes, "I cannot help, agreeing with the severest satirist, considering the sex as the weakest as well as the most oppressed half of the species" (35). And several passages in *A Vindication* do seem to agree with "the severest satirist[s]" of women. While analyzing the "sexual weakness that makes woman depend upon man," for example, Wollstonecraft scorns "a kind of cattish affection which leads a wife to purr about her husband as she would about any man who fed and caressed her" (175). If the female looks subhuman in her cattiness here, elsewhere she appears sinful in her cunning trickery. To castigate those made "inferiour by ignorance and low desires," Wollstonecraft describes "the serpentine wrigglings of cunning" that enable women to "mount the tree of knowledge, and only acquire sufficient to lead men astray" (173). Like their foremother, Eve, women bear the responsibility for the fall of man, and they do so because of their misuse of knowledge. Predictably, one of Wollstonecraft's favorite Greek allusions is to Eve's prototype, Pandora.

And a number of other passages in *A Vindication of the Rights of Woman* concur with the severest satirists of the weaker sex, whom Wollstonecraft actually echoes. Take, for example, the following attack on the institution of marriage as a commodities market:

> It is acknowledged that [women] spend many of the first years of their lives in acquiring a smattering of accomplishments; meanwhile strength of body and mind are sacrificed to libertine notions of beauty, to the desire of establishing

themselves,—the only way women can rise in the world,—by marriage. And this desire making mere animals of them, when they marry they act as such children may be expected to act: —they dress; they paint, and nickname God's creatures. —Surely these weak beings are only fit for a seraglio! (10)

Not only does Wollstonecraft paraphrase Hamlet's angry speech to Ophelia—"You jig, you amble, and you lisp; you nickname God's creatures and make your wantonness your ignorance"; by relegating the feminine woman to a seraglio, she also glosses his refrain—"get thee to a nunnery": both nunnery and seraglio were common euphemisms for whorehouse. But the word "seraglio"—a Turkish or Eastern lodging for the secluded harem of Islamic noblemen—captures Wollstonecraft's disdain for a feminine lassitude so degenerate, so threatening to Western civilization that it must be marked as what Edward Said would call a kind of "Orientalism."

If we compare Wollstonecraft's portrait of the feminine here with the notoriously severe eighteenth-century satirists of the weaker sex, it becomes clear that she shares with them Hamlet's revulsion. Judge Wollstonecraft's emphasis on libertine notions of beauty, for example, in terms of Pope's famous lines in his "Epistle to a Lady"—"ev'ry Woman is at heart a Rake" and "Most women have no characters at all"—as well as his insistence that the best woman is "a contradiction" in terms, "a softer man." Consider her picture of female animality and dilettantism in relation to Swift's monstrous Goddess of Criticism in *The Tale of the Tub*, a symbol of ignorance portrayed as part cat, part ass. Compare Wollstonecraft's vision of feminine hypocrisy and prostitution to Swift's attacks in his mock pastorals on dressing and painting, debased arts that conceal syphilitic whores; or place her indictment that unaccomplished women "nickname God's creatures" up against Dr. Johnson's comparison between a woman preaching and a dog dancing. Finally, examine Wollstonecraft's childish wives in terms of the Earl of Chesterfield's definition of women as "children of a larger growth."[8]

Why does Wollstonecraft's text so eerily echo those composed by masculinist satirists?[9] A number of critics have noted problems, tensions, and repressions in the *oeuvre* produced by Wollstonecraft.[10] In particular, these scholars claim that, by appropriating an Enlightenment rhetoric of reason, Wollstonecraft alienated herself and other women from female sexual desire. While it is certainly the case that throughout *A Vindication of the Rights of Woman*, Wollstonecraft elevates friendship between the sexes over romantic and erotic entanglements (which she condemns as ephemeral or destructive),

I would view this motif not merely as a repression of sexuality but more inclusively as a symptom of the paradoxical feminist misogyny that pervades her work, only one sign of the ways in which Wollstonecraft's feminism operates vis-à-vis feminization and by no means an eccentric fault of her philsophizing. For, as Cora Kaplan has insightfully remarked, "There is no feminism that can stand wholly outside femininity as it is posed in a given historical moment. All feminisms give some ideological hostage to femininities and are constructed through the gender sexuality of their day as well as standing in opposition to them" ("WN" 29).

If feminist expository prose necessarily situates itself in opposition to self-demeaning modes of feminization even as it is shaped by them, what Moira Ferguson describes as Wollstonecraft's propensity "to find women culpable of their vanity, their acceptance of an inferior education, their emphasis on feeling," her tendency to "locate herself outside what she deem[ed] self-demeaning behavior," takes on not only personal but also political and philosophical import (97). Indeed, the tensions at work in Wollstonecraft's text dramatize, on the one hand, the ways in which "feminisms give some ideological hostage to femininities," as Kaplan puts it, and, on the other hand, the ironies embedded in the stage of patrilineal affiliation that Sandra Gilbert and I have examined in the aesthetic paradigm we call "the female affiliation complex" (*WW* 165–224).

To take the first subject first, is it possible to view Wollstonecraft's description of the fever of femininity in *A Vindication of the Rights of Woman* as a portrait of any middle-class woman of her age, indeed as a *self*-portrait? Could the disgust at fallen, fated, or fatal females be *self*-disgust? In the words of Emma Goldman, the "sexually starved" Wollstonecraft was "doomed to become the prey of more than one infatuation" and her "insatiable hunger for love" led not only to a tragic desire for the married painter Fuseli but also to the two suicide attempts resulting from her tempestuous involvement with the philanderer Gilbert Imlay (254–5). Wollstonecraft was so overcome by passion for Fuseli that she had suggested a ménage à trois to his shocked wife; after discovering Gilbert Imlay's actress-mistress, she soaked her skirts so as to sink into the water after she threw herself from Putney Bridge. Did anyone better understand slavish passions, the overvaluation of love, fickle irrationality, weak dependency, the sense of personal irrelevance, and anxiety about personal attractiveness than Wollstonecraft herself?

Thus Virginia Woolf, considering the various ways in which Wollstonecraft "could not understand . . . her own feelings," believed that the eighteenth-century polemicist made theories every day, "theories by which life should be lived," but "Every day too—for she was no pedant, no cold-blooded theorist—something was born in her that thrust aside her theories and forced her to model them afresh" (269–70). From the perspective of Goldman's and Woolf's essays, therefore, the misogyny of *A Vindication* dramatizes the self-revulsion of a woman who knew *herself* to be constructed as feminine and thus it exhibits a kind of "antinarcissism."[11] Indeed, what both Goldman and Woolf implicitly ask us to confront is the disparity between the feminist feats of *A Vindication of the Rights of Woman* and the gothic fates inflicted on Wollstonecraft's fictional heroines in *Mary, a Fiction* (1788) and *Maria* (1798).

Of course the subtitle of *Maria—The Wrongs of Woman*—establishes it as a counterpart or extension of *A Vindication of the Rights of Woman*, as does the gloomy insight of its heroine when she asks, "Was not the world a vast prison, and women born slaves?" (27). Curiously, however, both novels negate or traverse the argument of *A Vindication*, which, after all, condemns precisely the conventions of sentimental fiction *Mary* and *Maria* exploit. For the enflamed, volatile emotions Wollstonecraft castigates as weakness, folly, and madness in *A Vindication* infuse, motivate, and elevate the heroines of both novels. After weeping, fainting, and bemoaning her love for a dead friend and a dead lover, the admirable paragon of sensibility who is the central character of *Mary* exclaims, "I cannot live without loving—and love leads to madness" (102). Just as rapturous and tearful, the heroine of *Maria* exhibits the passion denounced throughout *A Vindication* in a narrative that at moments seems not to caution against romance so much as to consecrate it: "So much of heaven" do the lovers of *Maria* enjoy together "that paradise bloomed around them. . . . Love, the grand enchanter, 'lapt them in Elysium,' and every sense was harmonized to joy and social extacy" (51).

But the startling slippages in Wollstonecraft's thinking about heterosexuality are accompanied by equally dramatic strains in her meditations on the bonds between women. Though historians of homosexuality have been led by Wollstonecraft's emotional relationships with Jane Arden and Fanny Blood to argue that the female intimacies celebrated in *Mary* should be situated on what Adrienne Rich calls a "lesbian continuum," several passages in *A Vindication of the Rights of Woman* inveigh against the "grossly familiar" relationships spawned in female communities.[12] Women "shut up together in nurseries, schools, or convents" engage in "nasty customs," share "secrets" (on subjects "where silence ought to reign"), and indulge in "jokes and hoiden tricks" (128). Wollstonecraft the novelist valorizes the nurturing comfort and intensity of female intimacies; however, Wollstonecraft the philosopher hints at the obscene debaucheries of such contacts.

The odd juxtapositions between the *Vindication* and the novels imply that the misogynist portrait of the feminine penned by the feminist may, in fact, represent Wollstonecraft's efforts to negotiate the distance between desire and dread, what she thought she should have been and what she feared herself to be. In other words, *A Vindication of the Rights of Woman* presents a narrative voice of the feminist-philosopher and a fictive profile of femininity that interact to illuminate a dialogue between self and soul, the culturally induced schizophrenia of an antinarcissist. And in some part of herself, Wollstonecraft seemed to have understood this very well. In October 1791, after she had begun composing *A Vindication of the Rights of Woman* and while she was sitting for a portrait a friend had commissioned, she wrote that friend the following lines: "I do not imagine that [the painting] will be a very striking likeness; but, if you do not find me in it, I will send you a more faithful sketch—a book that I am now writing, in which *I* myself . . . shall certainly appear, head and heart" (*CL* 202–3).

Just this dialectic—between head and heart, between a hortatory philosophic voice and a debased self-portrait of femininity—characterizes the feminist misogyny Wollstonecraft bequeathed to her literary descendants, including feminist polemicists writing today. Partially, it was informed by Wollstonecraft's inexorable entrapment inside a patrilineal literary inheritance. In *The War of the Words*, Sandra Gilbert and I argued that women writers before the late nineteenth century necessarily affiliated themselves with an alien and alienating aesthetic patrilineage. But this is even more true for the author of feminist expository prose than it is for the woman poet or novelist who, like Elizabeth Barrett Browning, "look[ed] everywhere for [literary] grandmothers and [found] none" (231–2) because, instead of looking for aesthetic grandmothers, Wollstonecraft set out to debate the most powerfully paternal influences on her own culture: Moses and St. John, Milton and Rousseau, Pope and the authors of conduct and etiquette books.[13]

As a genre, feminist expository prose inevitably embeds itself in the misogynist tradition it seeks to address and redress. Representing the masculinist voice in order to controvert its messages, one chapter of *A Vindication*—brilliantly analyzed by Patricia Yaeger—proceeds by lengthily quoting Rousseau's portrait of womanhood "in his own words, interspersing [Wollstonecraft's] comments and reflections" (74–5). Thus, another dialectic emerges beyond the one between the individual author's head and heart, specifically in *A Vindication* the conversation between Wollstonecraft and Rousseau and more generally in the expository prose of her descendants the dialogic relationship between the histories of feminism and misogyny.

"It Takes One to Know One": the "One" in my subtitle is meant to indicate that it takes a feminist to know a misogynist, and vice versa. The terms of their engagement—as they bob and weave, feint and jab, thrust and parry in their philosophical fencing match or boxing ring—are particularly important to understand because, although feminism historically has not been the condition for misogyny's emergence, the pervasive threat of misogyny brought into being feminist discourse. To the extent that there can be (need be) no feminism without misogyny, the sparring of this odd couple—the feminist, the misogynist—takes on a ritualized, stylized quality as they stroll through the corridors of history, reflecting upon each other and upon their slam dancing. A full description of the choreography of their steps remains beyond the scope of this chapter; however, a brief study of the eccentric dips and swirls executed by these curiously ambivalent partners at the beginning and end of this century can begin the task Judith Butler sets feminist critique, namely understanding "how the category of 'woman,' the subject of feminism, is produced and restrained by the very structures of power through which emancipation is sought" (*GT* 2).

Like Mary Wollstonecraft's, Olive Schreiner's feminist prose stands in a vexed relationship to her fiction: specifically, her polemical *Woman and Labour* (1911)—calling for "New Women" and "New Men" to enter "a new earth"—contrasts with a novel that obsesses over the self-pitying masochism of those who dream of altered sexual arrangements, just as it broods with nauseated fascination on the horrible tenacity of traditional women (272, 282).[14] The would-be author of an introduction to *A Vindication*, Schreiner formulated her demands for female liberation as an attack not on men but on women and specifically on what she called "the human female parasite—the most deadly microbe . . . on the surface of any social organism" (82). In *Woman and Labour*, which functioned as "the Bible" for first-wave feminists, the idle, consuming "parasite woman on her couch" signals "the death-bed of human evolution" (132–3).[15] Strangely, too, Schreiner seems to blame the limits of evolution on female anatomy when she speculates that the size of the human brain could only increase "if in the course of ages the *os cervix* of women should itself slowly expand" (129–30).

Just as discomforting as the thought of an *os cervix* having to extend so as to produce larger human heads may be the less biologistic but comparable woman-blaming in Schreiner's second-wave descendants. Perhaps Ann Douglas's *The Feminization of American Culture* (1977) furnishes the best case among the pioneers in Women's Studies. For here, nineteenth-century women's "debased religiosity, their sentimental peddling of Christian belief for its nostalgic value," and their "fakery" manage to "gut Calvinist orthodoxy" of its rigorous intellectual vitality (6). So aware was Douglas herself about faulting women for the fall (the "feminization") of American culture that she used her introduction to defend herself against the charge that she had "sid[ed] with the enemy" (12). Though Douglas claimed to be motivated by a "respect" for "toughness," this (implicitly male) toughness seems entwined with self-hatred: "I expected to find my fathers and my mothers," she explains about her investigations into the past (8); "instead I discovered my fathers and my sisters" because "The problems of the women correspond to mine with a frightening accuracy that seems to set us outside the processes of history" (11).

About the immersion of Douglas's contemporaries in the literary history of the fathers, we might ask, what does it mean that a generation of readers was introduced to the works of Henry Miller and Norman Mailer through the long quotations that appeared in Kate Millett's important text *Sexual Politics* (1970)? In this respect, Millett's work typifies a paradox that persists in a branch of feminist criticism that, following in the wake of *A Vindication*, tackles the problematics of patriarchy by examining sexist authors (from Milton to Mailer) or by exploring male-dominated genres (pornography, the Western, adventure tales, men's magazines, film noir). No matter how radical the critique, it frequently falls into the representational quandary of *A Vindication of the Rights of Woman*: replication or even recuperation. Throughout the feminist expository prose of the nineteen-seventies, the predominant images of women constellate around the female victim: foot-binding and suttee, clitoridectomy and witch-burning appear with startling frequency; the characters of the madwoman, the hysteric, the abused whore, the freak, and the female eunuch abound.

From *The Troublesome Helpmate* (1966), Katharine Roger's groundbreaking history of misogyny in literature, to my own work with Sandra Gilbert, moreover, feminist literary criticism has demonstrated that the most deeply disturbing male-authored depictions of women reveal with exceptional clarity the cultural dynamics of gender asymmetries. Thus, although Sandra Gilbert and I usually focus on the female tradition, it seems striking that our most extended meditations on male authors center on such infamous masculinists as Milton, Rider Haggard, Freud, D. H. Lawrence, and T. S. Eliot, rather than, say, John Stuart Mill, George Meredith, or George Bernard Shaw, all self-defined friends of the women's movement. When questioned about our reliance on Freud, we tend to respond by emphasizing how we have sought to disentangle the *de*scriptive powers of his insights into the sex/gender system from the *pre*scriptive overlay contained in the values he assigns aspects or stages of that system.

Perhaps this speculation tells us as much about the masculinist tradition as it does about the intervention of feminism. Can we extend it by proposing that misogynist texts often elaborate upon feminist insights, but within structures of address or rhetorical frames that—in different ways, to different degrees—vilify, diminish, or dismiss them? To return to *Hamlet* or, for that matter, *Othello* and *King Lear*, can it be that Shakespeare's portraits of femicidal heroes lay bare the causes and dynamics of woman-hating, albeit in plots that equivocate about the value placed upon such an emotion? To return to Freud, didn't his description of psychosexual development in Western culture make possible the radical revisions of a host of feminist theorists, ranging from Joan Rivière and Karen Horney to Shulamith Firestone, Juliet Mitchell, Gayle Rubin, Nancy Chodorow, and Adrienne Rich? In other words, if Wollstonecraft's *Vindication* embeds within it a misogynist text, do Shakespeare's *Hamlet*, Milton's *Paradise Lost*, Rousseau's *Confessions*, and Freud's "Female Sexuality" contain antithetical feminist subscripts?[16]

The idea of feminist misogyny might thereby explain a host of critical controversies over the ideological designs of individual authors or texts. For at the current time probably every "major" writer in the canon, possibly every touchstone work, has been claimed by one scholar or another as prototypically feminist *and* quintessentially masculinist. Nor is this surprising, given that each individual's "language," according to the foremost theorist of this issue, "lies on the borderline between oneself and the other." As Bakhtin's most evocative description of the "overpopulation" of language explains,

> The word in language is half someone else's. . . . It exists in other people's mouths, in other people's contexts, serving other people's intentions; it is from there that one must take the word, and make it one's own. (293–4)

"Expropriating" language from the purposes or designs of others, "forcing it to submit to one's own intentions and accents": this is the "complicated process" in which feminists and misogynists necessarily engage so their discourses necessarily intersect in numerous ways, undercutting or supplementing each other over time, contesting what amounts to a complex nexus of ideas, values, perspectives, and norms, a cultural "heteroglossia" of gender ideologies and power asymmetries. Like the concept of black self-hatred and Jewish anti-Semitism, feminist misogyny might bring to critical attention the interlocutionary nature of representation; that is, the crucially different effects of the sentence "I am this" and "You are that."[17]

Inevitably, as the interaction between "I am this" and "You are that" implies, feminist consciousness today still bears the marks of its having come into being through interactions with a masculinism that has been shaped, in turn, by women's independence movements, a phenomenon that explains a number of anomalies: that Mary Daly, not Norman Mailer, entitled a volume *Pure Lust* (1984) and coined the phrase "fembot," for instance; that Norman Mailer, not Kate Millett, wrote *The Prisoner of Sex* (1971); that after Kate Millett's *Sexual Politics*—an analysis of masculine domination, feminine subordination—she published *The Basement* (1979), a gothic meditation on the sexual subordination and ultimate annihilation of a young girl by a power-crazed, sadistic *woman*.[18] Similarly, feminist misogyny amplifies the eerie reverberations set in motion by Germaine Greer's decision to follow *The Female Eunuch* (1970) with *Sex and Destiny* (1984). The former sprinkles quotations from *A Vindication* throughout a plea for a "revolution" in consciousness that requires that women refuse to bow down to "the Holy Family," reject the desexualization of their bodies, and protest against the manifold ways "our mothers blackmailed us with self-sacrifice" (335, 12, 157). However, the latter champions the family as the best social organization for women and children; touts chastity, coitus interruptus, and the rhythm method as optimal birth control methods; and nostalgically hymns the praises of the nurturance provided in so-called primitive cultures, specifically lauding "Mediterranean mothers [who] took their boy babies' penises in their mouths to stop their crying" (248).

Feminist misogyny in Mary Wollstonecraft's *oeuvre* may also help us understand why Andrea Dworkin has supplemented her antipornography expository prose with a gothic novel that could be said to be pornographic: *Ice and Fire* (1986) stands in as vexed a relation to *Intercourse* (1987) as *Mary* and *Maria* do to *A Vindication*. Dworkin the antipornography polemicist condemns sexual intercourse in our culture as "an act of invasion and ownership undertaken in a mode of predation: colonializing, forceful (manly) or nearly

violent" (*163*). However, her novel *Ice and Fire* includes two types of sexually explicit scenes that contravene this definition, one in which "a girl James
Dean" (72) uses men to invade or colonize her self—

> When a man fucks me, she says, I am with him, fucking me. The men ride her
> like maniacs. Her eyes roll back but stay open and she grins. She is always them
> fucking her, no matter how intensely they ride   (54–5)

—and the second in which the female narrator takes on the office of instruct-
ing her male lover on how to invade or colonize her:

> I teach him disrespect, systematically. I teach him how to tie knots, how to use
> rope, scarves, how to bite breasts: I teach him not to be afraid: of causing pain.
> (104–5)

To be sure, when the masochistic speaker here explains about her abusive lover "Reader, I married him" and when "Reader, he got hard" metamorphoses into "he got hard: he beat me until I couldn't even crawl" (101),
we are meant to understand that Dworkin is returning to the romance tradition of Charlotte Bronte's *Jane Eyre* ("Reader, I married him") so as to
uncover its abusive sexual politics (104). Nevertheless, the question remains,
if the antipornography ordinance Dworkin framed with Catherine McKin-
non were deemed constitutional, would she be able to publish this kind of
fiction? How can it be that her heroines resemble the actresses in the snuff
films she seeks to outlaw, women bent on finding sexual fulfillment in their
own destruction?

More generally, the feminist misogyny that pervades Dworkin's work
typifies the uncanny mirror dancing that repeatedly links feminist polemicists
to their rivals and antagonists. In 1975 the feminist-linguist Robin Lakoff published her ground-breaking *Language and Woman's Place*, a description of
the genderlect she called "women's language": euphemism, modesty, hedg-
ing, polite forms of address, weak expletives, tag questions, empty adjectives
and intensives, and hypercorrect grammar were said to characterize women's
speech. Curiously, her findings accorded with those of Otto Jesperson, whose
1922 study *Language: Its Nature, Development, and Origin* proved that women
were timid, conservative, even prudish language-users and thus incapable of
linguistic inventiveness. As I intimated earlier, another odd coupling could be
said to exist between Jacques Lacan, who viewed women as inexorably exiled

from culture, and the French feminists Luce Irigaray and Hélène Cixous, who valorize female fluidity, multiplicity, sensuality, and libidinal *jouissance*. Are all these feminists dancing with wolves?

"Feminism," Nancy Cott reminds us in much less heated or metaphorical terms, "is nothing if not paradoxical":

> It aims for individual freedoms by mobilizing sex solidarity. It acknowledges diversity among women while positing that women recognize their unity. It requires gender consciousness for its basis, yet calls for the elimination of pre-scribed gender roles. (49)

Just as aware of internal differences, Jane Gallop locates tensions within the psychology of feminism that explain the questions with which I began, the query of Ann Snitow's friend ("how can someone who doesn't like being a woman be a feminist?") as well as Snitow's response ("Why would anyone who likes being a woman *need* to be a feminist?"): "The feminist," according to Gallop, "identifies with other women but also struggles to rise above the lot of women. Feminism both desires superior women and celebrates the common woman" (*A* 138).

Over the past two decades the stresses described by Cott and Gallop, along with professional competition inside the academy and social setbacks outside it, have given rise to internecine schisms in Women's Studies, divisions widened by feminists faulting other feminists as politically retrograde or even misogynist: activists and empiricists denounced theorists and vice versa; lesbian separatists castigated integrationists; "prosex" and antipornography advocates clashed; class and race divided feminists, as did competing methodologies based on sexual difference or sexual equality, as did contested definitions of womanhood arising from cultural or poststructuralist thinkers.[19] In-fighting reached a kind of apex in literary criticism as various histories began to appear, some featuring feminist critiques of feminism that served intentions not always hospitable to academic women. Here the Toril Moi of *Sexual/Textual Politics* (1985) can officiate over feminist woman-bashing: Moi dismisses American Women's Studies scholars as "patriarchal" because of their naive faith in the authority of the female subject and the unity of the work of art while she touts as her heroine Julia Kristeva, who "refuses to define 'woman' " and judges the belief that one "is a woman" to be "absurd" (163, 165).[20] With friends like these, does feminism need enemies?

This atmosphere in which women need to beware women is probably what has led me to see feminist misogyny now and not, say, back in the seventies. As "constructionists" such as Moi continue to vilify "essentialists," both groups segue into defensive and offensive steps that recall nothing so much as the rhythms of competing nationalities satirized in Sheldon Harnick's song "Merry Little Minuet":

> The whole world is festering with unhappy souls.
> The French hate the Germans, the Germans hate the Poles,
> Italians hate Yugoslavs, South Africans hate the Dutch,
> And I don't like anybody very much. (Glazer 217–8)

Does the price of institutionalization—of Women's Studies' inclusion in the academy—consist of our reduction to a plethora of jostling fields or approaches in which unhappy souls war for precedence with even more ferocity than they do in longer established areas or departments?

Have we attained our maturity in an age of ethnic purges and nationalistic frays that in our own domain take the form of battle dances that cause us to lose sight of our common aim to expropriate language and its users of overpopulated intentions hostile to women's health and welfare? When strutting our stuff with each other, among ourselves (and who, after all, are "we," given our institutional, generational, ethnic, and methodological differences?), have we lost sight of the ways in which unsympathetic outsiders or hostile institutions can appropriate or coopt our internal debates, transforming self-critiques into assaults against our larger project? A brouhaha over Katie Roiphe's book epitomizes such difficulties. When in *The Morning After: Sex, Fear, and Feminism on Campus* Roiphe—a self-defined feminist— attacked Take Back the Night, antipornography, and sexual harassment activists for reenforcing Victorian stereotypes of predatory men and victimized women, it seemed eerily appropriate that she aligned herself with Ishmael Reed by entitling one of her chapters "Reckless Eyeballing": just as Reed's masculinist novel *Reckless Eyeballing* lambastes Alice Walker for promoting a knee-jerk, racist suspicion about the criminality of African-American men (and in the process illuminates the culturally diverse constructions of the feminist-misogynist dialogue), Roiphe's chapter presents contemporary feminists as retrograde zealot-puritans who would criminalize all men and indeed all forms of heterosexuality.[21]

Questioning another feminist critique of other feminists, namely constructionists' wholesale dismissal of essentialists, Diana Fuss has argued that "the political investments of the sign 'essence' are predicated on the subject's complex positioning in a particular social field, and . . . the appraisal of this investment depends not on any interior values intrinsic to the sign itself but rather on the shifting and determinative discursive relations which produced it" (*ES* 20).[22] Similarly, about feminist misogyny I think that—instead of furnishing us with yet another label to brand each other—it should make us sensitive to the proliferation of sexual ideologies, to the significance of who is deploying these ideologies and with what political effect, even as it breeds a healthy self-skepticism born of an awareness of our own inexorable embeddedness in history. Since we cannot escape how culture makes us know ourselves, we need to understand that even as our own theorizing engages with the social relations of femininity and masculinity, it is fashioned by them. Ultimately, then, the game of "Can you really tell?" reminds us that claims and counterclaims in the feminist-misogynist dialogue cannot be appraised without some consideration of the complex social identities, rhetorical frameworks, and historical contexts upon which they are predicated.

To adopt Gallop's words once again, "I am as desirous of resolving contradictions as the next girl, but I find myself drawing us back to them, refusing the separations that allow us to avoid but not resolve contradiction" (*A* 139). On the list of paradoxes she and other thinkers have enumerated, I would write the one so telling and compelling in the work of Mary Wollstonecraft. For the contradiction-in-terms that her life and letters dramatizes continues to fashion the discourses through which many have struggled to vindicate the rights of men and women. As I think this, I seem to see them lining up for a succession of pas de deux; or is it a Virginia Reel? a do-si-do? a last tango? a merry little minuet?—Rousseau and Wollstonecraft, Havelock Ellis and Olive Schreiner, Freud and Woolf, Sartre and Beauvoir, Mailer and Millett or Dworkin, Lacan and Irigaray or Cixous, Reed and Walker. But out of whose mouth does a voice issue to save the waltz by declaring, "Your turn to curtsy, my turn to bow"? And who takes the lead, if (when?) we turn to tap dance or shuffle along with one another?

8

A Chapter on the Future

In an outline for a cultural history left unfinished at the time of her death, Virginia Woolf moved from the Middle Ages through the nineteenth century and then enjoined herself, "Skip present day. A Chapter on the future."[1] Consider not only the unmitigated chutzpah of appropriating a provisional project that feminism's most important progenitor concocted for her own investigations, but also of daring to deploy it in an effort to conceptualize exactly what a literary historian knows nothing about! After the editors of the series in which this collection appears asked me to skip to the future in some concluding remarks about feminist criticism's prospects, can you marvel that I said, "I don't want to go in there by myself"? A hastily conceived questionnaire sent to an unscientifically selected cohort group seemed the only solution, and so I mailed out a cover letter—some forty, in fact—with ten queries meant to take the temperature of my peers, to solicit their views on the strengths and weaknesses of feminist criticism today, to find out how they experienced their own institutionalization, to learn whether early practitioners envisioned an ongoing relationship to the field, to ask them what words they wanted to speak to their successors. Even if I received few replies, I figured that I'd learn something about my generation's reaction to what the present moment holds.

While waiting for responses, I found myself mulling over the total picture emerging from the various chapters of this book. What sorts of quarrels have we had, what kinds will we need to have in the twenty-first century? In my introduction, I claimed there was no plot to the volume, but now perhaps I see the outlines of a story about the development of feminist criticism. That each of the typologies proposed by identity categories in the first four essays of this volume—African-American women artists, lesbian writers, Jewish-American feminists, female professors—spawned a host of quite various characters demonstrates the volatility conferred on those categories by poststructuralist modes of inquiry and, of course, by the bewildering complexities of life as well as art. If we view the emergence and interaction of identity politics and poststructuralism as the defining markers of turn-of-the-century feminist studies, what can we discern about their impact on each other?

When identity politics appeared to multiply the term "women," its advocates proposed placing gender along side racial identity, sexual identity, religious identity, and caste identity (to take the categories I have used to organize the first section of this book; others would do as well). But even as political agency became associated with these terms (providing platforms for supporters of African-American women artists, lesbian writers, Jewish-American feminists, female professors), these new categories were stretched or undermined by poststructuralist analyses as well as a complex of other factors: the fiction of race was replaced by the mutability of color; queer theory undermined faith in any fixed lesbian identity; a canny people, Jews "always already" knew we could never agree on what constitutes Jewishness (remember the old adage: three Jews, four opinions?); not a unified group, the professoriate clearly contained women of divergent stations and allegiances.

Yet because proponents of identity politics imagined groups of people allied by a sense of solidarity and acting together for social and political justice, they foregrounded the ways in which poststructuralist thinkers (followers of Lacan, Derrida, or Foucault) tended to isolate individuals within powerful psychological, linguistic, or social systems that deprived human beings of authority. Poststructuralists thus abrogated ideals—of moral responsibility as well as benevolent social relations—deemed necessary in feminism. Seyla Benhabib puts it this way:

> The view that the subject is not reducible to "yet another position in language,"
> but that no matter how constituted by language the subject retains a certain
> autonomy and ability to rearrange the significations of language, is a regulative

principle of all communication and social action. Not only feminist politics, but also coherent theorizing becomes impossible if the speaking and thinking self is replaced by "authorial positions," and if the self becomes a ventriloquist for discourses operating through her or "mobilizing" her. (*SS* 216)

Similarly critical of poststructuralism's "turning from the material side of life," Martha Nussbaum believes that its feminist advocates subscribe to the retrograde idea "that there is little room for large-scale social change, and maybe no room at all" (38): an "exaggerated denial of precultural agency" (41) makes for an "empty politics" or "a dangerous quietism" (43).

About identity politics: the agency made possible by lending political clout to hyphenated collectives has been qualified by a reliance on illusory or reductive categories which erase or censure alternative identifications of and connections between people. About poststructuralism: the epistemological sophistication that calls into question the coherence of illusory or reductive modes of being or knowing has been founded on an ahistorical insistence on determinist discursive mechanisms that reify and isolate identity formations while demoting politics into what Bruno Latour terms "pure simulacrum" (62). The activist agenda of identity politics brackets poststructuralist claims, whereas poststructuralism's critique of a unified subject subverts activist agendas.

Both these liabilities have been foregrounded for feminists by cultural studies scholars, with their attention to specific aesthetic contexts of creation, production, and reception.[2] In addition, both drawbacks will become more obvious as feminists take on what I suspect will be our next major tasks: gendered approaches to the complex consequences of rapidly expanding scientific technologies and the globalization of culture in the twenty-first century. Curiously, moreover, even as advocates of identity politics and of poststructuralism contested the basis of each others' claims, they colluded to invalidate generalizations about "women," which they viewed as a speciously universalized term. Claims of radicalism notwithstanding, this skepticism made both groups vulnerable to those distressed by a lack of critical attention to the social justice issues feminist academics derived from their origins in the women's movement. In a sort of shorthand, one might say that discourse about "who I can say I am" displaced language about "what we should do." How can scholars get beyond these impasses? What possible methodologies will surface to deal with such problems?

Perhaps the future of feminist studies will depend on finding what Benhabib considers the "true negation of identity logic [that] would imply a relation to an 'other' who could at every point remind the self that it was not a mere projection or extension of the self, but an independent being, another self" (*CNU* 221) and also on getting beyond what Amanda Anderson calls the "systematic anti-cogito that characterizes the poststructuralist sensibility ('The system thinks me, therefore I am not')" (221).[3] For Anderson, who turns to Habermas, this entails beginning to understand "the possibility of an intersubjective perspective that would define the human subject not as purely autonomous and self-present, nor as a mere place on intersecting grids, but rather as constituted through its ongoing relations to others as they are mediated by language, social systems, and history" (220). "It is arguable," Nancy Fraser claims in a related statement, "that the current proliferation of identity-dereifying, fungible, commodified images and significations constitutes as great a threat to women's liberation as do fixed, fundamentalist identities" ("FA" 71). When she wonders whether some conceptualizations of identity faulted for their oppressively imperialistic cast have functioned in certain historical settings as emancipatory efforts, she, too, raises the prospects of moving beyond the limits of Judith Butler's formulations ("FA" 69).

Further addressing the crucial problem "dissimulated in Butler's argument" about the nonidentity of "women," namely, "whether there are real conflicts of interest among women of different classes, ethnicities, nationalities, and sexual orientations," Fraser speculates:

> Certainly, there *are* conflicts when interests are defined relative to present forms of social organization. . . . The hard question feminist movements need to face is one Butler's proposal elides: Can "we" envision new social arrangements that would harmonize present conflicts? And if so, can "we" articulate "our" vision in terms that are sufficiently compelling to persuade other women—and men— to reinterpret their interests? ("FA" 70–71)

According to Fraser, this articulation might involve "conceiving subjectivity as endowed with critical capacities *and* as culturally constructed"; developing "a view of collective identities as at once discursively constructed *and* complex, enabling of collective action *and* amenable to mystification, in need of deconstruction *and* reconstruction" ("FA" 71–2). If, as I have argued in the pages of this book, certain deployments of identity politics and poststructuralism have threatened to produce feminist knowledge purchased at the price of power, a sustained and skeptical engagement with their interaction can re-empower our common enterprise.

Unlike these heady and difficult philosophical tasks, a more obvious (already evident) fall-out from the recent evolution of feminist studies has to be specialization in scholarship. It is impossible for any single human being to "keep up in the field" because that field contains so much work under each of the rubrics with which gender has been combined. To read widely in gender and race, gender and sexuality, gender and religion, gender and class would mean not having time to teach, no less eat, sleep, or walk around in the world. Even within the comforting confines of a specific, nationally defined historical period, it may be difficult to stay abreast of engendered racial, sexual, religious, and class approaches to, for example, English Romanticism or the post-World War II cultural industries of South Korea. Whereas in the past we had experts in feminist criticism, now we have people devoted to what Adrienne Rich has called a politics of location: "I don't want to write that kind of sentence now, the sentence that begins, 'Women have always,' " Rich has explained. "If we have learned anything in these years of late twentieth-century feminism, it's that that 'always' blots out what we really need to know: when, where and under what circumstances has the statement been true?" (10) Another consequence of the fragmentation which specialization signifies remains more baffling, for while earlier works of or on feminist studies tended to rely on large-scale generalizations accessible to undergraduates, the specificity and complexity of recent scholarly writing render it formidable to students. One challenge we face, then, consists in keeping criticism teachable so that pedagogic interactions can continue to enrich our scholarship and undergraduates can discover forms of feminism that will enhance their lives outside the classroom.

When things fall apart and the center does not hold, acrimony may be inevitable, calling into question the fiction of stability that the institutionalization of feminism promulgates and testifying to the vertiginous effects of the interactions between identity politics and poststructuralism. The Fall 1997 issue of *differences*, entitled *Women's Studies on the Edge*, attests to growing anxiety among intellectuals, people who played major roles in the institutionalization of feminist studies, about the the some six hundred programs in Women's Studies and Gender Studies that have developed since the seventies. Biddy Martin, a professor of German Studies and Women's Studies at Cornell (who currently also serves as a dean), begins with the "insularity" of Women's Studies faculty, "the exclusionary work that identity categories do," the "righteousness" of feminists engaged in "often routinized ways of representing race, class, sex, and transnationalism," but also the "excesses of 'social constructionism,' " and thus a defensive "resistance . . . to the notion that 'biology' might play any role at all in the construction of subjectivity" (102–8). She then goes on to contrast "parochial" ideological struggles within the field (113) to the curiosity and risk-taking that might translate current "contestation" into future "exploration" (119). Given the "turf wars" and "dogma," however, Martin concludes, "I do not believe that Women's Studies as now institutionalized can become the site for the kinds of interdisciplinary intellectual interactions that will compel the imaginations of our faculties and students" (129–30).

An equally startling repudiation surfaces in "The Impossibility of Women's Studies," an essay by Wendy Brown, a professor of Women's Studies and Legal Studies at the University of California, Santa Cruz. According to Brown, the "theory wars, race wars, and sex wars notoriously ravaging women's studies in the 1980s" meant that theorists as well as those scholars interested in race and sex were colonized "to preserve the realm" (83). Unlike a discipline based upon a "genre of inquiry," a field "organized by social identity" remains "especially vulnerable to losing its raison d'etre when the coherence or boundedness of its object of study is challenged" (86). By emphasizing gender over nationality, race, sexuality, caste, and class in the construction of subjects, practitioners in Women's Studies experience "the difficulty of analytically grasping the powers constitutive of subjection" (92).[4] Future insurrectionary work, which must attend to a whole network of complex forces converging on identity, "will no longer have gender at its core and is in that sense no longer women's studies" (95). Indeed, to the extent that feminists "adhere to a founding and exclusive preoccupation with women and feminism," Brown believes, "they will further entrench themselves as conservative barriers to the critical theory and research called for by the very scholarship they incited and pedagogical practices they mobilized over the past two decades" (95). Since, according to Brown, the most stimulating thinking goes on outside Women's Studies, she advocates a return to "mainstreaming" (moving gender-related courses back into the general curriculum of the traditional disciplines).[5]

Despite Martin's and Brown's dire forecasts about Women's Studies, the picture for feminism paradoxically brightens, given the audacity of these articles. Not grounded in the neoconservative stereotyping that usually accompanies attacks on women within academe, Martin and Brown seek to throw out the bathwater to save the baby. Their commitment to interdisciplinary research bringing gender to bear on other and differently structured forms of difference suggests that they seek to preserve the excitement of feminism's intellectual vigor from the loss of ardor that unavoidably accompanies institutional legitimation (especially in a period of retrenchment). Like African-American Studies programs, also established with a specifically political agenda, Women's Studies continues to have passionate, smart advocates within higher education, people attempting to deal productively with the marginalization of work on sexuality and race as well as with sectarianism.[6] To the extent that a defender like Shirley J. Yee surmises that "the porousness of borders . . . has been and will continue to be both a source of strength and distinctiveness and a point of potential vulnerability" (61), however, she ends up agreeing with Martin and Brown. Permeable boundaries appear to be what many advocates of future research believe will ensure the liveliness of future scholarship and pedagogy as well as their institutional and intellectual instability.[7]

As I intimated in my introduction, one resonant model for what happens when things fall apart and the center does not hold—more specifically, for the critical condition of feminist studies—consists of the supernova. When a star explodes, a "new" (nova) star appears visible in the sky. "Actually," Timothy Ferris explains, "what's new is not the star but its titanic demise, set off when thermonuclear fuel at its core is exhausted, causing the star to collapse and then resound in a literally disastrous detonation" (55). Conspicuous in the galaxy, because supernovas appear where no star had previously been seen, they serve what Ferris calls "galactic ecology": "they cook light atoms into heavy ones and then spew these back into space; all the gold in the universe, among other elements, originated in this way" (56). They also function as what Ferris calls "standard candles": if their brightness could be ascertained, it might be used to establish the expansion rate of the universe.

Should we think of gender as the thermonuclear fuel that propelled the establishment of feminist criticism, it might be said that its usefulness as a single, investigative category (usually applied in a Western national context) was quickly consumed by the astonishingly rapid production of scholarship and teaching during the seventies and early eighties. Brilliant and combustible, the collapse of a core—a commonly agreed upon center for feminism in the academy—released spin-off fields, area studies that provoked lively scholarly activity. If not "galactic ecology," then a sort of intellectual ecology works to transform feminist ideas and spew them forward into feminism's discontinuous futurity. As a kind of "standard candle," the studies of feminists—in all the intensity of their interactions—measure the expansion of multidisciplinary venues of scholarship. The one word that hinders such an analogy is "disas-

trous"—as in Ferris's description of "a literally disastrous detonation"; however, his "literally" reminds us that what looks disastrous (as in a calamity) can
at times be read etymologically as a "dis" or reversal of "astro" (a star) that
transforms its matter into the precious elements of the universe. Just as ejected
materials continue to transmute after the supernova's explosion, feminist
methodologies will generate fusion reactions with a host of other approaches
to lay the groundwork for innovative modes of inquiry. Gender, recombined
with the matter of many disciplines, will shape the progress and interaction of
the humanities and the sciences. At the same time this volatile energy signals a
dispersal or diaspora, the danger of a dissipating "feminist core" in academia,
which may require institutional and pedagogic safeguards as well as fresh justi-
fications for its continued (though inevitably transformed) missions.

Not merely an extension of its origins or of the middle passages mapped
in the pages of this book, feminism's long-range future as rendered in the
image of the supernova promises a violent eruption of the "nonidentical,"
"nonsequential excess" Robyn Wiegman forecasts when she asks us to imagine a time inconsistent with the past and present, unencumbered by the bag-
gage—of belatedness or replication or diminishment—bequeathed by the
generational "maternal plot," which conceptualizes the first generation of academic feminists as mothers handing on a legacy to be sustained by their academic daughters.[8] According to Wiegman and to Judith Roof, "the maternal
plot" places a dreary burden on future descendants of bearing the past into the
future. But such a story of academic feminism's history is also a drag for the
so-called mothers, caretakers now presumed to be in need of caretaking.
Besides, what good mother wants belatedness or replication or diminishment
for her offspring? So often confined within the family romance, women rightly skeptical of its dynamics need not embrace it as a paradigm of the history
of feminist studies. Millennial in its apocalyptic connotations and thus nicely
suited to the turn of the century, the supernova as one alternative metaphor
suggests that feminist studies have begun to fuel dispersed discoveries where
none had been apparent before.

Titanic power in the process of fissuring: certainly, though the respondents to my questionnaire quite reasonably focused on the near rather than the
far future, many agreed that the very success of feminist criticism has paradoxically produced the critical condition we currently face. Indeed, attentive to the
problems posed by an impending diasporic feminism, they caution against a
too hasty and thus rash capitulation to a dispersion that at the present time
might jeopardize the professional breakthroughs we have just begun to achieve.

For most of my contemporaries, the accomplishment of feminist criticism relates directly not only to academic acceptance of its intellectual authority and institutionalization but to the end of the isolation early practitioners experienced when they were either the token woman in their department or their research and teaching were not granted scholarly respect. In her response to my questionnaire, Gayatri Chakravorty Spivak measures attainment by the histories that will be written about turn-of-the-century feminist inquiry: "That it has won a place for itself in any account of literary criticism, even by non-feminist people, seems to be a major strength." According to Judith Kegan Gardiner, "The institutionalization of feminists, and of Women's Studies in the academy, means we have a base of support for teaching and connecting with students, building programs and research to benefit women and others, cohering with like-minded faculty across disciplines and generations, and making further demands upon the institution." For Ann Rosalind Jones, institutionalization signifies "responsibilities for programs and majors, tenure battles."

On a more personal note, Sandra Gilbert points out one major consequence that also holds true for others, namely, that the academic legitimacy of the field gives her a "platform" as well as "prestige—and a range of material as well as intellectual awards—that, paradoxically enough, I might not have gained had I steered a more conservative course in my career." (Janet Todd admits that while institutionalization "allowed me access to good jobs in the States," it "made me virtually unemployable in the UK in 1980. Now that the most antagonistic have come onto the bandwagon here, I'm back in the mainstream—but old.") Achievement is often expressed in terms of my peers' pleasure in—as Nina Baym puts it—"the extremely welcome presence of many more women in English departments" and thus "much less isolation." "I can relax a little now that others have been hired and tenured," Ruth Perry exclaims, and "it is a relief to have a few colleagues." Carolyn Heilbrun expresses a related sentiment with poignant brevity: "I found friends."

Institutional obstacles still abound, though. A university administrator, Shari Benstock cogently outlined some of them in her correspondence with me. Pedagogic difficulties continue to hamper teachers. "Although we have better delivery systems for getting feminist scholarship into the classroom than we did twenty years ago, most of us still rely on some version of the course pack that was all we had in the 1970s." She feels "we need quicker access to classroom materials than handbooks and anthologies can provide: this dynamic field of scholarly production is moving on electronic time." Also an obstacle, many undergraduate women and men, refusing to identify themselves as feminists, tend to "think of feminists as women of their mothers' generation, angry women resentful of men," even though "battles for equivalent pay" still need to be waged. In addition, Benstock sees "daily how difficult it is to change reward systems and dominant ideologies. On hiring and tenure issues, women are still in the minority; sexual harassment is still part of everyday life."

Mapping the intellectual terrain, Shari Benstock lists a number of conversations as particularly important in the history of feminist criticism: differences among American, French, and British feminisms; the pornography debates; textuality and sexuality (or how gender is inscripted); arguments about psychoanalysis; discussions of discourse (Peggy Kamuf) and experience (Nancy K. Miller); approaches dissenting against the white, middle-class feminism of the seventies (race, sexual orientation, class); colonial and postcolonial research on the material conditions of women's lives; sexuality and the embodiment of gender. The methodological and political debates Gayatri Chakravorty Spivak has found especially significant swirl "about postmodernism and politics. About black and white feminism. About Western feminism and its relationship to the world. About woman as essence and social construction. About difference and identity. About a specifically 'feminine' writing."

A coeditor of *The Feminist Memoir Project: Voices from Women's Liberation*, undertaken to defend "against historical amnesia," Rachel Blau DuPlessis contrasts an earlier "feminism of production" with a forthcoming "feminism of reception." Gesturing toward the work of Susan Stanford Friedman, Blau du Plessis welcomes the rise of a "kind of culturalist criticism," which manifests growing interest in "the interplay of a variety of social sites and situations." Instead of "a binarist mindset (women v. men)," this "feminism of reception" will encourage scholars to investigate "how gender modes—and all other modes of social situatedness—contribute to the production and dissemination and reception of artworks." To Marianne Hirsch, the most challenging work today "tries to maintain gender and women in focus even while thinking about race and class." Particularly stimulating are those fields of inquiry in which "gender no longer imposes itself as an obvious and absolutely necessary form of analysis—trauma and the Holocaust, for example." Several correspondents believe that, whereas identity politics and essentialism played a principal role in the past, analyses of masculinities, of nonfeminist women, of popular media, and of the cultures produced by changing technologies of science and transnational capitalism will take center stage in our future discussions.

Since the people I consider my cohorts did most of their work in English departments or American Studies programs, it is hardly surprising that a number of them feel threatened by some of the alterations wrought during the eighties and nineties, in particular what they view as the marginalization of literature and literary history. Two factors contribute to this worry. First the hegemony of so-called theory: when theorists only refer to and write about other theorists, theory itself becomes evacuated of historical and aesthetic specificity. Although several participants in this dialogue listed Lesbian Studies and queer theory as a source of energy, Alicia Ostriker feels that the "takeover of theory, and especially of queer theory, to the extent that it exists in a self-reflecting vacuum independent of the lives women and men actually live, is to me a deeply serious problem." Too much current work "seems jargony, pretentious and fundamentally anti-literary" to Sandra Gilbert, though she continues to "read in/about particular authors, especially women poets, with great delight." In part a consequence of the eminence of philosophy in feminist studies today, the marginalization of literature could have drastic pedagogic results in classes sponsored by literature programs, according to Nina Baym: "students will vote with their feet and depart our courses." More positive about theory than some others, Catharine Stimpson lists as the chief problem in the field "a knee-jerk suspicion of theory combined with theory's often dense prose."

For a number of respondents, however, the proliferation of ideologically driven modes of censorship, what Alicia Ostriker calls "party lines and catch phrases" and Nina Baym terms "regrettable p.c. policing," is either linked to the hegemony of theory or to the rise of area studies. The second problem, then, involves the substantial shift of interest toward Black, Postcolonial, and Gay Studies, with a resulting tilt toward recent periods: for if minority, third-world, and lesbian subjects are privileged, what happens to those historical periods in which they were not able to produce cultural artifacts? Will white, heterosexual Anglo-Protestant women be too easily dismissed, given what Nina Baym terms "an increasingly exclusive interest in the contemporary" or, as Sandra Gilbert puts it, will the divide widen between those "who continue to believe in a commonality between women that transcends the divisions shaped by race/class/sexual orientation and those who see such divisions as inexorably separating women from each other"? Like Sandra Gilbert, Martha Vicinus feels that "too much emphasis" has been placed "on differences and not enough on what might actually work to bring us together, to improve our teaching and to help our understanding of literature." In addition, she notes that "too many broad generalizations [are] made on the basis of too little read-ing and research" because "weaker students know the answers already (the Victorians were racist and sexist, etc; women writers had a tough time, etc.), while stronger ones pick certain texts over and over."

Janet Todd frets that "there has been such a takeover of feminist criti-cism/women's studies by race/gender and postcolonialism that few seem to be taking women's studies seriously." "The energy" in the field, Shari Ben-stock explains, "is coming from other disciplines (history, ethnography, anthropology). Postcolonial is a good example: questioning what we mean by 'race,' 'ethnicity,' 'nationality,' 'class' as concepts themselves." For this reason, she believes that "feminist criticism will continue but not as a separate field, rather as a strain within intertwined disciplines and scholarly endeavors." Gay-atri Chakravorty Spivak appears to agree that feminist criticism "must undo itself as a single issue, but"—she cautions—"with enough patience and atten-tion to detail": "it will lose itself to become part of the mainstream, yet there will always be a specifically self-identified group of feminists." However, this sort of "undoing" distresses Martha Vicinus, who finds younger women "more interested in making their mark within their departments/fields than in Women's Studies or interdisciplinary journals": "personally," she adds, "it has meant a fair amount of 'kicking at older mothers'—i.e., younger colleagues, who can't act out against their departments, act out against senior feminist scholars and expect only support in return."

To a startling extent, many of my contemporaries related "regrettable p.c. policing" as well as the overvaluation of theory to their major concern, the depoliticizing of academic feminism during a conservative period in American history when affirmative action, abortion, welfare, gay rights, and the women's movement came under attack. Although earlier feminists "hardly achieved all (or even most) of our original goals," Sandra Gilbert explains, "too many of our colleagues appear to have lost touch with that reality-connection, in some cases because they cannot agree on a monolith-ic 'Real World' (or indeed any real world) and in others because the very incorporation of the field into mainstream academia coopts its scholars into strivings that seem more 'academic' (in the pejorative sense) than practi-cal." After explaining that "one major strength is feminism's relatively secure institutionalization," Annette Kolodny concludes that "secure insti-tutionalization is also the biggest problem because that apparent security has effectively disengaged many (happily, not all) feminist practitioners from continued activism both on and off campus." Similarly, Ruth Perry admits, "feminism's success in the academy means that for some young women choosing to do feminist criticism is a marketing strategy rather than a political-intellectual urge that they can't resist."

As may be evident from the critics quoted here, a number of the people to whom I sent questionnaires did not respond—less a sign of disinterest (to my mind) than of their efforts to follow the sage advice of Professor Erma Bombeck and "Just Say No" to one more demand made on their already limited free time. But among those who did reply and with uncertainty about the future, Sandra Gilbert best expresses this generation's sense of perplexity: "So much of women's history tends to involve 'a sleep and a forgetting' that I fear the same consciousness-raising revolutions may have to happen over and over again before truly definitive changes are implemented." Always wonderfully attuned to the geopolitical context of intellection, Gayatri Chakravorty Spivak answered the question "What sentences would you like to speak to the next generation of feminist critics?" with her own funny, but smart query: "Where?"

Others, whose rejoinders assume that the "where" is here on the concluding pages of this volume, form a chorus with which it seems appropriate to end a meditation about an enterprise very much in process. In regard to my imagining of the supernova, their refrain reminds us that this stupendous phenomenon remains light years away from the everyday material conditions of most of our colleagues' and students' lives. Although diasporic feminists are sowing seeds of thought in far-flung intellectual realms, recollection of our political origins can provide one precaution against too quick a repudiation of our commonality and the privations of exile such a defection could bring about. Lest our enterprise fizzle out while still indispensable, my wary cohorts implicitly approach the critical condition of feminist studies not through a metaphor like that of the supernova but instead through the image of delicate, new growth in need of attentive nuturing. For they caution vigilance, lest feminist scholars lose supports we still require. Like the groups discussed in these pages—African-American women artists, lesbian writers, Jewish-American feminists, female professors—those of us engaged in feminist studies comprehend our collectivity as "amenable to mystification," to use Fraser's words, but also "enabling of action." Neither matricidal rage nor later-life despair but instead a chary obstinacy characterizes these voices, which react to dizzying changes in the field by insisting on the need to formulate a sufficiently compelling "we" to articulate "our" divergent visions so that histories of feminism as well as feminism itself will continue to be reinvented.

Carolyn Heilbrun: "Let's stop fighting each other. Let's relate criticism to politics. Let's not be ashamed or fearful of privileging women in our work: all women. Let's live with the risks of being feminists."

Annette Kolodny: "Please forge coalitions with other progressive causes and social activists to work together for progressive social change; focus on the campus but also on the community, the nation, and the international scene.

Please become models for your students of socially and politically activist intellectuals.

Please help turn the national discourse from the center right, where it's now settled, to a discourse that includes better government (not smaller government); caring about the poor, the sick, the disabled, the children, the addicted; preserving affirmative action; universal quality health care for everyone, based on a single-payer system; curbing corporate greed; protecting the environment globally—not just locally or nationally."

Martha Vicinus: "Read as widely as possible in primary sources; love literature for its own virtues. Criticism—and your own critical voice—will come if you don't fall too quickly into one paradigm.

Also, given the lack of a viable and visible political movement 'out there,' it will be interesting to see if feminist criticism turns to the much-needed task of selling the humanities and criticism to the general public, and, indeed, to our students. I think this is the most urgent current political task at hand."

Ruth Perry: "Feminism this go-round started out as an attempt to make a better world; righting women's wrongs was just the opening wedge for social justice for all. Make the personal political again."

Janet Todd: "Use rather than abuse the past. There are more important things than fashion and career success."

Jane Tompkins: "Don't try to sound like anyone but yourself. Never disavow or betray your own experience."

Ann Rosalind Jones: "Follow the energies of political groups in protest and you won't turn into academic dodos."

Shari Benstock: "There is no such thing as 'postfeminism' in the academy, or in life. The issues of rights and representation for all peoples are always before us, always requiring our commitment to first imagining—and then striving to put in place—a future free of prejudice and censorship and hatred."

Judith Kegan Gardiner: "Be willing to label your convictions feminist. Beware of the cynical manipulation of cynicism, of those who tell you that feminism is outmoded, whether they say it lost or won. I think it's important to retell our stories of accomplishment and of the efforts to make changes and the struggles for institutionalization."

Catharine Stimpson: "Know history and take risks. These are compatible activities."

It gives me great pleasure to record these sentences, not because I agree with all of them but because they register the passionate commitment my peers continue to make to intergenerational bonding and to the ongoing evolution of feminism's future. If I were to answer my own question, the sentences I would like to speak to the next convoy of feminist critics would remain as contradictory as they have been throughout this book. For, on the one hand, I'd wish to strengthen their resolve by reminding them how much we have already achieved ("we've come a long way") and, on the other, I'd want to strengthen their resolve by reminding them how much needs to be done ("the more things change, the more things stay the same").

Indeed, after reading the responses of my contemporaries, my own metaphor of the supernova fills me with trepidation. Yes, in a zillion years, it may be that the core that is feminist studies within the academy can disperse in manifold directions; but, in the here and now, don't we still need institutional safeguards (imperfect though they admittedly are) to protect the *vita nova* (new life) of our recent development? Since most establishments of the humanities are so besieged at the present time, it behooves feminist academics not to collude with any measures that would further marginalize our quite diverse scholarly and pedagogic projects. What we should do, then, is stage even what might seem to be our irreconcilable differences, our most factious quarrels, with sufficient lucidity and ardor to draw students and the general public into understanding their significance to the society at large as well as to the smaller academic community. Given a feminism that has become critical—ensconced within higher education as scholarship often specialized and fractious—feminists need to engage our bold political history to accentuate not the clinical or disparaging meaning of the word "critical" but its sense of compelling urgency and irreverent vitality.

Notes

2. Women Artists and Contemporary Racechanges

1. Rich's term is discussed by Elizabeth Spelman in *Inessential Woman* (128–9).

2. See Michel Feher in *Blacks and Jews* (275–6), for his model of "cosmopolitanism [which] criticizes identity politics and liberal universalism both." See also David A. Hollinger, *Postethnic America*.

3. Thus the back of a paperback book asks the following questions: "Can an African American male be a feminist? Can a straight female teacher satisfactorily lead a classroom discussion about the poems of Allen Ginsberg?" See *Who Can Speak? Authority and Critical Identity*, ed. Judith Roof and Robyn Wiegman.

4. What Rey Chow considers "the white liberal enthusiasm for 'peoples of color' that is currently sweeping through North American academic circles" (29) smacks of a fetishized primitivism or tokenism. She goes so far as to link multiculturalism's idealized image of a representative Other with the foundations of fascism in the 1930s (xxiii). On the social construction of race, see Anthony Appiah, "The Uncompleted Argument: Du Bois and the Illusion of Race."

5. Ringgold's rage against Stokely Carmichael's sentiment that "The only position of women . . . is prone" and her anxieties about her daughters' acceptance of such a view are expressed in "From *Being My Own Woman*" (301).

6. "In general," Bill Readings explains further, "the effect of multiculturalism is necessarily to homogenize differences as equivalently deviant from a norm" (113).

7. In feminist criticism, the growing areas of Chicana and Asian-American Studies have produced a significant body of work over the past five years. My own focus on African-American artists has been shaped, on the one hand, by my earlier work in *Racechanges* and, on the other, by the belief I share with many thinkers that American history has made the situation of African-Americans quite distinct from that of other ethnic and racial groups.

8. I discuss this shift from mockery to mimicry to mutuality throughout *Racechanges*.

9. Margaret Homans contrasts the propensity of African-American male writers to focus on figuration and social construction with the tendency of African-American women writers to deal with literal biological definitions of race: see " 'Racial Composition.' "

10. This statement opposes others by Piper: "I would never simply say [I was] Black because I felt silly and as though I was co-opting something, i.e., the Black Experience, which I never had. I've had the Gray Experience." See Judith Wilson's excellent summary of Piper's career changes: "In Memory of the News and of Our Selves"; this quote appears on page 42. In an essay about her Jewishness entitled "Hadassah Arms," Nancy K. Miller describes a number of scenes in which anti-Semitic comments were made in her hearing and her subsequent confusion about how to react since the assumption had been made that she was not Jewish (158).

11. The concept of "female female impersonation"—the idea that women put on a masquerade of femininity—is discussed in chapter 2 of Sandra M. Gilbert and Susan Gubar, *Letters from the Front*, the final volume of *No Man's Land*.

12. Recent performances of whiteness by artists such as Shannon Jackson seek to dramatize its racially marked significance. Jackson describes her performance in *White Noises* as an attempt "to enact a kind of white liberal consciousness, publicizing it as a conflicted and ubiquitous state of self-righteousness, guilt, entitlement, romanticization, objectification, and self-censorship" (53).

13. Eddie Murphy has a funny skit called "White Like You" in which white make-up allows him to see beyond the facades erected before black people, to understand that whites bond with and support each other as if members of a club or conspiracy.

14. See her "Passing for White, Passing for Black" (235).

15. Lazarre herself is "warmed by the love and friendship" of the remark, but "also knows its message is false." In a later passage she describes her horror of being categorized as a "honkey" and her pleasure at a friend calling her a "nigger": "But these particular stripes—black shadows on the white background of my permanently privileged skin—will have to be earned over and over again as I begin to live in a Black world as much as a white one" (38).

16. Gates's essay on " 'Authenticity,' or the Lesson of *Little Tree*" analyzes the complex rhetorical issues raised here, as does Werner Sollors in his discussion of "ethnic transvestism" (252)

17. Elizabeth Abel gives a different but excellent reading of this story in "Black Writing, White Reading."

18. Lazarre discusses the incarceration statistics (96). Piper has returned to the image of the hypersexualized black man repeatedly: not only in "Mythic Being" but also in the installation *Four Intruders Plus Alarm System*, in which she projected slides of black men as thieves and interlopers. African Americans constitute around 12

percent of the population; however, in 1992, 44.8 percent of all persons arrested for violence crimes were black. According to Randall Kennedy, "Blacks made up 55.1 percent of those arrested for homicide, 42.8 percent of those arrested for rape, and 69.9 percent of those arrested for robbery" (22–23).

19. Walter Benn Michaels "insists that our actual racial practices, the way people talk about and theorize race, however 'antiessentialist,' can be understood only as the expression of our commitment to the idea that race is *not* a social construction" and that "if we give up that commitment, we must give up the idea of race altogether" (125).

20. Adrian Piper approached the issue of color divested of race in her book of photographs aptly entitled *Colored People* (1991). In this collection of self-portraits, sixteen subjects (equal numbers of people of color and euroethnics, women and men) took eight different shots of themselves, "each expressing facially the corresponding colloquial metaphor of color as mood." Presumably Piper herself used crayons to color them in: "Tickled Pink," "Scarlet with Embarrassment," "Purple with Anger," "Blue," "Green with Envy," "Jaundiced Yellow," "White with Fear," "Black Depression." Childlike strokes that often do not stay within the lines emphasize the coloring book analogy even as they connect people fixed and framed by what we ordinarily consider fleeting feelings. Here color, like a filter placed on a stage light, is a psychological state individuals can enter or leave, not always at will. Replacing the dualism of white versus black is the spectrum of primary and mixed colors, none privileged as a state of plenitude or stasis.

21. See Deborah R. Geis's elaboration of this reading. She discusses the black blood on the sheets in *Movie Star* as a linking of writing, wounding, and menstrual bleeding (177).

22. For background on Deavere Smith's earlier performances among communities undergoing certain transitions and therefore asking for her services, see Sandra L. Richards, "Caught in the Act of Social Definition." Carol Martin points out that Deavere Smith originally mimed people who were the members of her audience and at the same time maintained her own visibility as an actress. "The PBS/American Playhouse production of *Fires* directed by George C. Wolfe (Artistic Director of the Public Theatre) moved even further away from the audience-as-source origin of Smith's work" (89) and she almost completely extinguished her identity with each new character.

23. *Twilight*, dealing with the civil disturbances after the 1992 Rodney King verdict, goes beyond the Jewish/black context to include many different immigrant, ethnic, and Euro-American types of people.

24. Octavia Butler's *Kindred* plays with the idea that a black contemporary woman is the last in a long line going back to a white slavemaster, whom she visits in

a sort of spiritual time-travel; Alice Walker returns to the idea of reincarnation in *The Temple of My Familiar*: the elderly Miss Lissie recalls being several black women throughout history but also a white man and a large cat. See Margaret Homans's discussion of the significance of this passage: " 'Racial Composition' " (86).

25. From the period of the witchcraft trials to Madame Blavatsky (an early twentieth-century spiritualist) and Madame Sosostris (a fictive character who holds all the cards in Eliot's *The Waste Land* [1922]), the image of the woman as prophetess, medium, or spiritualist has saturated Western culture, as Deavere Smith surely knows.

26. As Anne Anlin Cheng put it about Deavere Smith's theater, "the representation, mimicry even, may be employed as a kind of *performative* counteroccupation, whereby the act of placing oneself in the other's place exposes one's vulnerability to that performed other" (58).

27. I am disagreeing here with Carol Martin, who has called Anna Deavere Smith's shape-shifting "a morph without aid of digitization" (83). The computer program Morph (for metaMORPHosis) mixes features on the cover of *Time* magazine (special issue, Fall 1993) to illustrate America's "New Face" in the 1990s, a multicultural picture of "Eve" combining the features of Anglo-Saxons, Middle Easterners, Africans, Asians, Southern Europeans, and Hispanics. Far from being drawn to people of mixed backgrounds and far from emphasizing the melding of various people, Deavere Smith has explained that she is attracted to individuals who "wear their beliefs on their bodies—their costumes. . . . Crown Heights is no melting pot and I really respect that" ("WBY" 187).

28. The first phrase is Barbara Johnson's ("Response" 42) and the second is meant to evoke the recent genocide in Yugoslavia.

29. With its telling title, Lorraine O'Grady's *The Space Between* typifies this work. Two separate documents are contrasted in its diptych-like installation: on the one hand, a chronicle of O'Grady's earlier performances in the New York art world of the persona "Mademoiselle Bourgeoise Noire" (a debutante in a cape constructed of 180 white gloves, wrapped in a beauty pageant banner, with a cat-o'-nine-tails peeking out beneath) and, on the other, her *Miscegenated Family Album* (a series of sixteen photographic images of the artist's deceased sister, Devonia, paired with pictures of the ancient Egyptian Queen Nefertiti). Although "Mademoiselle Bourgeoise Noire" originally appeared at museum openings to protest the exclusion of African-American women artists, she simultaneously empowered O'Grady's parodic approach to the decorous, ladylike self-fashioning some middle-class African-American women used to refute the purported promiscuity of black females (a myth propagated—as the whip hints—during slave times to legitimize the sexual exploitation of black women by their white masters). *Miscegenated Family Album* explores a personal and a collective grief. Seven years before Martin Bernal's *Black Athena*,

O'Grady mourned the loss of her sister by juxtaposing her with one of the most beautiful ancient images and also with African-Americans' loss of Egyptian ancestry because of racist definitions of what constitutes the African heritage.

Both the hyperpropriety of "Mademoiselle Bourgeoise Noire" and the absence of allusions to interracial sex in a work called *Miscegenated Family Album* call attention to O'Grady's resistance to normative literary treatments of the miscegenation plot. O'Grady makes this point retrospectively in "Nefertiti/Devonia Evangeline" (64).

30. After the enervated white senator Bulworth has turned into an energetic black-talking rapper (reminiscent of Norman Mailer's "White Negro"), he sees interracial love as a solution to racism. Yet it remains difficult to understand how an "open-ended program of procreative racial deconstruction" will solve the overrepresentation of African-Americans as victims of crime, their underrepresentation in universities, and their higher degrees of unemployment. The worst moment in the movie occurs when gorgeous young Nina (played by Halle Berry) falls in love with this white man some forty years her senior, exclaiming "Don't you know you're my nigger." Bulworth gets shot—just like the other great leaders of the race whose pictures we have seen during the opening credits (Martin Luther King, Robert Kennedy, Malcolm X). Beatty's film hints that the libidinal black folks portrayed in the picture need a great white hope like Bulworth/Beatty as their savior.

31. The first instance I encountered of this sort of cultural miscegenation appeared in Patricia Williams's meditation in *The Rooster's Egg* on a document she had seen attesting to the property value of her enslaved great-great-grandmother and specifically on how her understanding of this document shifted after she viewed colorful canvases painted by a survivor of the concentration camps (209). I discuss her palimpsestic vision of her ancestor within the human-shaped blank spots of the paintings, a revelation that resolutely refuses to reduce the Jewish to the African-American experience or conflate them, in *Racechanges* (257–8).

32. As Ringgold put it to one audience, "What I am doing here is rewriting history. It's too bleak as it is" (*DL* 61).

33. No wonder that the "mise-en-scène" of the chapel in Vence reminds Ringgolds's daughter Michele Wallace of "Momma Jones's Funeral at the Abyssinian Baptist Church in Harlem in 1981" (*DL* 24).

34. I am, of course, drawing on Laura Mulvey's work on the male gaze and on John Berger's on the female as an object surveyed.

35. According to Wallace, "*Les Demoiselles* might be seen as illustrating the occasional advantage of art over institutionalized history or science in that it seems to represent the desire to both reveal and repress the scene of appropriation as a conjunction of black/female bodies and white culture—a scene of negative instruction between black and white art or black and white culture" (*OT* 45).

36. Although African-American men and women as well as white women participated in the modernist movements of Europe and America, for the most part they remained marginalized in and by them. By presenting the reciprocity between whites and blacks, men and women, Ringgold makes the case for a fully democratized, miscegenated modernism that never, in fact, existed. See Houston A. Baker, *Modernism and the Harlem Renaissance*.

37. Ringgold writes movingly about her struggles with Michele Wallace in her autobiography *We Flew Over the Bridge*, especially during the period when *Black Macho and the Myth of the Superwoman* appeared: "She gave me no credit as a role model for learning how to be both a woman and a political activist. There is no greater defeat to a woman who is a mother than to have her value as a mother denied" (94). She goes on to explain that many of her works of art attempted to "make up for some of the closeness I missed in my relationships with my daughters. Through art I tried to create the peace we could not achieve in real life" (96). At the same time, she pays tribute to Wallace's contributions on behalf of black artists at the "Black Popular Culture" conference she organized in 1991: "It is moments like this in which a mother can feel real proud of a daughter, and know for sure she's done something right" (95).

38. As I mentioned earlier in this essay, *U.S. Postage Stamp* also highlights the difference between gender and our cultural language of gender. Ringgold's awareness of the masculinism at work in the Black Power movement generates our self-consciousness about reading the faces as male.

39. Afsaneh Najmabadi argues that "new categories—no matter how many times hybridized and how provisionally performative—continue to construct (new) zones that produce the kind of confining pressures from which I have been trying to escape by arguing for the desirability of unavailable intersections, by resisting acts of inclusion premised on recognizability" (74). When she claims that "disclaiming categories as identities need not become politically paralyzing" (74), she raises the most pertinent point made on their behalf, namely that they are necessary for the purposes of political agency.

40. Jane Lazarre captures in words the efforts of many of her and Ringgold's contemporaries to replace Du Bois's metaphor of the "color line" with an image of fabric woven of many differently colored threads in various patterns. Having set herself the task "of making a tapestry of words," Lazarre describes one self-portrait:

> Every few blues there will be a grey. Every four greys, a deep red. But the pattern is visible only for a moment and then, as it was intended to do, it assumes a collective identity again. A tweed—a greyish, brownish, bluish tweed. Some color with no precise name. (135)

About the fact that the biological sciences no longer help us understand race, while they still contribute to our understanding of gender and sexuality, Auslander points out that "in another century," perhaps "bodily distinctions may disappear or differences of 'maleness' or 'femaleness' may come to seem as biologically trivial as biological differences of 'Jewishness' or 'African-Americanness' " (21).

3. Lesbian Studies 101 (As Taught by Creative Writers)

1. This phenomenon is punctuated by the recent appearance of the *Lesbian Review of Books*.

2. I am grateful to Bonnie Zimmerman's essay "Lesbians Like This and That" for bringing the Brossard quotation I use as an epigraph to my attention. Also linking visionary power with lesbianism, Audre Lorde declared, "there is, for me, no difference between writing a good poem and moving into sunlight against the body of a woman I love" (58).

3. For this reason, Sandra Gilbert and I reprinted Hacker's poem and Brown's stories in our *Norton Anthology of Literature by Women*, second edition. Should we bring out a third edition, I would certainly argue for the inclusion of Winterson's extremely teachable story. Because the first and last texts with which I deal in this essay are so short, I have omitted page references altogether.

4. See especially *Winter Numbers* (1994) with its prefatory "Against Elegies" and its later sequence about the fate of the Jews of France.

5. In a 1980 interview with Karla Hammond, Hacker explained: "It is important for women writers to reclaim the tradition, to rediscover and redefine our place in it and lay claim to our considerable contributions, innovations, and inventions." Later she mentions Adrienne Rich, Judy Grahn, and earlier women writers who have influenced her, adding that "Elizabeth Bishop is a poet whom I read fairly early on and whose work I still admire" (22, 24).

6. See Faderman, *Surpassing the Love of Men* and *Odd Girls and Twilight Lovers*; Smith Rosenberg, "The Female World of Love and Ritual"; Case, "Toward a Butch-Femme Aesthetic"; Carby, "It Just Be's Dat Way Sometimes: The Sexual Politics of Women's Blues"; and Newton, "Mythic Mannish Lesbian" as well as her "Just One of the Boys." None of these images of the lesbian can be equated with Gloria Anzaldúa's view of her queerness as "two in one body, both male and female" or "the *hieros gamos*: the coming together of opposite qualities within" (19).

7. Much has been written critically about Rich's "Compulsory Heterosexuality and Lesbian Existence," especially about its erasure or blurring of the sexuality of

lesbians and of gay men; however, it continues to be an influential text in lesbian intellectual history. See Carolyn Dever (19–41).

8. Johnson writes about the lesbometer in the context of her finding Nella Larsen's novel *Passing* more erotic than Toni Morrison's *Sula*. A good example of this type of approach appears in Paula Bennett, "The Pea That Duty Locks: Lesbian and Feminist-Heterosexual Readings of Emily Dickinson's Poetry" (104–25); Bennett argues that heterosexual critics overemphasize Dickinson's relationship to male tradition and men, whereas "the privileging of homoeroticism affects our interpretation of Dickinson's erotic poetry" (106).

9. Bonnie Zimmerman's groundbreaking "What Has Never Been" explains that the critic in search of a lesbian canon "will need to consider whether a lesbian text is one written by a lesbian (and if so, how do we determine who is a lesbian?), one written about lesbians (which might be by a heterosexual woman or a man), or one that expresses a lesbian 'vision' (which has yet to be satisfactorily outlined)" (208). See Lillian Faderman's critique of Zimmerman in "What Is Lesbian Literature?" and especially her emphasis on the need for lesbian writers to encode or camouflage their meanings before the literature produced in the period I am discussing or their tendency to sacrifice the integrity of the work for the antihomophobic message it sought to teach (51, 54–5).

10. See Diana Fuss's excellent work on the ways in which the hetero-/homobinary erases differences among lesbian women (*ES* 110).

11. Why do we assume these women's heterosexuality from various social configurations, when we require that their homosexuality depend on overt evidence of sexual consummation? This point is made most directly by Martha Vicinus, who argues for "the possibilities of the 'not said' and the 'not seen' " as tools for Lesbian Studies: "It is ironic that 'lesbianism' continues to depend upon the evidence of sexual consummation, whereas heterosexuality is confirmed through a variety of diverse social formations" (*LS* 2, 3).

12. "Lesser" here is meant to gesture toward the "greater" lives of the men of genius to whom they were connected. The quote is an allusion to the book entitled *Lesser Lives* that Diane Johnston wrote about Jane Carlyle, the wife of the Victorian sage Thomas Carlyle.

13. Lowell's "The Sisters" (1925) lists her predecessors as a passionate but suicidal Sappho, a hyperconventional Elizabeth Barrett Browning, and a weirdly eccentric Emily Dickinson, concluding that this "queer lot" leave the twentieth-century American descendant feeling "sad and self-distrustful." In part Lowell uses the word "queer" to refer to the anomaly of being "double-bearing, / With matrices in body and in brain." Sandra Gilbert and I discuss twentieth-century women writers' relationship to their female precursors in *No Man's Land*, volume 1, chapter 4.

14. This is a hotly debated issue, whether lesbian textuality ought to be conflated with or subsumed under the metafictional parodies, pastiches, disruptions, and deconstructions of postmodernism. See Linda Hutcheon, Elizabeth A. Meese, and Marilyn R. Farwell.

15. Whereas the "ho(m)mo-sexual" economy, which conceptualizes all forms of sexuality on the basis of male anatomy, transmutes the clitoris into a little penis, the vagina into a lack, Winterson's Picasso paints "with [her] clit" and has "had all the brushes [she] needs" (417). This is a joking allusion to Renoir who painted with his penis. It is worth mentioning about Irigaray's comments that they threaten to flatten heterosexuality out into a single, stable economy.

16. See Leigh Gilmore on Wittig's and Winterson's "refusal of the patriarchal regime of names" (230).

17. After a breakup that Sappho attributes to her own habits of silence and avoidance, she remains faithful to the ideal of eros her relationship with Picasso represents:

> For seven years she and I had been in love. Love between lovers, love between mother and child. Love between man and wife. Love between friends. I had been all of those things to her and she had been all of those things to me. (419–20)

Even the most pessimistic of lesbian texts participates in this ecstatic hymn to lesbian love. How evocative this passage is of the first lesbian novel in English, Radclyffe Hall's *The Well of Loneliness* (1928) in which Stephen Gorden believes herself "all things to Mary; father, mother, friend and lover, all things; and Mary all things to her—the child, the friend, the beloved, all things" (314).

18. I approached this subject first in "Sapphistries," which deals with this "fantastic collaboration" twentieth-century literary women perform with the progenitor of song.

19. See Laura Doan's "Jeanette Winterson's Sexing the Postmodern" for an interesting meditation on how postmodernism and feminism mesh in the novels (137–55).

20. I will be quoting from "Some Psychological Consequences of the Anatomical Distinction Between the Sexes" (1925) and "Female Sexuality" (1931), both in *Sexuality and the Psychology of Love*. In chapter 4 of *The War of the Words* Sandra Gilbert and I use this same passage in Freud to elaborate what we call "an affiliation complex" that shapes lines of influence between women and men of letters.

21. In the *Norton Anthology of Literature by Women*, p. 1830 and in Swensen. See also Sylvia Plath's poem "Cut" about slicing off the top of a finger—

How you jump—
Trepanned veteran,
Dirty girl,
Thumb stump (236)

—and Marge Piercy's "The Friend" in which a man speaks to a woman:

he said, cut off your hands.
they are always poking at things.
they might touch me.
I said yes.

22. Grosz also asks, "Do women have a phantom phallus?" in *Volatile Bodies* (73). Clearly the fantasy of having a penis has informed recent lesbian literature, as a passage from *Susie Bright's Sexual Reality* indicates:

What if I were a man? Then, of course, I'd have a penis. My friend Sarah Schulman wrote a story about a lesbian who wakes up one day with a penis. She ends up cruising in Central Park and meets a guy in the bushes who goes down on her. "Ann had always wanted to say 'suck my cock' because it was one thing a lot of people said to her, but she never said to anyone."
   I'd like to say that, too.   (27)

I first became a dildo booster to alleviate the fears of some lesbian feminists that they would become magically heterosexualized by a toy phallus. (28)

Also pertinent to this topic is the astonishing photograph entitled "Lynda Benglis ad" that appeared in *Artforum* in November 1974 and is reprinted in *New Feminist Criticism*, ed. Joanna Frueh, Cassandra L. Langer, and Arlene Raven (35). Benglis poses wearing only sunglasses, lipstick, and earrings, her body greased and with one hand holding a huge dildo sticking up from her pubic hair. Colleen Lamos discusses the "dildo as the mime of the phallus/penis, a 'fake or bad copy' of the penis, but a derivative that shows the 'original' penis is a reiterated and vain attempt to pass itself off as the phallus" (95).

23. Of course, Freud believed that fetishism was a male phenomenon. A substitute for the mother's penis that the little boy once believed in, the fetish allows the boy to believe that castration has not happened. Often the fetishized objects—fur or velvet or shoes—are related to what the boy has seen before he witnesses the mother's castration. However, a number of feminists—Naomi Schor and Elizabeth

Grosz among them—have agreed with de Lauretis about the phenomenon of women's fetishism, though they have theorized it differently. Heather Findlay analyzes the prominence of contemporary debates about "dildo fantasies" and psychoanalytic theory of fetishism in "Freud's 'Fetishism' and the Lesbian Dildo Debates."

24. Actually, the two characters could also be viewed as male homosexuals, although the signature of the author and the title of the collection tend to steer readers away from such an interpretation.

25. The narrator of *The Autobiography of Alice B. Toklas* counters Miss Etta Cone's remark that "she could forgive but never forget" with the comment, "as for myself I could forget but not forgive" (68). For an early critique of the ways in which feminism perpetuated an unrealistic vision of lesbianism as "a 'perfect' vision of egalitarian sexuality," see Amber Hollibough and Cherríe Moraga.

26. As a dominator, Califia sees handcuffs, dog collars, whips, bondage, tit clamps, and enemas as "metaphors for the power imbalance" (162). "I devise and mete out appropriate punishments for old irrational 'sins.' I trip up the bottom, I see her as she is, and I forgive her and turn her on and make her come, despite her feelings of unworthiness or self-hatred or fear. We are all afraid of losing, of being captured and defeated. I take the sting out of that fear. A good scene doesn't end with orgasm—it ends with catharsis" (163). For an overview of the pro and con feminist criticism on lesbian sadomasochism, see B. Ruby Rich, "Feminism and Sexuality in the 1980s."

27. In "Separating Lesbian Theory from Feminist Theory," Cheshire Calhoun explains that the butch/femme role-playing that runs contrary to feminist politics may be affirmed by lesbian politics. Rather than following the lead of feminists viewing lesbian S/M as a recycling of patriarchal sexual violence against women, lesbian thinkers might stress the importance of its denaturalizing of heterosexuality through outlawed performances that divorce masculinity and femininity from the bodies of heterosexual couples.

28. Biddy Martin also argues against an essential or homogenized lesbian identity, finding in autobiographical texts by Cherríe Moraga and Gloria Anzaldúa attempts "to attend to the irreducibly complex intersections of race, gender, and sexuality, attempts that both directly and indirectly work against assumptions that there are no differences within the 'lesbian self' and that lesbian authors, autobiographical subjects, readers, and critics can be conflated and marginalized as self-identical and separable from questions of race, class, sexuality, and ethnicity" (*LI* 277).

29. Colleen Lamos, in "The Postmodern Lesbian Position," believes that the "demise of lesbian feminism" attests to "a queer lesbian culture that blurs distinctions between masculine and feminine and between gay and straight sexuality" (94).

In addition, she argues that "the postmodern lesbian is not another lesbian but the end of lesbianism as we know it—as a distinct, minority sexual orientation" (99).

30. On the rise of lesbian chic in Lesbian Studies, see Sonya Andermahr, " 'There's Nowt So Queer as Folk' " (13–14). She attributes to the influence of queer theory a rethinking of beleaguered identity politics among lesbian theorists: "Instead of focusing on the authenticity of the lesbian/gay subject and looking for evidence of homosexuality in culture, queer offers an interpretive strategy which focuses on the construction of 'the normal', allowing us to trace the shifting boundaries of 'deviance' " (16).

31. In her response in the Winter 1999 issue of *Critical Inquiry* to my essay "What Ails Feminist Criticism?" Robyn Wiegman writes about the "lost literary object," claiming that the aesthetic has been displaced from the center of Women's Studies scholarship (372, 374).

4. Eating the Bread of Affliction: Judaism and Feminism

1. The Passover Haggadah, Deluxe Edition, Compliments of the Coffees of Maxwell house, was used for many years by many synagogues and families. All subsequent page references in the text pertain to this edition of the Haggadah. According to Burton L. Visotsky, a professor at the Jewish Theological Seminary in New York, "Maxwell House has probably done more to codify Jewish liturgy than any force in history" (in Allen R. Myerson, 14–15).

2. My colleague Alvin Rosenfeld has pointed out to me that my phrase "Jewish non-Jew" deviates from Isaac Deutscher's "non-Jewish Jew"; however, I have kept it here to emphasize through the adjectival an inescapable history, not a claimed identity.

3. For a very different reaction to Khaled, see Letty Cottin Pogrebin, *Deborah, Golda, and Me* (158–9).

4. See, for example, Charlotte Baum, Paula Hyman, and Sonya Michel, *The Jewish Woman in America* and Elizabeth Koltun, ed., *The Jewish Woman: New Perspectives*. Many of the authors included in these anthologies and in *On Being a Jewish Feminist* discuss exclusionary aspects of Judaism: the partition separating women from men in the synagogue, for example; the prohibiting of women from saying Kaddish at the grave; the injunction of *kol ishah*, whereby a female singing voice is considered sexually arousing to men and thereby forbidden in worship; and perhaps most alarmingly, the discussion in talmudic tractate *ketubot* of whether a woman should be considered a virgin for the purposes of her marriage contract if a man had intercourse with her when she was under three years old.

Others examine disturbing Torah passages: the episode in which two strange men under threat of sexual molestation by the male inhabitants of Sodom are offered by Lot his two virgin daughters (Gen. 18:4–8); the law that a jealous husband who suspects his wife "has defiled herself" may require a priest to administer "the water of bitterness"—sacral water mixed with earth from the floor of the tabernacle—that will distend her belly and make her "curse among her people," unless she miraculously remains unharmed, thereby proving her innocence (Num. 5:11–28); the description of the war with the Midianites, in which the Israelites' booty amounts to "675,000 sheep, 72,000 head of cattle, 61,000 asses, and a total of 32,000 human beings, namely, the women who had not had carnal relations" (Num. 31:32–35). To be sure, as Alvin Rosenfeld has pointed out to me, such proof-texts may place the feminist critic in the role of a fundamentalist, for any interpretation of them as constituting Jewish thought omits the entire corpus of the oral Torah.

More recently, *Twiced Blessed*, ed. Christie Balka and Andy Rose, provides crucial insights on the contradictions between Jewish traditions and homosexual existence, as does Eve Kosofsky Sedgwick in *Epistemology of the Closet* (75–82).

5. At the time at least one commentator noticed the disparity between the number of Jewish feminist critics studying literature and the paucity of Jewish woman writers: see Carole Zonis Yee, "Why Aren't We Writing about Ourselves?" (131). Lillian Robinson has pointed out to me that "the cover of Showalter's *The New Feminist Criticism*, where your collaborator is the only gentile on the list, is an especially striking example" of how many feminist critics are Jewish. She adds that "another cover, this one listing the five co-authors of *Feminist Scholarship: Kindling in the Groves of Academe*, includes four Jewish women and one Gentile. (It may be of some sociological interest that the four Jews are named DuBois, Kelly, Kennedy, and Robinson, and the only Gentile, Carolyn Korsmeyer, is married [to a Jewish scholar].)"

6. See Sandra M. Gilbert, "For the Muses," "The Dressmaker's Dummy," and "Anna La Noia," in *Emily's Bread* (17, 21, 50); the section entitled "The Summer Kitchen" in *Blood Pressure* (51–85); and "*Piacere Conoscerla*: On Being an Italian-American," in *From the Margin* (116–20).

7. In an eccentric and nonscientific manner, my questionnaire went out to feminist critics who had not established their professional identities on any Jewish scholarly subject. I am grateful throughout this essay for the wonderful responses sent to me by Elizabeth Abel, Nina Auerbach, Rachel Brownstein, Rachel Blau DuPlessis, Judith Frank, Jane Gallop, Judith Kegan Gardiner, Annette Kolodny, Nancy K. Miller, Alicia Ostriker, Adrienne Rich, Lillian Robinson, Naomi Schor, Susan Suleiman, and several respondents who wished to remain unnamed. All undocumented quotations from these critics were taken from these questionnaires.

8. Earlier in this essay, Heilbrun admits, "Having been a Jew had made me an outsider. It had permitted me to be a feminist," but she goes on to explain that "if Jews were outsiders, women were outsiders among Jews" (20–1).

9. Judith Kegan Gardiner, who grew up in Chicago, writes, "My father used to tell me bedtime stories about Freudian theory."

10. I would like to thank Deborah Reichler for providing me with copies of several such feminist Haggadahs. Also see E. M. Broner, Penina V. Adelman, and Aviva Cantor Zuckoff.

11. This is a theme running through Helen Epstein's excellent *Children of the Holocaust*.

12. It wasn't until reading Sander Gilman's *Jewish Self-Hatred* that I knew this phrase to come from Heine's "The New Jewish Hospital in Hamburg" (composed in 1842):

A hospital for poor, sick Jews,
for people afflicted with threefold misery,
with three evil maladies;
poverty, physical pain, and Jewishness.

The last named is the worst of all the three:
the thousand-year-old family complaint,
the plague they dragged with them from the Nile valley,
the unhealthy faith from ancient Egypt.

Incurable, profound suffering! No help can be looked for
from steam-baths, showerbaths, or all the implements
of surgery, or all the medicines
which this house offers its sick inmates.   (384).

13. See her memoir as well as "My War in Four Episodes."

14. See also Beauvoir's comment that "Just as in America there is no Negro problem, but rather a white problem, just as 'anti-Semitism is not a Jewish problem; it is our problem'; so the woman problem has always been a man's problem" (118–19).

15. Judith Frank, who describes herself as "bitter" about Judaism and Israeli culture, says of this feeling identifiable as a Jew in a gentile context: "It gives me a certain amount of wry pleasure, but also a certain belligerence about my style of talking and arguing: I'm prone to a kind of aggressiveness, even vulgarity, when speaking among my genteel colleagues."

16. In other words, I did not send my questionnaire out to self-identified Jewish feminists such as Evelyn Torton Beck, Melanie Kaye/Kantrowitz, or Irena Klepfisz. However, their books are essential background reading on the subject of women and Judaism.

17. Esther Ticktin proposes a "new *halakhah*" on the basis of this Passover text in "A Modest Beginning," in *The Jewish Woman*, ed. Elizabeth Koltun (129–35).

18. Melanie Kaye/Kantrowitz, Irena Klepfisz, and Grace Paley make a similar point in "An Interview with Grace Paley," in *The Tribe of Dina* (329).

19. See Elly Bulkin, Minnie Bruce Pratt, and Barbara Smith on "competition for victim status" and "oppression privilege" (75, 99).

20. Elizabeth Abel explained on the questionnaire: "I do think that my current attraction to black women's writing is shaped by my Jewishness; there's some identification at work here that's only starting to become clear to me."

21. See Irena Klepfisz, "*Yom Hashoah, Yom Yerushalaym*: A Meditation," (260–85). I am indebted to Adrienne Rich for sending me several copies of *Bridges*, which is published by New Jewish Agenda and is committed to combining "the traditional Jewish values of justice and repair of the world with insights honed by the feminist, lesbian and gay movements" (Editorial Mission statement).

22. See Moses' poem in Deut. 32:7, 10, 13.

23. See James Baldwin, "The Price of the Ticket" and "Negroes Are Anti-Semitic Because They Are Anti-White."

5. The Graying of Professor Erma Bombeck

1. Jill Dolan expresses best the elation I, too, feel about this transformation: "I can still remember my pleasure and surprise at finding I *was not* the only one, or that I could have conversations and arguments over whatever I perceived as my differences. The institutionalization of feminism has meant a move away from this fearful singularity, a move from frustrating isolation, to the empowerment of community, to the power of *position* in academic systems" (3). Using data collected in the academic year 1989–90, Helen S. Astin and Lynda Malik conclude that "significant gains have been made" in academia, largely because of the women's movement, but "American academic women continue to lag behind men with respect to their overall participation, status and rewards" (192).

2. Pointing out that fully two-thirds of part-time and nontenure-track writing faculty are women, Eileen E. Schell documents their lack of benefits, job security, and chances for promotion. "In the humanities, for every woman in a full-time position, there are approximately two women occupying part-time positions since women represent 67 percent of all part-time faculty and only 33 percent of the full-time faculty in the humanities" (5). My essay, then, exposes problems for a relatively elite group.

3. In their 1988 book *Women of Academe*, Nadya Aisenberg and Mona Harrington point out that, despite the greatly increased numbers of women in higher educa-

tion, women who enter the profession "are not gaining full professional authority" (4). What they call "the two tiered structure of professional authority" meant that "in 1983, women made up about 26 percent of the full-time faculty at four-year colleges and universities, but only about 10 percent of the full professors." If "looking at universities, . . . only about 6 percent of the full professors were women" (5).

According to Catharine R. Stimpson, "In 1987 the American Association of University Professors regretfully reported that non-tenure track positions are increasing, and women are more apt to be in them than men" ("What" 59). Bettina J. Huber demonstrates that women "continue to be underrepresented at the full-professor level" in 1990 (61): "In the aggregate, women in the modern languages are, and will continue to be, underrepresented at this final plateau because throughout the 1980s they were disadvantaged at every post-Ph.D. career stage" (63).

About the overextension of African-American women in and out of their home institutions, Nellie Y. McKay states: "Because there are still so few of them, they are overburdened with committee and professional world at home and abroad. . . . Most are overworked and overextended" ("Literature and Politics" 93). In agreement with her, Ann duCille explains that "black women academics . . . see themselves consumed by exhaustion, depression, loneliness, and a higher incidence of such killing diseases as hypertension, lupus, cancer, diabetes, and obesity" (p. 119). Chandra Talpade Mohanty believes that, "while the highly visible bartering for Third World 'stars' serves to suggest that institutions of higher education are finally becoming responsive to feminist and Third World concerns, this particular commodification and personalization of race suggests there has been very little change since the 1970s—both in terms of a numerical increase of Third World faculty and our treatment in white institutions" ("On Race and Voice" 202–3). On the barriers to further advancement for Asian-American women, see Deborah Woo.

4. A 1985 introduction to a book on reentry women puts the economic problems this way: "Today the academic picture is catastrophic for all unemployed and indentured academicians, female and male. Institutions of higher education are feeling the consequences of the baby boom of the 1950s, of the planned parenthood of the 1960s, of financial recessions, and of dwindling federal funds for college students and universities in the 1970s and 1980s" (Thompson and Roberts 2).

5. Looking at the severe contraction of the academic job market since the mid-1970s as well as the simultaneous decline in majors as undergraduates shifted to fields with vocational utility, Bettina J. Huber explains "that just as women were starting to join the faculty ranks in significant numbers, the doors of the academy were swinging shut" (58).

6. Valerie Miner believes that most women feel "especially competitive with women," though they are suffused with guilt because of this (184). Jane Gallop argues

that "feminism makes it worse," by which she does not mean that "if we give up feminism these problems would be less bad. But feminism produces the expectation that it should be different, and so when it isn't different it's much more painful—and therefore worse" (129). Because "feminists were too optimistic about how quickly we could change" the system, we have been "dishonest with ourselves about the investments we had in things like 'competition and prestige'" (131). Diane Elam contends that women's "solidarity" in the academy was mythic and "What is perhaps new is how crucial the question of power *within* feminism has become" ("WA" 67).

7. Diane Elam is excellent on this point. Also of interest is the "intergenerational polylogue" the editors of *differences* set up. See Christian et al. (52–108).

8. According to Ellen Messer-Davidow, "Today, feminist studies is institutionalized nationwide as some 630 Women's Studies programs offering majors, minors, and graduate degrees, feminist subfields in most disciplines, local and national curriculum transformation projects, more than 80 feminist research centers, national associations of feminist scholars, feminist committees and scholarly divisions in virtually every disciplinary association, and thousands of feminist presses, book series, and journals" (*DF*, forthcoming).

9. According to the authors of *Feminist Scholarship*, an "either/or answer" to the debate between those advocating "the autonomy of women studies versus its integration into the disciplines" should be jettisoned for a both/and response (Du Bois et al. 201–2).

10. Shirley J. Yee provides an excellent overview on the issues at stake when Women's Studies is renamed Gender Studies and herself argues for keeping "The 'Women' in Women's Studies" (46–64). For startling critiques of the field from people holding positions in Women's Studies, see Biddy Martin's and Wendy Brown's contributions to *differences* and the last chapter of this book.

11. Barbara Johnson agrees: "just at the moment when women (and minorities) begin to have genuine power in the university, American culture responds by acting as though the university itself is of dubious value" (*FD* 3).

12. Carol Christ documents the overproduction of Ph.D. degrees in English departments: "Between 1988–9 and 1994–5, the number of jobs advertised annually in the *Job Information List* declined by forty-four percent; during the same period the number of Ph.D.s granted increased by fifty percent" (59).

13. Biddy Martin makes a point pertinent to all faculty today, perhaps especially women: "The mixed messages we get and pass on to each other about distinctions in merit, status, visibility, and influence need to be fully acknowledged and then abandoned in favor of serious discussions about how to introduce into the institution greater differentiation in views of and rewards for different strengths and functions" ("Success and Its Failures" 105).

14. In "Know-How," Ellen Messer-Davidow summarizes the voices of a number of feminists who "have begun to ask whether, in institutionalizing ourselves, we have reproduced the academic organization and reproduction of knowledge we once sought to change" (281). She goes on to argue that "The apparatus we have built will constrain us *if* we allow it to absorb us in traditional academic activities; or it will empower us . . . *if* we use it to amplify feminist social change" (301). In a subsequent study she claims that "the venues feminists appropriated and built anew—academic conferences and publications, Women's Studies courses and programs—turned female studies toward scholarship" even as they "balkanized feminists in the academy, divided us from nonacademic feminists and progressives, and reconstituted social change as an artifact of our esoteric discourses" (*DF*, forthcoming).

15. The report "Assessing Faculty Publication Productivity: Issues of Equity" that was released by the Education Resource Information Center (ERIC) Clearinghouse at George Washington University in May 1998 found that "Women tend to teach undergraduates rather than graduate students, are less likely to have earned the Ph.D. from a top-notch program, and are more often in untenured posts." These factors contribute to the fact that 43 percent of women in academe have never published an article, compared with 23 percent of men. Other factors related to this asymmetry include the tendency to cite only the lead author of an article, the fact that articles (as a venue for publication) predominate in the hard sciences (where the percentage of women is lowest), and the complications of raising children. "Even when they do publish, many women don't reap the same rewards as men. 'When compared to men, women-authored papers are less widely read, the payoff in terms of salary is lower, and more publications are required to be promoted,' the report says." All quotes are taken from a column entitled "Footnotes" in *The Chronicle of Higher Education* (June 12, 1998): A12.

16. "Data from the AAUP and other sources show no reduction in tenure disparity in recent decades. In 1976–77, 64 percent of male professors had tenure, while 44 perfect of female professors did. In 1995–96, 72 percent of men were tenured, but only 48 percent of women were. In other words, the tenure gap was 20 percent points in 1976–77 and 24 percentage points in 1995–96. (The persistence of the gap is not attributable to increasing percentages of women in assistant-professor positions.)" (Valian 52).

6. What Ails Feminist Criticism?

1. In books such as Christina Hoff Sommers's *Who Stole Feminism?* and Jean Curthoys' *Feminist Amnesia*, feminist criticism has come under attack by those who wish to see Women's Studies programs dismantled. Needless to say, I write as part

of the enterprise, not outside it, in the hopes of strengthening feminism within the academy.

2. Obviously, I cannot fully disengage myself from the generational argument. As Marianne Hirsch has pointed out, "There is a certain generation of feminist theorists who have really gotten it from all sides: Elaine Showalter, Nancy Chodorow, Sandra M. Gilbert and Susan Gubar, Carol Gilligan. . . . When you go to a conference and get attacked by other feminists—and I don't just mean criticized, I mean trashed—the whole tone and range of the project changes and certain work gets disallowed" (364–65). Consider, also, Janet Todd's remark: "It seems to me that my middle-aged generation has necessarily handed over the centre (if there can be one in what are still the margins) to the younger, whose aims and references are different because their experience of life and the state of the discipline are very different. But the older can still comment and prod and grumble as they have always done" ("AAD" 243–4). Yet the generational model "means privileging a kind of family history that organizes generations where they don't exist, ignores intra-generational differences and inter-generational commonalities, and thrives on a paradigm of oppositional change" (72), as Judith Roof has shown in "Generational Difficulties."

3. To be sure, as Evelyn Fox Keller has pointed out, "A focus on the supposed coherence of seventies feminism obscures the fact that, from its earliest days, feminist theory was in fact characterized by a marked multiplicity in its goals, and in its stated functions" (382); however, I am arguing that there was more solidarity and coherence in the seventies than in its later evolution.

4. If *The Madwoman in the Attic* seems unusually gothic in this context, both its subtitle—*The Woman Writer and the Nineteenth-Century Literary Imagination*—and the title of the collection of essays Sandra Gilbert and I edited that same year—*Shakespeare's Sisters*—participate in the exuberant universalizing so common in the late seventies and viewed with so much suspicion today. I have placed Barbara Christian's work in this stage (not that of the next) in part because of its early date of publication (1980) but also in part because it used the rhetoric of recovery.

5. Jeannette Foster's 1956 *Sex Variant Women in Literature* was reprinted by Diana Press in 1975, and by 1977 Audre Lorde published a piece entitled "Poetry Is Not a Luxury" about the need to "come more into touch with our own ancient, noneuropean consciousness of living" (*SO* 36). By 1981 the "Lavender Menace," Ti-Grace Atkinson, and Adrienne Rich's "Compulsory Heterosexuality and Lesbian Existence" had sparked critical debates between straight and gay women, while Gayatri Chakravorty Spivak had taken the French feminists to task for their inadequate awareness of an "international frame." See Dever and Spivak's "French Feminism" in *In Other Worlds* (134–53).

6. As Sandra Gilbert and I learned when revising the *Norton Anthology of Literature by Women* for its second edition, even in the ten years that separated this publication from its first appearance in 1985, a host of discoveries—writers such as Mary Wroth, Eliza Haywood, Helen Maria Williams, and Anne Spencer—dramatized the difference the period of recovery has made in the Anglo-American literature classroom and in our mapping of the various literary periods of production.

7. I am taking issue with Toril Moi's view that Anglo-American empiricism stood in opposition to theoretical French feminism because I see both camps involved in comparable endeavors. In her frequently reprinted "The Laugh of the Medusa," Hélène Cixous began by using Derrida's notion of hierarchized binary oppositions to censure Western culture's identification of masculinity with activity, rationality, culture, and logos; of femininity with passivity, sensitivity, nature, and pathos. Then she attempted to excavate an *écriture féminine* composed of "white milk" in a "language of 1,000 tongues which knows neither enclosure nor death" (889). Similarly, in her influential *Speculum*, Luce Irigaray castigated the "specular logic of the same" in philosophical traditions established from Plato to Hegel and Freud that situate woman outside representation. For Irigaray, *le parler femme* described in "This Sex Which Is Not One" constitutes a recoverable and infinitely fluid style that is "*always in the process of weaving itself, of embracing itself with words, but also of getting rid of words in order not to become fixed, congealed in them*" (29). On British input into feminist criticism in this period, see Janet Todd's *Feminist Literary History* as well as the special issue of *Tulsa Studies in Women's Literature* on Anglo-American criticism (12, 2 [Fall 1993]).

8. This is the title of Johnson's essay on the institutionalization of deconstruction in *A World of Difference*.

9. This is especially the case vis-à-vis the first two stages. As the procedure of critique is usually practiced, after all, one expects the interpreter to find the text either feminist or misogynist in its sexual ideologies. With recovery, often the woman writer being excavated is claimed to be central because of the highly charged (again, feminist or misogynist) sexual ideologies of her productions, or the standards of evaluation by which she had been judged are said to be skewed by generic and gendered criteria inappropriate to her accomplishment.

10. See Carol Gilligan's description of her dismay at seeing herself disparaged by feminists as an advocate of the "Victorian angel in the house" and "pious maternalism" (26). Gayle Greene writes about how feminists in the eighties established credentials by "demonstrating how feminism fits in with or around Lacan, Derrida, Lyotard, or how we're superior to our benighted compatriots (Showalter and Gilbert and Gubar are the favorite targets)" (17). Describing a 1987 conference in which she witnessed "the raw hostility" of attendees, Susan Bordo admits feeling "dismayed at

the anger that (white, middle-class) feminists have exhibited toward the work of Gilligan and Chodorow" (*UB* 233).

When Dale Bauer confesses, "most feminist professors I know have to fight on a daily basis the temptation to give up. The level of frustration can be overwhelming," she stresses the difficulties of keeping the discipline "vital precisely at the time society, the economy, and conventional politics are making it increasingly difficult for us to thrive" ("PC" 65). In relation to the vulnerability of African-American women within the humanities, Ann duCille writes about "the startling number of brilliant black women scholars who have produced only one book or no book" in part because they have been "used up as role models [who] . . . find themselves chewed up" (97).

11. Tania Modleski's *Feminism Without Women* addresses related points about the hazards of attempting to establish a political movement for women without the category of "women" or with that category saturated by a misogynist intellectual history.

12. Of course, doris davenport's analysis never attains the sophistication of the subsequent African-American and postcolonial thinkers I consider; however, the volume in which she appears played an important role in the intellectual history I am tracing.

The rancor of early black feminists has to be understood in terms of the unraveling of the Black Power movement and the perception that white feminists were coopting the language of Civil Rights. For another example of it, see Lorraine Bethel's poem "What Chou Mean *We*, White Girl?" in *Conditions Five*, which is equally angry in its dedication "TO THE PROPOSITION THAT ALL WOMEN ARE NOT EQUAL; I.E. IDENTICALLY OPPRESSED":

so this is an open letter to movement white girls:
Dear Ms Ann Glad Cosmic Womoon,
We're not doing that kind of work anymore
educating white women [.] (88)

In particular, Bethel rages against white feminist lesbians "who would be scorned as racist dogs if they were/heterosexual white men/instead of white lesbians hiding behind the liberal veneer of/equal bedroom opportunity" (90). Unlike this indignant work, *Common Differences: Conflicts in Black and White Feminist Perspectives* by Gloria I. Joseph and Jill Lewis insists on "the importance of Black women and White women connecting their specific understandings of oppression to an understanding of the political totality that thrives on these oppressions" (14).

13. Audre Lorde's strategic position as a black lesbian poet made her exceptionally influential in ways that most histories of this period have not yet fully documented. See *Sister Outsider* as well as *Zami*.

14. Although Michele Wallace judges bell hooks's *Ain't I a Woman* a "fine job of providing the historical overview of black feminist thought" (*"FWBT"*21), she condemns hooks's later writing as "self-indulgent and undigested drivel that careens madly from outrageous self-pity, poetic and elliptical, to playful exhibitionism, to dogmatic righteous sermonizing" (22). In another recent review Wallace criticizes the absence of documentation in hooks's books: "The only person being empowered by her failure to use footnotes and bibliography is her. Footnotes and bibliographies take extra time to prepare and cost more money. Not only that, the reader might get a better idea of when hooks, herself, is 'eating the other' " ("AWS" 8). On competition and distrust between powerful black female intellectuals and artists, see hooks's "Third World Diva Girls."

15. A similar point is made by Barbara Smith in her essay "Toward a Black Feminist Criticism" when—after protesting the absence of black women writers in feminist criticism—she finds "the idea of critics like Showalter *using* Black literature . . . chilling, a case of barely disguised cultural imperialism" (172).

16. Consider the thirty-five pages of response to Annette Kolodny's "Dancing Through the Minefields" printed by *Feminist Studies* in 1982, attacking Kolodny's supposed racism, heterosexism, classism (described by Nancy K. Miller in *Getting Personal* [83]). In *Risking Who One Is*, Susan Suleiman reprints a letter from Raquel Portillo Bauman, a Chicana mother, who complains that Suleiman's 1989 essay on "Maternal Splitting" excluded not only Bauman's experiences but also those of her Mexican and Mexican-American grandmothers and her black mother-in-law. Suleiman notes in her response Bauman's assumption that her ethnicity somehow makes her more representative of "the 'real' experiences of minority women" and thus more accurate about them than the supposedly "advantaged" scholar writing from a psychoanalytic perspective could ever be. "Are racial or ethnic allegiances more significant and ultimately more important, than allegiances among women?" Suleiman then asks ("MI" 62). "Does one have to choose between allegiances rather than try to combine them?" In short does being identified as a Hispanic or a black mean one cannot also identify as a woman with women from other traditions?

17. Politically correct identity politics that troubled Women's Studies teachers in the classroom could not be easily addressed in public since the media had already attached the label of "PC" to *all* feminists within the academy, absurdly linking the teaching of Alice Walker to the decline of cultural literacy and the destruction of Western civilization. See the satire *Masterpiece Theatre* that Sandra Gilbert and I wrote on this and related subjects.

18. Bordo's point seems pertinent in this regard: "It is striking to me that there is often a curious selectivity at work in contemporary feminist criticism of gender-based theories of identity. The analytics of race and class—the two other giants of modernist social critique—do not seem to be undergoing quite the same deconstruction" (*UW* 229).

19. Pam Morris's rhetoric of self-blame, which appears in *Literature and Feminism*—

> My inevitably western-orientated critical discourse can itself be regarded as a colonizing and expansionist language, appropriating the writing of "black" women for my own academic purposes. To construct black feminist writing as the object of my "knowledge" would be to engage in one of the most typical forms of colonial linguistic oppression (175)

—leads directly to a quoting of Gayatri Chakravorty Spivak on "the immense distance separating privileged 'first-world' feminists and the great majority of women in the 'third-world' " (175). Perhaps a passage in Dympna Callaghan's "The Vicar and the Virago" can best stand for the common use of Spivak against white feminists:

> Lacking the reassurance of absolute hegemonic subjective and social identities (which, by definition, can never be secure enough), significant feminist theoretical texts can be understood as playing out a white identity crisis that, despite all assertions to the contrary, reinstates white hegemony via a complicity with what Gayatri Chakravorty Spivak has called "the persistent constitution of the Other as the Self's shadow" (198).

Spivak herself rejects the standard demonization of white feminists—"There is nothing necessarily meretricious about the Western feminist gaze," she declares (*OTM* 182)—and she has "found politically very troubling" the tendency of "[m]ore and more people" to find in her "a very convenient marginal, capital M" (*PC* 156).

20. How else compute Spivak's recognition of the advantages accruing to her from her traveling and teaching (when she speaks of her own "*carte d'identité* in Western Europe and Britain" [*TPC* 16] or "a *carte d'entrée* into the elite theoretical *ateliers* in France" [*IOW* 221]) with her meditation on the transcendental purity of third-world critics who "live in a First World country, but have kept ourselves clean from citizenship so that we can have a voice that we can suggest you cannot hear" (*DW* 216)? Spivak's attention to the disenfranchised and her identity as a third-world critic sponsor her mockery of deluded first-world scholars who perform "the 'poor little rich girl

speaking *personal* pain as victim of the *greatest* oppression' act that multiculturalist capitalism—with its emphasis on individuation and competition—would thrust upon us" (*OTM* 139). This rhetoric occurs again in an interview with Ellen Rooney when Spivak says, "I think the kind of antiessentialism that I like these days is in the work of Kalpana Bardhan. If you read her, you probably wouldn't see what I was talking about" (*OTM* 17).

In my approach to Spivak, I am indebted to Shirley Geok-lin Lim's discussion of "the kind of bad faith and reasoning inherent in Third World intellectualization within the hegemony of the First World" (283). Also of use is Robert Young's insight that "the paradox of Spivak's own work remains: it seems as if the heterogeneity of the Third World woman can only be achieved through a certain homogenization of the First" (167).

21. See also Deborah E. McDowell's list of the ways in which the program of black feminist critics diverged from that of poststructuralists; i.e., when black feminists asserted the significance of black women's experience, poststructuralists dismantled the authority of experience.

22. This is why, as Diane Elam puts it, "feminism must be willing to understand the necessity of indeterminacy" (*FD* 31). Elam's view that feminist analysis should be "a deconstruction of representation that keeps the category of women incessantly in question, as a permanently contested site of meaning" (41), underscores the efforts of poststructural thinkers to reject universalisms at work in feminist analysis. In this regard, one might think of some of the work produced by Catherine Belsey, Mary Jacobus, Peggy Kamuf, Alice Jardine, and Mary Poovey.

23. Emboldened by Monique Wittig's argument that "Lesbian is the only concept I know of which is beyond the categories of sex (woman and man), because the designated subject (lesbian) is *not* a woman, either economically, or politically, or ideologically" (20), Butler argued that the categories of woman, man, and sex had to be debiologized; however, she distinguished herself from Wittig by claiming that the latter "subscribes to that metaphysics of substance that is responsible for the production and naturalization of the category of sex itself" (*GT* 20).

That any reliance on the "metaphysics of substance" was demonized by poststructuralists appears evident in the pollution metaphors used by Caroline Ramazanoglu: "the possibility of biological nature, or material bodies, playing some part in explanation of gender difference runs under the fields of feminism like a camouflaged sewer in which the unwary may trip and so be contaminated without fully realising their danger. . . . Many feminists . . . have found the odour of biological essentialism clinging to them" (7).

24. See Linda Charnes on how Butler's "jargon-clotted and, at times, numbingly redundant prose" echoes Foucault's "heavily Latinate, juridical, phallogocentric,

often plodding, and by now, institutionally 'authoritative' prose" in her insightful discussion of how Butler's "critical style matters" (138–9).

25. In this regard, to be sure, Butler represents a series of sophisticated thinkers—Barthes, Bakhtin, Foucault, Lacan, Derrida, Žižek, Levinas—whose treatises have profoundly influenced the writing of literary criticism. Pedagogically, what will their effect be on those dissertators—not a negligible group—who decide to model their prose on Butler's or Lacan's, even though their knowledge of, say, Wittig and Freud derives only from Butler's or Lacan's take on those precursors?

26. Not all these subject-verb disagreements follow the pattern of dual nouns with singular verbs. See *Gender Trouble*, pp. 91 and 126. In *Bodies That Matter*, see pp. 48, 55, 87, 125, 126, 127, 207, 224, and 236; "Against Proper Objects," pp. 2, 8, and 16; "Feminism By Any Other Name," pp. 31 and 33; and "Imitation and Gender Insubordination," pp. 23 and 27.

27. My first thought on seeing what Butler would call "the iterability" of this usage was to wonder, where was the copyeditor when her manuscripts arrived at the publisher's or journal's office? Have economic pressures on publishers caused them to withdraw this important safety net from writers? Or has the star system so dismantled the normative manner of refereeing that anything goes for an elite group of academicians? If so, should we count as one of the problems facing feminist criticism the effects of this star system on a depressed marketplace? For, at the institutional level, marked disparities (in work loads, professional status, and reward systems) between the few at the top and those laboring in what we tellingly call "the trenches" have contributed to a divisive atmosphere that affects all practitioners in the humanities at the present time.

28. Pertinent to this discussion is Butler's admission that "it takes a certain suspicion toward grammar to reconceive the matter [of an "I" that performs gender] in a different light" (*BTM* 7). Consider, too, the comment in "Imitation and Gender Insubordination": "In my view, the self only becomes a self on the condition that it has suffered (*grammar fails* us here, for the 'it' only becomes differentiated through that separation), a loss which is suspended" (emphases mine, 27). Yet if Butler purposefully generates ungrammatical structures, one would expect her to foreground that strategy more consistently throughout her texts.

29. The grammatical problem also proves the truth of Kate Soper's admonition that an "emphasis on the discursive formation of our corporeal existence . . . ceases to be productive if it is pressed at the expense of proper recognition of the impossibility of dispensing with any reference to a pre-discursive reality" (32–3). On the essentialism of always viewing essentialism as reactionary, see Fuss (*ES* 21). On the limits of poststructural views of subjectivity, see George Levine's introduction and Irving Howe's essay in *Constructions of the Self*.

30. Although I have set aside the issue of Nietzsche's masculinism, it seems pertinent that he prefaced his remark about God and grammar with the sentence " 'Reason' in language—oh, what an old deceptive female she is!" (483). My question about the ideals at risk in Butler's brand of poststructuralism reflects a growing interest in ethics among philosophers and literary critics today.

31. "Denial of the unity and stability of identity is one thing," Susan Bordo remarks. "The epistemological fantasy of *becoming* multiplicity—the dream of limitless multiple embodiments, allowing one to dance from place to place and self to self—is another" (*UW* 228–9). Judith K. Gardiner links anti-essentialism with "a fear of mortality" that "springs less from the stable facts of human embodiment than from a current crisis precipitated by the fear of meaninglessness, which is related for the left, even more than for the right, to a crisis of values" (90).

32. In her "Afterword," Amanda Anderson unravels the consequences of Spivak's turn to a "strategic essentialism" that her own assumptions make illogical.

33. See Miller, "Public Statements, Private Lives: Academic Memoirs for the Nineties." Jane Tompkins, Deborah McDowell, bell hooks, Alice Kaplan, Annette Kuhn, Shirley Geok-lin Lim, Susan Suleiman, Marianna Torgovnick, Bonnie Zimmerman, and Marianne Hirsch are just a few representative writers in this genre. Needless to say, others have accused autobiographical critics of the narcissism symptomatic of an evacuated subject or of displacing critical disagreements rather than engaging them directly.

34. The constructedness of the self or even its fictive escapades do not discount or erase its actuality in personal criticism, especially in the work of renewal individuals must accomplish under sometimes tragic, sometimes difficult circumstances. We are given to believe that these authors experience their own authenticity, if only at certain intense moments of being when social practices are benign, or downright beneficial. Furthermore, though socially formed and highly unstable, though performative and multiple, the self nevertheless appears able to rebel against at least some of those pernicious factors that brought it into being. In this regard, feminist autobiographical criticism ironically underscores the way in which the antitotalizing theory of poststructuralists actually totalizes all selves as passive products of discursive power-knowledge regimes that are, in turn, assumed to be nothing but malign. See George Levine's introduction and Irving Howe's essay in *Constructions of the Self*.

35. I am agreeing with Gayle Greene, when she senses "a self-defeating tendency" in feminist critics' "fierce self-scrutiny" and identifies it as "a kind of professional/pedagogical anorexia" (17).

36. Feminist criticism has shifted away from the earlier default position of whiteness to generate a vast amount of scholarship on the literary history of women of color. A growing number of white women are now participating with women of color in African-American and Postcolonial feminist studies; however, optimism

about this event needs to be qualified by several points made by Anne duCille. Her "uneasy antagonism" toward certain senior scholars—untrained in African-American studies but nevertheless publishing in the field—is related to her awareness that "black culture is more easily intellectualized (and canonized) when transferred from the danger of lived black experience to the safety of white metaphor" (88, 87, 91). She also points out that the influx into African-American Studies by white feminists is related to "white feminist restlessness with an already well-mined female literary tradition" (93).

37. A recent effort to inject feminist rhetoric with more anger against social injustice and with a stronger sense of community has been undertaken by younger women known as "Riot Grrrls" (advocates of punk rock feminism) (Rosenberg and Garafalo).

7. Feminist Misogyny; or, The Paradox of "It Takes One to Know One"

1. Both Lacan passages are discussed by Jane Gallop, in *The Daughter's Seduction* (34, 45).

2. Throughout this paragraph, I am indebted to Henry Louis Gates Jr., who questions the efficacy of the "Can you really tell?" test with reference primarily to the ethnicity of the author in his *New York Times Book Review* essay on " 'Authenticity.' "

3. Tania Modleski cogently argues about this and other so-called "postfeminist" theorists that "for many 'women' the very term arouses a visceral, even phobic reaction" (*FWW* 16).

4. See Timothy J. Reiss, "Revolution in Bounds: Wollstonecraft, Women, and Reason" (11–50).

5. Sandra Gilbert and I have examined the seeming eccentricity of the literary women of Wollstonecraft's generation, the problem they pose to conventional definitions of the period, in " 'But Oh! That Deep Romantic Chasm: The Engendering of Periodization.' " For an interesting discussion of Beauvoir's much-quoted point, as well as Monique Wittig's revisionary response to it, see Judith Butler, *Gender Trouble* (111–12).

6. Equally telling, as Elissa S. Guralnick points out, Wollstonecraft couples the term "woman" with bashaws, despots, kings, emperors, soldiers, and courtiers, all of whom exercise "illegitimate power" and thus "enjoy the degradation of the exalted" (308–16).

7. Along similar lines, Joan B. Landes argues that Wollstonecraft subscribes to an ideology of republican motherhood that views women's civic role as one performed inside the home, ascribes to men unbridled physical appetites, sets up a model of female duty, and displays an adherence toward male linguistic control that aligns her with the male philosophers of her day (129–38).

8. For a general discussion of the misogyny in these eighteenth-century texts, see my "The Female Monster in August Satire."

9. Ironically, then tragically, Wollstonecraft's detractors exploited precisely the images she shared with her philosophical opponents. She was depicted as one of the "philosophizing serpents in our bosom," a "hyena in petticoats," lampooned in *The Unsex'd Females: A Poem* as a "Poor maniac," ridiculed in a review in the *European Magazine* as a "philosophical wanton," and mocked in *The Shade of Alexander Pope on the Banks of the Thames* as "passion's slave." Similarly, her *Memoirs and Posthumous Works* was judged to be "A Convenient Manual of Speculative Debauchery," and in 1801 the author of "The Vision of Liberty" intoned, "Lucky the maid that on her volume pores / A scripture, archly fram'd, for propagating w—s": see Ralph M. Wardle (318, 321, and 322), as well as Janet Todd, "Introduction," in *A Wollstonecraft Anthology* (16–19).

10. Besides Poovey's and Landes's studies, see Mary Jacobus and Cora Kaplan, as well as Janet Todd, who reviews all these critics in *Feminist Literary History* (103–10). On Wollstonecraft's making "genius a machismo male," see also Christine Battersby (98).

11. I am relying here on a term proposed by Hélène Cixous in "The Laugh of the Medusa" (878).

12. Adrienne Rich, "Compulsory Heterosexuality and Lesbian Existence." On Wollstonecraft, see Jeannette Foster, *Sex Variant Women in Literature* (56–60) and Lillian Faderman, "Who Hid Lesbian History?" (117). Interesting in this regard is the misogyny in lesbian literature that can be traced back to Radclyffe Hall's portraits of "feminine" women in *The Well of Loneliness*, many of whom strike her mannish Stephen Gordon as manipulative, materialistic, and frivolous. "Grossly familiar": Wollstonecraft, *Vindication*, 127.

13. In *The War of the Words* Sandra Gilbert and I discuss the woman writer's "turn toward the father" (171–81). The two female precursors Wollstonecraft admires are Hester Mulso Chapone and Catharine Sawbridge Macaulay Graham, both discussed quite briefly in *A Vindication* (105–6 and 137).

14. The long, slow death of the New Womanly Lyndall in *The Story of an African Farm* (1883) contrasts throughout the novel with the obesity, stupidity, voracity, racism, and cruelty of the traditional woman Tant' Sannie. Like Wollstonecraft, too, Schreiner publicly protested against female dependency on men but suffered repeated thralldom to men in her private life.

15. On Schreiner's plans to produce an introduction to *A Vindication* and on *Woman and Labour* as a "Bible," see Joyce Avrech Berkman, *Olive Schreiner: Feminism on the Frontier* (7, 10, and 2).

16. In an introduction to the republication of her first book, Sandra M. Gilbert explains her own attraction to D. H. Lawrence's works and that of women readers from

Katherine Mansfield and H.D. to Anaïs Nin by envisioning Lawrence as "a proto French feminist": see Gilbert, *Acts of Attention* (xix). It is interesting in this regard that Rachel Blau DuPlessis's often reprinted essay "For the Etruscans" evokes D. H. Lawrence's *Etruscan Places*: see Blau DuPlessis, *The Pink Guitar: Writing as Feminist Practice* (1–19).

17. According to Barbara Johnson, in a subtle analysis of the impact of racial stereotypes on racial identity, "questions of difference and identity are always a function of a specific interlocutionary situation—and the answers a matter of strategy rather than truth": see Johnson, "Thresholds of Difference" (285).

18. On "fembot," see Mary Daly, *Pure Lust* (93).

19. For background on such debates, see Joan Scott, "Deconstructing Equality-Versus-Difference" and Teresa de Lauretis, "Upping the Anti (sic) in Feminist Theory," both in Marianne Hirsch and Evelyn Fox Keller eds., *Conflicts in Feminism* (134–48 and 255–70).

20. Later Moi stated that her book was "written from a feminist perspective, or, in other words, from a perspective of political solidarity with the feminist aims of the critics and theorists I write about." In addition, she claimed that after "the reactionary backlash of the eighties," she found it "far more difficult to be sanguine about one's feminist position" and "would now emphasize much more the risks of being a feminist" (*FT* 95 and 102).

21. Katie Roiphe, *The Morning* (85). Significantly, Roiphe also aligns herself with John Irving and David Mamet (35 and 107). Yet in the opening of the book, she describes her own brand of feminism, which she inherited from her mother. On *Reckless Eyeballing* and Alice Walker, see Ishmael Reed, "Steven Spielberg Plays Howard Beach," in *Writin' Is Fightin'* (145–60).

22. See also Claire Goldberg Moses, " 'Equality' and 'Difference' in Historical Perspective," in *Rebel Daughters: Women and the French Revolution*, which argues that "The argument that feminist discourses of 'equality' and 'difference' are neither right nor wrong but relate to historically specific concerns or opportunities is further strengthened by noting the instability of these categories" (248).

8. A Chapter on the Future

1. See Sandra M. Gilbert and Susan Gubar, *Letters from the Front* (5), on Woolf's outline for *Reading at Random*.

2. Besides Susan Stanford Friedman's related comments in *Mappings* (102–4 and 184–90), see Amanda Anderson's outstanding analysis of the fatalism of poststructuralist conceptualizations that end up robbing subjectivity of indeterminacy and reciprocity (200–4.)

3. Perhaps, in other words, we will see the advent of what Susan Stanford Friedman calls a "migratory feminism" evolving within a "post/poststructuralist" future

(*M* 186). Amanda Anderson proposes Habermas's thinking as a solution to current stalemates, for he presents our "status as subjects who are constituted through intersubjective relations," yet "also placed in productive dialogue with an understanding of larger systems and histories" (223).

4. Nor can the problem be solved through "greater levels of specificity in the models themselves" (93), according to Wendy Brown. For "there are always significant elements of subjectivity and subjection that exceed the accounting offered by such lists" (94). In addition,

> this kind of excessive specificity sacrifices the imaginative reach of theory . . . and in this way repeats the very eclipse of sociohistorical powers it was intended to challenge: these powers become fixed as categories of analysis, rendered as adjectives and nouns, rather than historicized and theorized. Finally, this kind of specificity in identity description and analysis tacitly reiterates an understanding of power as only domination. (94)

5. Although Biddy Martin's and Wendy Brown's predictions about the future of Women's Studies sound grim, such dispatches undoubtedly partake of the bleak perspective of many diagnosticians of what Bill Readings called "the university in ruins": namely, the decline of the university's national cultural mission and the metamorphosis of institutions of higher education into market-driven, transnational corporations (complete with student-consumers, faculty-bureaucrats, staff-advertisers, and administrator-packagers), both of which undermine the centrality of humanistic disciplines.

6. In this same issue of *differences*, see Leora Auslander and Beverly Guy-Sheftall.

7. But what Dominick LaCapra calls "the fragility of disciplinary definitions" also characterizes English, history, and philosophy so that "It is today difficult to say precisely what a literary critic, historian, or philosopher is" (46). In other words, perhaps the confusion within Women's Studies and Gender Studies reflects more a general disarray in humanistic studies, less a crisis in its particular undertaking.

8. In her lecture entitled "Feminism's Apocalyptic Futures," at Indiana University (December 3, 1998), Robyn Wiegman described the maternal plot as a "doom and gloom" narrative of feminism's demise. I do not mean to suggest that Wiegman would accept my metaphor of the supernova; however, it does evade the pitfalls she locates in the maternal plot. See also Judith Roof's cogent arguments against using generations to measure feminism's enterprise in *Generations*.

Works Cited

Abel, Elizabeth. "Black Writing, White Reading: Race and the Politics of Feminist Interpretation." *Critical Inquiry* 19, 3 (Spring 1993): 270–98.

Abraham, Julie. *Are Girls Necessary?: Lesbian Writing and Modern Histories*. New York: Routledge, 1996.

Adelman, Penina V. *Miriam's Well: Rituals for Jewish Women Around the Year*, pp. 60–6. Fresh Meadows, N.Y.: Biblio, 1986.

Adler, Rachel. "The Jew Who Wasn't There: *Halakhah* and the Jewish Woman." In *On Being a Jewish Feminist: A Reader*, ed. Susannah Heschel, pp. 12–18. New York: Schocken, 1993.

Aisenberg, Nadya and Mona Harrington. *Women of Academe: Outsiders in the Sacred Grove*. Amherst: University of Massachusetts Press, 1988.

Andermahr, Sonya. " 'There's Nowt So Queer as Folk': Lesbian Cultural Studies." In *Straight Studies Modified: Lesbian Interventions in the Academy*, ed. Gabriele Griffin and Sonya Andermahr, pp. 8–23. London: Cassell, 1997.

Anderson, Amanda. *Tainted Souls and Painted Faces: The Rhetoric of Fallenness in Victorian Culture*. Ithaca: Cornell University Press, 1993.

Anzaldúa, Gloria. *Borderlands/"La Frontera": The New "Mestiza"*. San Francisco: Spinsters/Aunt Lute, 1987.

Appiah, Anthony. "The Uncompleted Argument: Du Bois and the Illusion of Race." *Critical Inquiry* 12, 1 (Autumn 1985): 21–37.

Appiah, Anthony K. and Amy Gutmann. *Color Conscious: The Political Morality of Race*. Princeton: Princeton University Press, 1996.

Astin, Helen S. and Lynda Malik, "Academic Women in the United States: Problems and Prospects." In *The Gender Gap in Higher Education*, a World Yearbook of Education 1994, ed. Suzanne Stiver Lie, Lynda Malik, and Duncan Harris. London and Philadelphia: Kogan Page, 1994.

Auslander, Leora. "Do Women's + Feminist + Men's + Lesbian and Gay + Queer Studies = Gender Studies?" *differences: A Journal of Feminist Cultural Studies* 9, 3, special issue on Women's Studies on the Edge (Fall 1997): 1–30.

Bakhtin, M. M. *The Dialogic Imagination*, ed. Michael Holquist, trans. Caryl Emerson and Michael Holquist. Austin: University of Texas Press, 1981.

Baker, Houston A. *Modernism and the Harlem Renaissance*. Chicago: University of Chicago Press, 1987.

Baldwin, James. "The Price of the Ticket" and "Negroes Are Anti-Semitic Because They're Anti-White." In *The Price of the Ticket: Collected Nonfiction, 1948–1985*, pp. ix–xx and 425–34. New York: St. Martin's, 1985.

Balka, Christie and Andy Rose, eds. *Twice Blessed: On Being Lesbian or Gay and Jewish*. Boston: Beacon, 1989.

Barrett Browning, Elizabeth. *The Letters*. Ed. Frederic G. Kenyon. 2 vols. New York: Macmillan, 1897. I: 231–32.

Battersby, Christina. *Gender and Genius: Toward a Feminist Aesthetics*. London: Women's Press, 1989.

Bauer, Dale M. "Personal Criticism and the Academic Personality." In *Who Can Speak? Authority and Critical Identity*, ed. Judith Roof and Robyn Wiegman, pp. 56–69. Urbana: University of Illinois Press, 1995.

Bauer, Dale M. Review-Essay. *The Women's Review of Books* 15, 5 (February 1998): 19–20.

Baum, Charlotte, Paula Hyman, and Sonya Michel. *The Jewish Woman in America*. New York: New American Library, 1976.

Beauvoir, Simone de. *The Second Sex*, trans. H. M. Parshley. New York: Knopf, 1953.

Beck, Evelyn Torton, ed. *Nice Jewish Girls: A Lesbian Anthology*. Boston: Beacon, 1989.

Bellafante, Gina. "Is Feminism Dead?" *Time Magazine*, June 19, 1998: 54–60.

Benglis, Lynda. Ad from *Artforum* (November 1974). Reprinted in *New Feminist Criticism: Art Identity Action*, ed. Joanna Frueh, Cassandra L. Langer, and Arlene Raven, p. 35. New York: HarperCollins, 1994.

Benhabib, Seyla. *Critique, Norm, and Utopia: A Study of the Foundations of Critical Theory*. New York: Columbia University Press, 1986.

Benhabib, Seyla. *Situating the Self: Gender, Community, and Postmodernism in Contemporary Ethics*. New York: Routledge, 1992.

Benn Michaels, Walter. "Autobiography of an Ex-White Man: Why Race Is Not a Social Construction." *Transition* 7, 1, special issue on The White Issue (May 1998): 122–43.

Bennett, Paula. "The Pea That Duty Locks: Lesbian and Feminist-Heterosexual Readings of Emily Dickinson's Poetry." In *Lesbian Texts and Contexts: Radical Revisions*, ed. Karla Jay and Joanne Glasgow, pp. 104–25. New York: New York University Press, 1990.

Berger, John. *Ways of Seeing*. London: British Broadcasting Corporation and Penguin, 1972.

Berkman, Joyce Avrech. *Olive Schreiner: Feminism on the Frontier*. St. Alban's, Vt.: Eden Women's Publications, 1979.

Berlant, Lauren. "The Female Complaint." *Social Text* 19/20 (Fall 1988): 237–59.

Bethel, Lorraine. "What Chou Mean *We*, White Girl." *Conditions Five*, the Black Women's Issue 2 (Autumn 1979): 86–92.

Bishop, Elizabeth. "One Art." *The Complete Poems 1927–1979*, p. 178. New York: Farrar Straus Giroux, 1983.

Blanchot, Maurice. *The Writing of the Disaster*, trans. Ann Smock. Lincoln and London: University of Nebraska Press, 1995.

Blau duPlessis, Rachel. *The Pink Guitar: Writing as Feminist Practice*. New York: Routledge, 1990.

Bombara, Toni Cade. *The Black Woman: An Anthology*. New York: New American Library, 1970.

Bordo, Susan. "Feminism, Foucault, and the Politics of the Body." In *Up Against Foucault: Explorations of Some Tensions Between Foucault and Feminism*, ed. Caroline Ramazanoglu, pp. 179–202. New York: Routledge, 1993.

Bordo, Susan. *Unbearable Weight: Feminism, Western Culture, and the Body*. Berkeley: University of California Press, 1993.

Bourne, Jenny. "Homelands of the Mind: Jewish Feminism and Identity Politics." *Race and Class* 29 (1987): 1–24.

Braidotti, Rosi. *Nomadic Subjects: Embodiment and Sexual Difference in Contemporary Feminist Theory*. New York: Columbia University Press, 1994.

Braun, Charlotte, Paula Hymen, and Sonya Michel. *The Jewish Woman in America*. New York: New American Library, 1976.

Bright, Susie. *Susie Bright's Sexuality Reality: A Virtual Sex World Reader*. Pittsburgh: Cleis, 1992.

Broner, E. N. "Honor and Ceremony in Women's Rituals." In *The Politics of Women's Spirituality: Essays on the Rise of Spiritual Power Within the Feminist Movement*, pp. 234–44. New York: Anchor, 1982.

Brossard, Nicole. *The Aerial Letter*, trans. Marlene Wildeman. Toronto: The Women's Press, 1988.

Brossard, Nicole. "Green Night of Labyrinth Park." In *Sexy Bodies: The Strange Carnalities of Feminism*, ed. Elizabeth Grosz and Elspeth Probyn, pp. 128–36. London: Routledge, 1995.

Brown, Rebecca. "Forgiveness." In *The Terrible Girls*. San Francisco: City Lights Books, 1992 and reprinted in *The Norton Anthology of Literature by Women*, ed. Sandra M. Gilbert and Susan Gubar, pp. 2368–72. New York: Norton, 1996.

Brown, Wendy. "The Impossibility of Women's Studies." *differences: A Journal of Feminist Cultural Studies* 9, 3, special issue on Women's Studies on the Edge (Fall 1997): 79–101.

Buber, Martin. *Eclipse of God*. New York: Harper Torchbooks, 1957.

Bulkin, Elly, Minnie Bruce Pratt, and Barbara Smith. *Yours In Struggle: Three Feminist Perspectives on Anti-Semitism and Racism*. Ithaca: Firebrand, 1988.

Butler, Judith. *Bodies That Matter: On the Discursive Limits of 'Sex'*. New York: Routledge, 1993.

Butler, Judith. "Feminism By Any Other Name." *differences: A Journal of Feminist Cultural Studies* 6, 2/3, special issue on More Gender Trouble (1994): 27–61.

Butler, Judith. *Gender Trouble: Feminism and the Subversion of Identity*. New York: Routledge, 1990.

Butler, Judith. "Imitation and Gender Insubordination." In *Inside/Out: Lesbian Theories, Gay Theories*, ed. Diana Fuss, pp. 13–31. New York: Routledge, 1991.

Butler, Octavia. *Kindred*, introduction by Robert Crossley. Boston: Beacon, 1988.

Calhoun, Cheshire. "The Gender Closet: Lesbian Disappearance Under the Sign of 'Women.' " In *Lesbian Subjects: A Feminist Studies Reader*, ed. Martha Vicinus, pp. 209–32. Bloomington: Indiana University Press, 1996.

Calhoun, Cheshire. "Separating Lesbian from Feminist Theory." *Ethics* 104 (April 1994): 558–81.

Califia, Pat. *Public Sex: The Culture of Radical Sex*. Pittsburgh: Cleis, 1994.

Callaghan, Dympna. "The Vicar and Virago: Feminism and the Problem of Identity." In *Who Can Speak? Authority and Critical Identity*, ed. Judith Roof and Robyn Wiegman, pp. 195–207. Urbana: University of Illinois Press, 1995.

Carby, Hazel. "White Woman Listen! Black Feminism and the Boundaries of Sisterhood." In *The Empire Strikes Back*, Center for Contemporary Studies, pp. 212–35. London: Hutchinson, 1982.

Carby, Hazel. "It Just Be's Dat Way Sometimes: The Sexual Politics of Women's Blues." In *Gender and Discourse: The Power of Talk*, ed. Alexandra Dundas Todd and Sue Fisher, pp. 227–42. Norwood: Ablex, 1988.

Carnegie Foundation for the Advancement of Teaching. "Women Faculty Excel as Campus Citizens." *Change* (September/October 1990): 39–43.

Case, Sue-Ellen. "Toward a Butch-Femme Aesthetic." Reprinted in *The Lesbian and Gay Studies Reader*, ed. Henry Abelove, Michèle Aina Barale, and David M. Halperin, pp. 294–306. New York: Routledge, 1993.

Castle, Terry. *The Apparitional Lesbian: Female Homosexuality and Modern Culture*. New York: Columbia University Press, 1993.

Charnes, Linda. "Styles That Matter: On the Discursive Limits of Ideology Critique." *Shakespeare Studies* 24 (1996): 118–47.

Cheng, Anne Anlin. "The Melancholy of Race." *The Kenyon Review* 19, 1 (Winter 1997): 49–61.

Chow, Rey. *Ethics After Idealism: Theory—Culture—Ethnicity—Reading*. Bloomington: Indiana University Press, 1998.

Christ, Carol. "Retaining Faculty Lines." In *Profession 1997*, ed. Phyllis Franklin, pp. 54–60. New York: The Modern Language Association of America, 1997.

Christian, Barbara et al. "Conference All." *differences: A Journal of Feminist Cultural Studies* 2, 3 (1990): 52–108.

Christian, Barbara. "The Race for Theory." *Feminist Studies* 14 (Spring 1988): 67–79.

Churchill, Caryl. *Top Girls*. Reprinted in *The Norton Anthology of Literature by Women*, ed. Sandra M. Gilbert and Susan Gubar, pp. 2153–202. New York: Norton, 1996.

Cixous, Hélène and Catherine Clément. *The Newly Born Woman*, trans. Betsy Wing. Minneapolis: University of Minnesota Press, 1986.

Coiner, Constance. "Silent Parenting in the Academy." In *Listening to Silences: New Essays in Feminist Criticism*, ed. Elaine Hedges and Shelley Fisher Fishkin, pp. 197–224. New York: Oxford University Press, 1994.

Cott, Nancy, "Feminist Theory and Feminist Movements: The Past Before Us." In *What Is Feminism?*, ed. Juliet Mitchell and Ann Oakley, pp. 49–62. New York: Pantheon, 1986.

Curthoys, Jean. *Feminist Amnesia: The Wake of Women's Liberation*. London: Routledge, 1997.

Daly, Mary. *Pure Lust: Elemental Feminist Philosophy*. Boston: Beacon, 1984.

De Lauretis, Teresa. *The Practice of Love: Lesbian Sexuality and Perverse Desire*. Bloomington: Indiana University Press, 1994.

De Lauretis, Teresa. "Upping the Anti (sic) in Feminist Theory." In *Conflicts in Feminism*, ed. Marianne Hirsch and Evelyn Fox Keller, pp. 255–70. New York: Routledge, 1990.

DePalma, Anthony. "Rare in Ivy League: Women Who Work as Full Professors." *The New York Times*, January 24, 1993, sec. 1, pp. 1, 23.

Deavere Smith, Anna. *Fires in the Mirror*. New York: Anchor, 1993.

Deavere Smith, Anna. *Twilight: Los Angeles, 1992*. New York: Anchor, 1994.

Deavere Smith, Anna. "The Word Becomes You: An Interview with Carol Martin." In *On and Beyond the Stage: A Sourcebook of Feminist Theatre*, ed. Carol Martin, pp. 185–204. New York and London: Routledge, 1996.

Derricotte, Toi. *The Black Notebooks*. New York: Norton, 1997.

Dever, Carolyn. "Obstructive Behavior: Dykes in the Mainstream of Feminist Theory." In *Cross-Purposes: Lesbians, Feminists, and the Limits of Alliance*, ed. Dana Heller, pp. 19–41. Bloomington: Indiana University Press, 1997.

Diamond, Elin. "Mimesis in Syncopated Time: Reading Adrienne Kennedy." In *Intersecting Boundaries: The Theatre of Adrienne Kennedy*, ed. Paul K. Bryant-Jackson and Lois More Overbeck, pp. 131–41. Minneapolis: University of Minnesota Press, 1992.

Dickinson, Emily. *The Poems of Emily Dickinson*. Ed. Thomas Johnson. 3 vols. Cambridge: The Belknap Press of Harvard University Press, 1955.

Doan, Laura. "Jeanette Winterson's Sexing the Postmodern." In *The Lesbian Postmodern*, ed. Laura Doan, pp. 137–55. New York: Columbia University Press, 1994.

Dolan, Jill. "Introductory Essay: Fathom Languages: Feminist Performance Theory, Pedagogy, and Practice." In *A Sourcebook of Feminist Theatre and Performance: On and Beyond the Stage*, ed. Carol Martin, pp. 1–20. London and New York: Routledge, 1996.

Douglas, Ann. *The Feminization of American Culture*. New York: Knopf, 1977.

Douglas, Ann. *Terrible Honesty: Mongrel Manhattan in the 1920s*. New York: Farrar, Straus and Giroux, 1995.

DuBois, Ellen Carol, Gail Paradise Kelly, Elizabeth Lapovsky Kennedy, Carolyn W. Korsemeyer, and Lillian S. Robinson. *Feminist Scholarship: Kindling in the Groves of Academe*. Urbana: University of Illinois Press, 1985.

DuBois, W. E. B. *Souls of Black Folk*. New York: Vintage/Library of America, 1990.

duCille, Ann. *Skin Trade*. Cambridge: Harvard University Press, 1996.

Dworkin, Andrea. *Ice and Fire*. New York: Weidenfeld & Nicolson, 1986.

Dworkin, Andrea. *Intercourse*. New York: Free Press, 1987.

Dworkin, Andrea. *Our Blood: Prophecies and Discourses on Sexual Politics*. New York: Harper and Row, 1976.

Eakin, Emily. "Whose Afraid of Elaine Showalter?" *LinguaFranca* 8, 7 (September 1998): 28–48.

Elam, Diane. *Feminism and Deconstruction: Ms. en Abyme*. London and New York: Routledge, 1994.

Elam, Diane. "Sisters Are Doing It To Themselves." In *Generations: Academic Feminists in Dialogue*, ed. Devoney Looser and E. Ann Kaplan, pp. 55–68. Minneapolis: University of Minnesota Press, 1997.

Ellis, Trey. "The New Black Aesthetic." *Callaloo* 12 (Winter 1989): 233–43.

Epstein, Helen. *Children of the Holocaust: Conversations with Sons and Daughters of Survivors*. New York: Penguin, 1979.

Fackenheim, Emil L. *The Jewish Bible after the Holocaust*. Bloomington: Indiana University Press, 1990.

Faderman, Lillian. *Odd Girls and Twilight Lovers: A History of Lesbian Life in Twentieth-Century America*. New York: Columbia University Press, 1991.

Faderman, Lillian. *Surpassing the Love of Men: Romantic Friendship and Love between Women from the Renaissance to the Present*. New York: William Morrow, 1981.

Faderman, Lillian. "What Is Lesbian Literature? Forming a Historical Canon." In

Professions of Desire: Lesbian and Gay Studies in Literature, ed. George E. Haggerty and Bonnie Zimmerman, pp. 49–71. New York: The Modern Language Association, 1995.

Faderman, Lillian. "Who Hid Lesbian Theory?" In *Lesbian Studies: Present and Future*, ed. Margaret Cruikshank, pp. 115–21. Old Westbury, N.Y.: Feminist Press, 1982.

Farwell, Marilyn R. "Heterosexual Plots and Lesbian Subtexts: Toward a Theory of Lesbian Narrative Space." In *Lesbian Texts and Contexts*, ed. Karla Jay and Joanne Glasgow, pp. 91–103. New York: New York University Press, 1990.

Farwell, Marilyn R. "Toward a Definition of the Lesbian Literary Imagination." *Signs* 14, 11 (1988): 100–18.

Farwell, Marilyn R. "The Lesbian Narrative: 'The Pursuit of the Inedible by the Unspeakable.' " In *Professions of Desire: Lesbian and Gay Studies in Literature*, ed. George E. Haggerty and Bonnie Zimmerman, pp. 156–68. New York: The Modern Language Association of America, 1995.

Faulkner, William. *Mosquitoes*. New York: Boni & Liveright, 1927.

Feher, Michel. "The Schisms of '67: On Certain Restructurings of the American Left, from the Civil Rights Movement to the Multiculturalist Constellation." In *Blacks and Jews: Alliances and Arguments*, ed. Paul Berman, pp. 263–85. New York: Delta, 1994.

Ferguson, Frances, "Wollstonecraft Our Contemporary." In *Gender and Theory: Dialogues on Feminist Criticism*, ed. Linda Kauffman, pp. 51–62. Oxford: Basil Blackwell, 1989.

Ferguson, Moira. "Mary Wollstonecraft and the Problematic of Slavery." *Feminist Review* 42 (August 1992): 82–102,

Ferris, Timony. "Seeing in the Dark." *The New Yorker*, August 10, 1998, pp. 55–61.

Fetterley, Judith. *The Resisting Reader: A Feminist Approach to American Fiction*. Bloomington: Indiana University Press, 1978.

Fiedler, Leslie. *Fiedler on the Roof: Essays on Literature and the Language of Revolution*. New York: David R. Godine, 1991.

Findlay, Heather. "Freud's 'Fetishism' and the Lesbian Dildo Debates." In *Lesbian Subjects: A Feminist Studies Reader*, ed. Martha Vicinus, pp. 151–66. Bloomington: Indiana University Press, 1996.

Finkel, Susan Kolker and Steven G. Olswang, "Child Rearing as a Career Impediment to Women Assistant Professors." *The Review of Higher Education* 19, 2 (Winter 1996): 123–39.

"Footnotes." *The Chronicle of Higher Education*, June 12, 1998, p. A12.

Foster, Jeannette. *Sex Variant Women in Literature*. Baltimore: Diana, 1976.

Fox Keller, Evelyn and Helene Moglen. "Competition: A Problem for Academic

Women." In *Competition: A Feminist Taboo?*, ed. Valerie Miner and Helen E. Longin, pp. 21–37. New York: The Feminist Press, 1987.

Fox Keller, Evelyn. "Practicing Conflict in Feminist Theory." In *Conflicts in Feminism*, ed. Marianne Hirsch and Fox Keller, p. 370. New York: Routledge, 1990.

Fraser, Nancy. "False Antitheses: A Response to Seyla Benhabib and Judith Butler." In Seyla Benhabib, Judith Butler, Drucilla Cornell, and Nancy Fraser, *Feminist Contentions: A Philosophical Exchange* (introduction by Linda Nicolson), pp. 59–64. New York: Routledge, 1995.

Fraser, Nancy. "Multiculturalism, Antiessentialism, and Radical Democracy." In *Justice Interruptus: Critical Reflections on the Postsocialist Condition*, pp. 173–88. New York: Routledge, 1997.

Friedan, Betty. *The Feminine Mystique*. New York: Dell, 1983.

Friedan, Betty. "How to Get the Women's Movement Moving Again." *New York Times Magazine*, November 3, 1985, pp. 26–28, 66–67, 89, 98, 106–7.

Friedman, Susan Stanford. " 'Beyond' Gynocriticism and Gynesis: The Geographics of Identity and the Future of Feminist Criticism." *Tulsa Studies in Women's Literature* 15 (Spring 1996): 13–40.

Friedman, Susan Stanford. *Mappings: Feminism and the Cultural Geographies of Encounter*. Princeton: Princeton University Press, 1998.

Friedman, Susan Stanford. "Relationship Epistemology and the Question of Anglo-American Feminist Criticism." *Tulsa Studies in Women's Literature* 12, 2 (Fall 1993): 247–62.

Freud, Sigmund. *Sexuality and the Psychology of Love*. New York: Collier, 1963.

Frueh, Joanna, Cassandra L. Langer, and Arlene Raven. *New Feminist Criticism: Art Identity Action*. New York: HarperCollins, 1994.

Frye, Marilyn. *Wilful Virgin: Essays in Feminism*. Freedom, Cal.: The Crossing Press, 1992.

Fuss, Diana. *Essentially Speaking: Feminism, Nature & Difference*. New York: Routledge, 1989.

Fuss, Diana. *Identification Papers*. New York: Routledge, 1995.

Gallop, Jane. *Around 1981: Academic Feminist Literary Theory*. New York: Routledge, 1992.

Gallop, Jane. *The Daughter's Seduction: Feminism and Psychoanalysis*. Ithaca: Cornell University Press, 1983.

Gallop, Jane. *Thinking Through the Body*. New York: Columbia University Press, 1988.

Gallop, Jane and Elizabeth Francis, "Talking Across." In *Generations: Academic Feminists in Dialogue*, ed. Devoney Looser and E. Ann Kaplan, pp. 103–31. Minneapolis: University of Minnesota Press, 1997.

Gardiner, Judith et al. "An Interchange on Feminist Criticism: On 'Dancing Through the Minefields.' " *Feminist Studies* 6 (Spring 1980): 1–25.

Gardiner, Judith. "Radical Optimism, Maternal Materialism, and Teaching Literature." In *Changing Subjects: The Making of Feminist Literary Criticism*, ed. Gayle Greene and Coppélia Kahn, pp. 83–96. London and New York: Routledge, 1993.

Gates, Henry Louis Jr. " 'Authenticity' and the Lesson of *Little Tree*." *The New York Times Book Review*, November 24, 1991, pp. 1, 9, 26–30.

Geis, Deborah R. " 'A Spectator Watching My Life': Adrienne Kennedy's *A Movie Star in Black and White*.' " In *Intersecting Boundaries: The Theatre of Adrienne Kennedy*, ed. Paul K. Bryant-Jackson and Lois More Overbeck, pp. 170–8. Minneapolis: University of Minnesota Press, 1992.

George, Diana Hume. " 'How Many of Us Can You Hold to Your Breasts?': Mother in the Academy." In *Listening to Silences: New Essays in Feminist Criticism*, ed. Elaine Hedges and Shelley Fisher Fishkin, pp. 22–44. New York: Oxford University Press, 1994.

Gilbert, Sandra M. *Acts of Attention: The Poems of D. H. Lawrence*. Ithaca: Cornell University Press, 1990.

Gilbert, Sandra M. *Blood Pressure*. New York: Norton, 1988.

Gilbert, Sandra M. *Emily's Bread*. New York: Norton, 1984.

Gilbert, Sandra M. *"Piacere Conoscerla."* In *From the Margin: Writings in Italian Americana*, ed. Anthony Julian Tamburri, Paolo A. Giordano, and Fred L. Gardaphe, pp. 116–20. West Lafayette, Ind.: Purdue University Press, 1991.

Gilbert, Sandra M. and Susan Gubar. *Masterpiece Theatre: An Academic Melodrama*. New Brunswick, N.J.: Rutgers University Press, 1995.

Gilbert, Sandra M. and Susan Gubar. *No Man's Land: The Place of the Women Writer in the Twentieth Century*. Vols. 1 (*The War of the Words*), 2 (*Sexchanges*), and 3 (*Letters from the Front*). New Haven: Yale University Press, 1988, 1989, 1994.

Gilbert, Sandra M. and Susan Gubar. " 'But Oh! That Deep Romantic Chasm': The Engendering of Periodization." *Kenyon Review* 13 (Summer 1991): 74–81.

Gilligan, Carol. "Getting Civilized." In *Who's Afraid of Feminism: Seeing Through the Backlash*, ed. Ann Oakley and Juliet Mitchell, pp. 13–28. New York: The New Press, 1987.

Gilman, Sander. *Jewish Self-Hatred: Anti-Semitism and the Hidden Language of the Jews*. Baltimore: Johns Hopkins University Press, 1986.

Gilmore, Leigh. "An Anatomy of Absence: *Written on the Body*, *The Lesbian Body*, and Autobiography without Names." In *The Gay '90s: Disciplinary and Interdisciplinary Formations in Queer Studies*, ed. Thomas Foster, Carol Siegel, and Ellen E. Berry, pp. 224–51. New York: New York University Press, 1997.

Glazer, Tom. *Songs of Peace, Freedom, and Protest*. New York: McKay, 1970.

Golden, Thelma. "My Brother." In *Black: Representations of Masculinity in Contemporary American Art*, ed. Thelma Gold, pp. 19–43. New York: Whitney Museum of American Art, distributed by Harry N. Abrams, 1994.

Goldman, Emma. "Mary Wollstonecraft: Her Tragic Life and Her Passionate Struggle for Freedom." In Mary Wollstonecraft, *A Vindication of the Rights of Woman: An Authoritative Text, Backgrounds, the Wollstonecraft Debate, Criticism*, ed. Carol H. Poston, pp. 249–56. New York: Norton Critical, 1988.

Gornick, Vivian and Barbara K. Moran. *Woman in Sexist Society: Studies in Power and Powerlessness*. New York: New American Library, 1971.

Gray, Paul. "Paradise Found." *Time Magazine*, January 19, 1998, pp. 62–8.

Greene, Gayle. "Looking at History." In *Changing Subjects: The Making of Feminist Literary Criticism*, ed. Gayle Greene and Coppélia Kahn, pp. 4–27. London and New York: Routledge, 1993.

Greer, Germaine. *The Female Eunuch*. New York: Bantam, 1971.

Greer, Germaine. *Sex and Destiny: The Politics of Human Fertility*. New York: Harper & Row, 1984.

Grosz, Elizabeth. "Refiguring Lesbian Desire." In *The Lesbian Postmodern*, ed. Laura Doan, pp. 67–84. New York: Columbia University Press, 1994.

Grosz, Elizabeth. *Volatile Bodies: Toward a Corporeal Feminism*. Bloomington: Indiana University Press, 1994.

Gubar, Susan. *Racechanges: White Skin, Black Face in American Culture*. New York: Oxford University Press, 1997.

Gubar, Susan. "The Female Monster in Augustan Satire." *Signs* 3 (Winter 1977): 380–94.

Gubar, Susan. "Sapphistries." In *The Lesbian Issue: Essays from Signs*, ed. Estelle B. Freedman, Barbara C. Gelpi, Susan L. Johnson, and Kathleen M. Weston, pp. 91–110. Chicago: University of Chicago Press, 1985.

Guillory, John. *Cultural Capital: The Problem of Literary Canon Formation*. Chicago: University of Chicago Press, 1993.

Gutmann, Amy. See Appiah, K. Anthony.

Guralnick, Elissa S. "Radical Politics in Mary Wollstonecraft's *A Vindication of the Rights of Woman*." In Mary Wollstonecraft, *A Vindication of the Rights of Woman: An Authoritative Text, Backgrounds, the Wollstonecraft Debate, Criticism*, ed. Carol H. Poston, pp. 308–16. New York: Norton Critical, 1988.

Guy-Sheftall, Beverly with Evelynn M. Hammonds. "Whither Black Women's Studies: Interview." *differences: A Journal of Feminist Cultural Studies* 9, 3 (Fall 1997): 31–45.

Hacker, Marilyn. "Ballad of Ladies Lost and Found." In *Assumptions*, pp. 87–92. New York: Alfred A. Knopf, 1985 and reprinted in *The Norton Anthology of*

Literature by Women, ed. Sandra M. Gilbert and Susan Gubar, pp. 2281–84. New York: Norton, 1996.

Hacker, Marilyn. "From Orient Point." In *Going Back to the River*, p. 36. New York: Random House, 1990 and reprinted in *The Norton Anthology of Literature by Women*, ed. Sandra M. Gilbert and Susan Gubar, p. 2285. New York: Norton, 1996.

Hacker, Marilyn. *Winter Numbers*. New York: Norton, 1994.

Hall, Radclyffe. *The Well of Loneliness*. New York: Avon, 1981.

Hantzis, Darlene M. and Devoney Looser. "Of Safe(r) Spaces and 'Right' Speech: Feminist Histories, Loyalties, Theories, and the Dangers of Critique." In *PC Wars: Politics and Theory in the Academy*, ed. Jeffrey Williams, pp. 222–49. New York: Routledge. 1995.

Hall, Radclyffe. *The Well of Loneliness*. New York: Avon, 1981.

Hammond, Paula. Interview with Marilyn Hacker, *Frontiers* 5, 3 (Fall 1980): 22–7.

Haraway, Donna. "A Manifesto for Cyborgs: Science, Technology, and Socialist Feminism in the 1980s." In *Feminism/Postmodernism*, ed. Linda J. Nicholson, pp. 190–233. New York: Routledge, 1990.

Hartman, Joan E. and Ellen Messer-Davidow, "Introduction." In *(En)Gendering Knowledge: Feminists in Academe*, ed. Hartman and Messer-Davidow, pp. 1–7. Knoxville: University of Tennessee Press, 1991.

Heilbrun, Carolyn. *Reinventing Womanhood*. New York: Norton, 1979.

Heilbrun, Carolyn. "Afterword." In *Changing Subjects: The Making of Feminist Literary Criticism*, ed. Gayle Greene and Coppélia Kahn, pp. 267–71. London and New York: Routledge, 1993.

Hirsch, Marianne and Evelyn Fox Keller. "Practicing Conflict in Feminist Theory." In *Conflicts in Feminism*, ed. Marianne Hirsch and Evelyn Fox Keller, pp. 370–86. New York: Routledge, 1990.

Hoff Sommers, Christina. *Who Stole Feminism?: How Women Have Betrayed Women*. New York: Simon & Schuster, 1994.

Hollibaugh, Amber and Cherríe Moraga, "What We're Rolling Around in Bed With: Sexual Silences in Feminism: A Conversation Toward Ending Them." *Heresies* 3 (1981): 58–62.

Hollinger, David A. *Postethnic America: Beyond Multiculturalism*. New York: Basic Books, 1995.

Homans, Margaret. " 'Racial Composition': Metaphor and the Body in the Writing of Race." In *Female Subjects in Black and White: Race, Psychoanalysis, Feminism*, ed. Elizabeth Abel, Barbara Christian, Helene Moglen, pp. 77–101. Berkeley: University of California Press, 1997.

hooks, bell. *Ain't I a Woman: Black Women and Feminism*. Boston: South End, 1981.

hooks, bell. "Third World Diva Girls: Politics of Feminist Solidarity." In *Yearning: Race, Gender, and Cultural Politics*, pp. 89–102. Boston: South End Press, 1990.

Howe, Florence. "Feminism and Literature." In *Images of Women in Fiction*, ed. Susan Koppelman Cornillon, pp. 253–77. Bowling Green, Ohio: Bowling Green University Popular Press, 1972.

Howe, Irving. "The Self in Literature." In *Constructions of the Self*, ed. George Levine, pp. 249–67. New Brunswick: Rutgers University Press, 1992.

Huber, Bettina J. "Women in the Modern Languages, 1970–1990." In *Profession 90*, ed. Phyllis Franklin, pp. 58–73. New York: The Modern Language Association of America, 1990.

Hull, Gloria T. "History/My History." In *Changing Subjects: The Making of Feminist Literary Criticism*, ed. Gayle Greene and Coppélia Kahn, pp. 48–63. London and New York: Routledge, 1993.

Hurston, Zora Neale. "How It Feels to Be Colored Me." In *I Love Myself When I Am Laughing . . . and Then Again When I Am Looking Mean and Impressive*, ed. Alice Walker, pp. 152–5. Old Westbury, N.Y.: Feminist Press, 1979.

Hutcheon, Linda. *A Poetics of Postmodernism: History, Theory, Fiction*. New York: Routledge, 1988.

Irigaray, Luce. *Speculum of the Other Woman*, trans. Gillian C. Gill. Ithaca: Cornell University Press, 1985.

Irigaray, Luce. *This Sex Which Is Not One*, trans. Catherine Porter with Carolyn Burke. Ithaca: Cornell University Press, 1985.

Jackson, Shannon. "*White Noises*: On Performing White, On Writing Performance." *The Drama Review* 42, 1 (Spring 1998): 49–65.

Jacobus, Mary. "The Difference of View." In *Women Writing and Writing about Women*, ed. Mary Jacobus, pp. 10–21. London: Croom Helm, 1979.

Johnson, Charles. *Oxherding Tale*. Bloomington: Indiana University Press, 1982.

Johnson, Barbara. "Response to Henry Louis Gates, Jr." In *Afro-American Literary Study in the 1990s*, ed. Houston A. Baker Jr., and Patricia Redmond, pp. 39–44. Chicago: University of Chicago Press, 1989.

Johnson, Barbara. *The Feminist Difference: Literature, Psychoanalysis, Race, and Gender*. Cambridge: Harvard University Press, 1998.

Johnson, Barbara. *A World of Difference*. Baltimore: Johns Hopkins University Press, 1987.

Johnson, Barbara. "Thresholds of Difference: Structures of Address in Zora Neale Hurston." *Critical Inquiry* 12, 1 (Autumn 1985): 278–89.

Joseph, Gloria I. and Jill Lewis, *Common Differences: Conflicts in Black and White Feminist Perspectives*. New York: Anchor/Doubleday, 1986.

Jouvre, Nicole Ward. *White Woman Speaks With Forked Tongue*. London and New York: Routledge, 1991.

Kaplan, Carla. *The Erotics of Talk: Women's Writing and Feminist Paradigms*. New York: Oxford University Press, 1996.

Kaplan, Cora. "Pandora's Box: Subjectivity, Class, and Sexuality in Socialist Feminist Criticism." In *Making a Difference: Feminist Literary Criticism*, ed. Gayle Greene and Coppélia Kahn, pp. 146–76. London: Methuen, 1985.

Kaplan, Cora. "Wild Nights: Pleasure/Sexuality/Feminism." In *Formations*, ed. Frederic Jameson et al., pp. 15–35. London: Routledge, 1983.

Kaye/Kantrowitz, Melanie and Irena Klepfisz. *The Tribe of Dina: A Jewish Women's Anthology*. Boston: Beacon, 1989.

Kennedy, Randall. *Race, Crime, and the Law*. New York: Pantheon, 1997.

Kennedy, Adrienne. *A Movie Star Has to Star in Black and White*. In *Adrienne Kennedy In One Act*, 79–104. University of Minneapolis Press, 1988. Reprinted in *The Norton Anthology of African-American Literature*, ed. Henry Louis Gates Jr. and Nellie Y. McKay, pp. 2081–94. New York: Norton, 1997.

Klepfisz, Irena. "*Yom Hashoah, Yom Yerushalaym*: A Meditation." In *Nice Jewish Girls: A Lesbian Anthology*, ed. Evelyn Torton Beck, pp. 260–85. Boston: Beacon, 1989.

Kofman, Sarah. *The Enigma of Woman: Women in Freud's Writing*, trans. Catherine Porter. Ithaca: Cornell University Press, 1985.

Kolodny, Annette. *Failing the Future: A Dean Looks at Higher Education in the Twenty-first Century*. Durham: Duke University Press, 1998.

Koltun, Elizabeth, ed. *The Jewish Woman: New Perspectives*. New York: Schocken, 1976.

Kuhn, Annette. *The Power of the Image: Essays on Representation and Sexuality*. London: Routledge & Kegan Paul, 1985.

LaCapra, Dominick. "The University in Ruins?" *Critical Inquiry* 25, 1 (Autumn 1998): 32–55.

Lamos, Colleen. "The Postmodern Lesbian Position: *On Our Backs*." In *The Lesbian Postmodern*, ed. Laura Doan, pp. 85-103. New York: Columbia University Press, 1994.

Landes, Joan B. *Women and the Public Sphere in the Age of the French Revolution*. Ithaca: Cornell University Press, 1988.

Larsen, Nella. *Quicksand and Passing*, ed. Deborah E. McDowell. New Brunswick: Rutgers University Press, 1986.

Latour, Bruno. *We Have Never Been Modern*, trans. Catherine Porter. Cambridge: Harvard University Press, 1993.

Lazarre, Jane. *Beyond the Whiteness of Whiteness*. Durham: Duke University Press, 1996.

Levine, George. "Introduction." In *Constructions of the Self*, ed. Levine, pp. 1–13. New Brunswick, New Jersey: Rutgers University Press, 1992.

Lim, Shirley Geok-lin. "Hegemony and 'Anglo-American Feminism': Living in the Funny House." *Tulsa Studies in Language and Literature* 12, 2 (Fall 1993): 279–87.

Lorde, Audre. *Zami: A New Spelling of My Name*. Freedom, California: The Crossing Press, 1994.

Lorde, Audre. "Uses of the Erotic: The Erotic as Power." In *Sister Outsider: Essays and Speeches*, pp. 53–59. Freedom, California: The Crossing Press, 1984.

Lowell, Amy. "The Sisters." Reprinted in *The Norton Anthology of Literature by Women*, ed. Sandra M. Gilbert and Susan Gubar, pp. 1271–75. New York: Norton, 1996.

Martin, Biddy. *Femininity Played Straight: The Significance of Being Lesbian*. New York: Routledge, 1996.

Martin, Biddy. "Lesbian Identity and Autobiographical Differences." In *The Lesbian and Gay Studies Reader*, ed. Henry Abelove, Michèle Aina Barale, and David M. Halperin, pp. 274–93. New York: Routledge, 1993.

Martin, Biddy. "Success and Its Failures." *differences: A Journal of Feminist Cultural Studies* 9, 3 (Fall 1997): 102-31.

Martin, Carol. "Bearing Witness: Anna Deavere Smith from Community to Theatre to Mass Media." In *A Sourcebook of Feminist Theatre and Performance: On and Beyond the Stage*, ed. Martin, pp. 81–93. London and New York: Routledge, 1996.

McDowell, Deborah E. "Recycling: Race, Gender, and the Practice of Theory." In *Studies in Historical Change*, ed. Ralph Cohen, pp. 246–63. Charlottesville: University of Virginia Press, 1993.

McKay, Nellie Y. "Literature and Politics: Black Feminist Scholars Reshaping Literary Education in the White University, 1970–1986." In *Left Politics and the Literary Profession*, ed. Lennard J. Davis and M. Bella Mirabella, pp. 84–102. New York: Columbia University Press, 1990.

McKay, Nellie Y. "Naming the Problem that Led to the Question 'Who Shall Teach African-American Literature?'; or, Are We Ready to Disband the Wheatley Court?" *PMLA* 113, 3 (May 1998): 359–69.

Meese, Elizabeth A. *(Sem)erotics: Theorizing Lesbian Writing*. New York: New York University Press, 1992.

Messer-Davidow, Ellen. "Know-How." In *(En)Gendering Knowledge: Feminists in Academe*, ed. Joan E. Hartman and Messer-Davidow, pp. 281–309. Knoxville: University of Tennessee Press, 1991.

Messer-Davidow, Ellen. *Disciplining Feminism: Episodes in the Discursive Production of Social Change*. North Carolina: Duke University Press, forthcoming.

Miller, Nancy K. *Getting Personal: Feminist Occasions and Other Autobiographical Acts.* New York: Routledge, 1991.

Miller, Nancy K. "Hadassah Arms." In *People of the Book: Thirty Scholars Reflect on their Jewish Identity* , ed. Jeffrey Rubin-Dorsky and Shelley Fisher Fishkin, pp. 154–68. Wisconsin: University of Wisconsin Press, 1996.

Miller, Nancy K. "Public Statements, Private Lives: Academic Memoirs for the Nineties." *Signs* 22, 41 (Summer 1997): 981–1013.

Millett, Kate. *Sexual Politics.* New York: Avon, 1971.

Miner, Valerie. "Rumors from the Cauldron: Competition among Feminist Writers." In *Competition: A Feminist Taboo?*, ed. Valerie Miner and Helen E. Longin, pp. 183–94. New York: The Feminist Press, 1987.

Modleski, Tania. *Feminism without Women: Culture and Criticism in a "Postfeminist" Age.* New York: Routledge, 1991.

Modleski, Tania. "Doing Justice to the Subjects: Mimetic Art in a Multicultural Society: The Work of Anna Deavere Smith." In *Female Subjects in Black and White*, ed. Elizabeth Abel, Barbara Christian, and Helene Moglen, pp. 57–76. Berkeley: University of California Press, 1997.

Mohanty, Chandra Talpade. "On Race and Voice: Challenges for Liberal Education in the 1990s." *Cultural Critique* 14 (Winter 1989/90): 179–208.

Mohanty, Chadra Talpade. "Under Western Eyes: Feminism, Scholarship and Colonial Discourses." In *Contemporary Postcolonial Theory: A Reader*, ed. Padmini Mongia, pp. 172–97. London: Arnold, 1996.

Moi, Toril. *Feminist Theory and Simone de Beauvoir.* Oxford: Basil Blackwell, 1990.

Moi, Toril. *Sexual/Textual Politics: Feminist Literary Theory.* London: Methuen, 1985.

Moraga, Cherrié and Gloria Anzaldúa, eds. *This Bridge Called My Back: Writings by Radical Women of Color.* New York: Kitchen Table, 1981.

Morgan, Robin, ed. *Sisterhood Is Powerful.* New York: Vintage, 1970.

Morris, Pam. *Literature and Feminism: An Introduction.* Oxford: Blackwell Publishers, 1993.

Morrison, Toni. *Beloved.* New York: New American Library, 1987.

Morrison, Toni. *The Nobel Lecture in Literature, 1993.* New York: Knopf, 1994.

Morrison, Toni. *Paradise,* New York: Knopf, 1998.

Morrison, Toni. "Recitatif." In *The Before Columbus Foundation Fiction Anthology*, ed. Ishmael Reed, pp. 445–64. New York: Norton, 1992.

Moses, Claire Goldberg. " 'Equality' and 'Difference' in Historical Perspective." In *Rebel Daughters: Women and the French Revolution*, ed. Sara E. Meltzer and Leslie W. Rabine, pp.231–54. New York: Oxford University Press, 1992.

Mulvey, Laura. *Visual and Other Pleasures.* Bloomington: Indiana University Press, 1989.

Myerson, Allen R. "Editions of the Passover Tale: This Year in Profusion." *New York Times*, April 4, 1993, sec. 4, pp. 14–15.

Najmabadi, Afsaneh. "Teaching and Research in Unavailable Intersections." *differences: A Journal of Feminist Cultural Studies* 9, 3, special issue on Women's Studies on the Edge (Fall 1997): 65–78.

Newton, Esther. "Just One of the Boys: Lesbians in Cherry Grove, 1960–1988." In *The Lesbian and Gay Studies Reader*, ed. Henry Abelove, Michèle Aina Barale, and David M. Halperin, pp. 528–41. New York: Routledge, 1993.

Newton, Esther. "The Mythic Mannish Lesbian: Radclyffe Hall and the New Woman." In *The Lesbian Issue: Essays from Signs*, ed. Estelle B. Freedman, Barbara C. Gelpi, Susan L. Johnson, and Kathleen M. Weston, pp. 7–26. Chicago: University of Chicago Press, 1984.

Newton, Judith. "Feminist Family Values; or, Growing Old—and Growing Up—with the Women's Movement." *Generations: Academic Feminists in Dialogue*, ed. Devoney Looser and E. Ann Kaplan, pp. 327–44. Minneapolis: University of Minnesota Press, 1997.

Nietzsche, Fredrich. *Twilight of the Idols*. In *The Portable Nietzsche*, ed. and trans. by Walter Kaufmann, pp. 463–564. Middlesex, England: Penguin, 1954.

Nightingale, Florence. *Cassandra*. In *The Norton Anthology of Literature by Women*, ed. Sandra M. Gilbert and Susan Gubar, pp. 837–44. New York: Norton, 1996.

Nussbaum, Martha C. "The Professor of Parody." *The New Republic* (Feb. 22, 1999): 37–45.

O'Grady, Lorraine. "Nefertiti/Devonia Evangeline." *Art Journal* 56 (Winter 1997): 64–5.

Olsen, Tillie. *Silences*. New York: Delacorte, 1978.

Ostriker, Alicia. "Entering the Tents." *Feminist Studies* 15 (Fall 1989): 541–48.

Ozick, Cynthia. "Notes Toward Finding the Right Question." In *On Being A Jewish Feminist*, ed. Susannah Heschel, pp. 120–51. New York: Schocken, 1983.

The Passover Haggadah, Deluxe Edition, Complements of the Coffees of Maxwell House. New York: General Foods Corporation, 1964.

Piercy, Marge. "The Friend." In *Hard Loving*, p. 24. Middletown, Conn.: Wesleyan University Press, 1969.

Piper, Adrian. *Colored People*. London: Book Works, 1991.

Piper, Adrian. *Out of Order, Out of Sight*. 2 vols. Cambridge, Mass.: MIT Press, 1996.

Piper, Adrian. "Passing for White, Passing for Black." In *New Feminist Criticism: Art Identity Action*, ed. Joanna Frueh, Cassandra L. Langer, and Arlene Raven. pp. 216–47. New York: HarperCollins, 1994.

Plaskow, Judith. *Standing Again at Sinai: Judaism from a Feminist Perspective*. San Francisco: Harper, 1990.

Plath, Sylvia. *Collected Poems*, ed. Ted Hughes. New York: Harper and Row, 1981.

Pogrebin, Letty Cottin. *Deborah, Golda, and Me: Being Female and Jewish in America*. New York: Crown, 1991.

Poovey, Mary. *The Proper Lady and the Woman Writer: Ideology as Style in the Works of Mary Wollstonecraft, Mary Shelley, and Jane Austen*. Chicago: University of Chicago Press, 1984.

Quinn, Rebecca Darkin. "An Open Letter to Institutional Mothers." In *Generations: Academic Feminists in Dialogue*, ed. Devoney Looser and E. Ann Kaplan, pp. 174–82. Minneapolis: University of Minnesota Press, 1997.

Ramazanoglu, Caroline. "Introduction." In *Up Against Foucault: Explorations of Some Tensions between Foucault and Feminism*, ed. Ramazanoglu, pp. 1–28. New York: Routledge, 1993.

Readings, Bill. *The University in Ruins*. Cambridge: Harvard University Press, 1996.

Reed, Ishmael. *Writin' Is Fightin': Thirty-Seven Years of Boxing on Paper*. New York: Atheneum, 1988.

Reiss, Timothy J. "Revolution in Bounds: Wollstonecraft, Women, and Reason." In *Gender and Theory*, ed. Linda Kauffman, pp. 11–50. Oxford. Basil Blackwell, 1989.

Rich, Adrienne. *An Atlas of the Difficult World: Poems 1988–1991*. New York: Norton, 1991.

Rich, Adrienne. *The Fact of a Doorframe: Poems Selected and New, 1950–1984*. New York: Norton, 1984.

Rich, Adrienne. "Compulsory Heterosexuality and Lesbian Existence." In *Women, Sex, and Sexuality*, ed. Catharine R. Stimpson and Ethel Spector Person, pp. 60–91. Chicago: University of Chicago Press, 1980.

Rich, Adrienne. "Notes Toward a Politics of Location." In *Women, Feminist Identity, and Society in the 1980s*, ed. Myriam Diaz-Diocaretz and Iris M. Zavala, pp. 5–22. Amsterdam/Philadelphia: John Benjamins, 1985.

Rich, Adrienne. "Split at the Root." In *Nice Jewish Girls: A Lesbian Anthology*, ed. Evelyn Torton Beck, pp. 67–84. Boston: Beacon, 1989.

Rich, Adrienne. "Sources." In *Your Native Land, Your Life*, pp. 1–27. New York: Norton, 1986.

Rich, Adrienne. "When We Dead Awaken: Writing as Re-Vision." In *On Lies, Secrets, and Silence: Selected Prose, 1966–1978*, pp. 33–49. New York: Norton, 1979.

Rich, B. Ruby. "Feminism and Sexuality in the 1980s." *Feminist Studies* 12, 3 (Fall 1986): 525–61.

Richards, Sandra L. "Caught in the Act of Social Definition: *On the Road* with Anna Deavere Smith." In *Acing Out: Feminist Performances*, ed. Lynda Hart and Peggy Phelan, pp. 35–53. Ann Arbor: University of Michigan Press, 1993.

Riley, Denise. *"Am I That Name?": Feminism and the Category of 'Women' in History.* Minneapolis: University of Minnesota Press, 1988.

Ringgold, Faith. *Dancing at the Louvre*, ed. Dan Cameron et al. Berkeley: University of California Press, 1988.

Ringgold, Faith. *We Flew Over the Bridge*. Boston: Little, Brown, 1995.

Ringgold, Faith. "From *Being My Own Woman*." In *Confirmation: An Anthology of African-American Women*, ed. Amiri Baraka and Amina Baraka, pp. 300–11. New York: Quill, 1983.

Roiphe, Katie. *The Morning After: Sex, Fear, and Feminism on Campus.* Boston: Little, Brown, 1993.

Roof, Judith. *Come As You Are: Sexuality and Narrative.* New York: Columbia University Press, 1996.

Roof, Judith. *A Lure of Knowledge: Lesbian Sexuality and Theory.* New York: Columbia University Press, 1991.

Roof, Judith. "Generational Difficulties; or, The Fear of a Barren History." In *Generations: Academic Feminists in Dialogue*, ed. Devoney Looser and E. Ann Kaplan, pp. 69–87. Minneapolis: University of Minnesota Press, 1997.

Roof, Judith and Robyn Wiegman. *Who Can Speak? Authority and Critical Identity.* Urbana: University of Illinois Press, 1995.

Rosenberg, Jessica and Gitana Garofalo. "Riot Grrrl: Revolutions from Within." *Signs* 23, 31 (1998): 809–41.

Roth, Moira. "Of Cotton and Sunflower Fields: The Makings of *The French* and *The American Collection*." In *Dancing at the Louvre*. Berkeley: University of California Press, 1998, ed. Dan Cameron et al., pp. 49–63. Berkeley: University of California Press, 1998.

Rorty, Richard. *Contingency, Irony, and Solidarity.* Cambridge: Cambridge University Press, 1989.

Rubin, Gayle. "The Traffic in Women: Notes on the 'Political Economy' of Sex." In *Toward an Anthropology of Women*, ed. Rayna R. Reiter, pp. 157–210. New York: Monthly Review Press, 1975.

Rukeyser, Muriel. *The Collected Poems.* New York: McGraw-Hill, 1982.

Ruthven, K. K. *Feminist Literary Studies: An Introduction.* Cambridge: Cambridge University Press, 1984.

Said, Edward. *Orientalism.* New York: Pantheon, 1978.

Schell, Eileen E. *Gypsy Academics and Mother-Teachers: Gender, Contingent Labor, and Writing Instruction.* Portsmouth, N.H.: Boyton/Cook, 1998.

Schor, Naomi. "Female Fetishism: The Case of George Sand." *Poetics Today* 61 (1985): 301–10.

Schreiner, Olive. *Woman and Labour.* London: Virago, 1978.

Schuster, Marilyn R. and Susan R. Van Dyne, "Curricular Change for the Twenty-first Century: Why Women" and "Changing the Institution." In *Women's Place in the Academy: Transforming the Liberal Arts Curriculum*, ed. Schuster and Van Dyne, pp. 3–12 and 89–97. Totowa, N.J.: Roman & Allanheld, 1985.

Scott, Joan. "Deconstructing Equality-Versus-Difference." In *Conflicts in Feminism*, ed. Marianne Hirsch and Evelyn Fox Keller, pp. 134–48. New York: Routledge, 1990.

Sedgwick, Eve Kosofsky. *Epistemology of the Closet*. Berkeley: University of California Press, 1990.

Shatz, Adam. "Black Like Me: Conceptual Artist Adrian Piper Gets Under Your Skin." *LinguaFranca* 8, 8 (November 1998): 39–54,

Showalter, Elaine. "A Criticism of Our Own: Autonomy and Assimilation in Afro-American and Feminist Literary Theory." In *The Future of Literary Theory*, ed. Ralph Cohen, pp. 347–69. New York: Routledge, 1989.

Showalter, Elaine. "Introduction: Twenty Years On." In *A Literature of Their Own*, expanded ed., pp. xi–xxxiii. Princeton: Princeton University Press, 1999.

Showalter, Elaine. "Toward a Feminist Poetics." In *The New Feminist Criticism: Essays on Women, Literature, and Theory*, ed. Showalter, pp. 125–43. New York: Pantheon, 1985.

Silver, Brenda R. "The Authority of Anger: *Three Guineas* as Case Study." *Signs* 16, 21 (1991): 340–70.

Smith, Barbara. "Toward a Black Feminist Criticism." In *The New Feminist Criticism: Essays on Women, Literature, and Theory*, ed. Elaine Showalter, pp. 168–85. New York: Pantheon, 1985.

Smith, Valerie. "Black Feminist Theory and the Representation of the 'Other.' " In *Changing Our Own Words: Essays on Criticism, Theory, and Writing by Black Women*, ed. Cheryl A. Wall, pp. 38–57. New Brunswick, N.J.: Rutgers University Press, 1989.

Smith Rosenberg, Carroll. "The Female World of Love and Ritual." *Signs* 1 (1975): 1–30.

Snitow, Ann. "A Gender Diary." In *Conflicts in Feminism*, ed. Marianne Hirsch and Evelyn Fox Keller, pp. 9–43. New York: Routledge, 1990.

Sollors, Werner. *Beyond Ethnicity: Consent and Descent in American Culture*, New York: Oxford University Press, 1986.

Spelman, Elizabeth. *Inessential Woman*. Boston: Beacon, 1988.

Spivak, Gayatri Chakravorty. *In Other Worlds: Essays in Cultural Politics*. New York: Routledge, 1988.

Spivak, Gayatri Chakravorty. *Outside in the Teaching Machine*. New York: Routledge, 1993.

Spivak, Gayatri Chakravorty. *The Post-Colonial Critic: Interviews, Strategies, Dialogues*, ed. Sarah Harasym. New York: Routledge, 1990.

Spivak, Gayatri Chakravorty. "A Response to 'The Difference Within: Feminism and Critical Theory." In *The Difference Within: Feminism and Critical Theory*, ed. Elizabeth Meese and Alice Parker, pp. 207–20. Amsterdam/Philadelphia: John Benjamins, 1989.

Soper, Kate. "Productive Contradictions." In *Up Against Foucault: Explorations of Some Tensions between Foucault and Feminism*, ed. Caroline Ramazanoglu, pp. 29–50. New York: Routledge, 1993.

Sprengnether, Madelon. "Generational Differences: Reliving Mother-Daughter Conflicts." In *Changing Subjects: The Making of Feminist Literary Criticism*, ed. Gayle Greene and Coppélia Kahn, pp. 201–10. London and New York: Routledge, 1993.

Stein, Gertrude. *The Autobiography of Alice B. Toklas*. In *Selected Writings*, ed. Carl Van Vechten, pp. 1–237. New York: Viking, 1962.

Steiner, George. *Extraterritorial Papers on Literature and the Language of Revolution*. New York: Atheneum, 1976.

Stimpson, Catharine R. "What Am I Doing When I Do Women's Studies?" In *Left Politics and the Literary Profession*, ed. Lennard J. Davis and M. Bella Mirabella, pp. 55–83. New York: Columbia University Press, 1990.

Stimpson, Catharine R. "Zero Degree Deviancy: The Lesbian Novel in English." *Critical Inquiry* 8, 2, special issue on Writing and Sexual Difference (Winter 1981): 363–79.

Stovall, Tyler. *Paris Noir: African Americans in the City of Light*. Boston: Houghton Mifflin, 1996.

Suleiman, Susan. *Budapest Diary*. Lincoln: University of Nebraska Press, 1996.

Suleiman, Susan. "Motherhood and Identity Politics: 'An Exchange.' " In *Risking Who One Is: Encounters with Contemporary Art and Literature*, pp. 55–63. Cambridge: Harvard University Press, 1994.

Suleiman, Susan. "My War in Four Episodes." *Agni* 33 (published at Boston University).

Suleri, Sara. "Woman Skin Deep: Feminism and the Postcolonial Condition." In *Identities*, ed. Kwame Anthony Appiah and Henry Louis Gates Jr., pp. 133–46. Chicago: University of Chicago Press, 1995.

Swensen, May, "Bleeding." In *Iconographs*, p. 13. New York: Scribner's, 1970 and reprinted in *The Norton Anthology of Literature by Women*, ed. Sandra M. Gilbert and Susan Gubar, p. 1830. New York: Norton, 1996.

Thompson, Irene and Audrey Roberts. *The Road Retaken: Women Reenter the Academy*. New York: The Modern Language Association of America, 1985.

Todd, Janet. *Feminist Literary History*. New York: Routledge, 1988.

Todd, Janet. "Anglo-American Difference: Some Thoughts of an Aging Feminist." *Tulsa Studies in Women's Literature* 12, 2 (Fall 1993): 241–62.

Todd, Janet. "Introduction." In *A Wollstonecraft Anthology*, ed. Janet Todd, pp. 1–24. New York: Columbia University Press, 1990.

Uchmanowicz, Pauline. "The $5,000–$25,000 Exchange." *College English* 57, 4 (1995): 426–47.

Valian, Virginia. "Sex, Schemas, and Success: What's Keeping Women Back?" *Academe: Bulletin of the American Association of University Professors* 84, 5 (September/October 1998): 50–55.

Van Dyne, Susan R. *Revising Life: Sylvia Plath's Ariel Poems*. Chapel Hill: University of North Carolina Press, 1993.

Vicinus, Martha. "Introduction." In *Lesbian Subjects: A Feminist Studies Reader*, ed. Martha Vicinus, pp. 1–14. Bloomington: Indiana University Press, 1996.

Vicinus, Martha. " 'They Wonder to Which Sex I Belong': The Historical Roots of the Modern Lesbian Identity." In *The Lesbian and Gay Studies Reader*, ed. Henry Abelove, Michele Aina Barale, and David M. Halperin, pp. 432–52. New York: Routledge, 1993.

Walker, Alice. "Everyday Use." In *In Love and Trouble: Stories of Black Women*, pp. 47–59. New York: Harcourt, Brace & Jovanovich, 1973.

Walker, Alice. *In Search of Our Mothers' Gardens*. San Diego: Harcourt Brace & Jovanovich, 1983.

Walker, Alice. *The Temple of My Familiar*. New York: Pocket Books, 1990.

Walker, Nancy A. *A Very Serious Thing: Women's Humor and American Culture*. Minneapolis: University of Minnesota Press, 1988.

Wallace, Michele. "Art for Whose Sake?" *The Women's Reivew of Books* 13, 1 (October 1995): 8.

Wallace, Michele. "*The French Collection*: Momma Jones, Mommy Fay, and Me." In *Dancing in the Louvre*, ed. Dan Cameron, et al., pp. 14–25. Berkeley: University of California Press, 1998.

Wallace, Michele. "For Whom the Bell Tolls: Why America Can't Deal with Black Feminist Intellectuals." *Voice Literary Supplement*, no. 140 (November 1995): 21–2.

Wallace, Michele. "Modernism, Postmodernism, and the Problem of the Visual in Afro-American Culture." In *Out There: Marginalization and Contemporary Cultures*, ed. Russell Ferguson, Martha Gever, Trinh T. Minh-ha, and Cornel West, pp. 39–50. New York: New Museum of Contemporary Art, 1990.

Wardle, Ralph M. *Mary Wollstonecraft: A Critical Biography*. Lawrence: University of Kansas Press, 1951.

Washington, Mary Helen. *Black-Eyed Susans: Classic Stories By and About Black Women.* New York: Anchor, 1975.

Weisstein, Naomi. "Psychology Constructs the Female." In *Woman in Sexist Society,* ed. Vivian Gornick and Barbara K. Moran, pp. 207–24. New York: New American Library, 1971.

West, Cornell. "Foreword." In Anna Deavere Smith, *Fires in the Mirror: Crown Heights, Brooklyn, and Other Identities,* pp. xvii–xxii. New York: Anchor, 1993.

Wiegman, Robyn. "Queering the Academy." In *The Gay '90s: Disciplinary and Interdisciplinary Formations in Queer Studies,* ed. Thomas Foster, Carol Siegel, and Ellen E. Berry, pp. 3–22. New York: New York University Press, 1997.

Wiegman, Robyn. Response to Susan Gubar, "What Ails Feminist Criticism?" *Critical Inquiry* 25 (Winter 1999): 362–79.

Williams, Linda. "A Provoking Agent: The Pornography and Performance Art of Annie Sprinkle." In *Writing on the Body: Female Embodiment and Feminist Theory,* ed. Katie Conboy, Nadia Medina, and Sarah Stanbury, pp. 360–79. New York: Columbia University Press, 1997.

Williams, Patricia J. *The Rooster's Egg: On the Resistance of Prejudice.* Cambridge: Harvard University Press, 1995.

Williams, Patricia J. *Seeing a Color-Blind Future: The Paradox of Race.* New York: Farrar, Strauss and Giroux, 1998.

Wilson, Judith. "In Memory of the News and Of Our Selves: The Art of Adrian Piper." *Third Text* 16/17 (1991): 39–62.

Wilson, Judith. "Optical Illusions: Images of Miscegenation in Nineteenth- and Twentieth-Century American Art." *American Art* 5 (1991): 89–107.

Winterson, Jeanette. "The Poetics of Sex." In *The Penguin Book of Lesbian Short Stories,* ed. Margaret Reynolds, pp. 412–22. London and New York: Viking, 1993.

Wittig, Monique. *The Straight Mind and Other Essays.* Boston: Beacon, 1992.

Wollstonecraft, Mary. *Maria; or, The Wrongs of Women.* New York: Norton, 1975.

Wollstonecraft, Mary. *Mary, a Fiction.* New York: Schocken, 1977.

Wollstonecraft, Mary. *Collected Letters,* ed. Ralph M. Wardle. Ithaca, N.Y.: Cornell University Press, 1979.

Wollstonecraft, Mary. *A Vindication of the Rights of Woman: An Authoritative Text, Backgrounds, the Wollstonecraft Debate, Criticism,* ed. Carol H. Poston. New York: Norton Critical, 1988.

Woo, Deborah. "The Gap Between Striving and Achieving: The Case of Asian-American Women." In *Race and Gender: An Anthology,* ed. Margaret Anderson and Patricia Hill Collins, pp. 191–200. Belmont, Cal.: Wadsworth, 1992.

Woolf, Virginia. "Journal of Mistress Joan Martyn." In *The Complete Shorter Fiction of Virginia Woolf,* ed. Susan Dick, pp. 33–62; New York: Harcourt, 1989.

Woolf, Virginia. "Mary Wollstonecraft." In Mary Wollstonecraft, *A Vindication of the Rights of Woman: An Authoritative Text, Backgrounds, the Wollstonecraft Debate, Criticism*, ed. Carol H. Poston, pp. 267–72. New York: Norton Critical, 1988.

Woolf, Virginia. *A Room of One's Own*. New York: Harcourt, Brace, 1981.

Woolf, Virginia. *Three Guineas*. New York: Harcourt, Brace & World, 1996.

Yaeger, Patricia. "Pre-Postmodernism: Academic Feminism and the Kitchen Sink." *The Journal of the Midwestern Modern Language Association* 27, 1, special issue on the Future of the Profession (Spring 1994): 4–25.

Yaeger, Patricia. "Writing as Action: *A Vindication of the Rights of Woman*." *Minnesota Review* 29 (Fall 1987): 67–80.

Yee, Carole Zonis. "Why Aren't We Writing about Ourselves?" In *Images of Women in Fiction*, ed. Susan Koppelman Cornillon, pp. 131–4. Bowling Green, Ohio: Bowling Green University Popular Press, 1972.

Yee, Shirley J. "The 'Women' in Women's Studies." *differences: A Journal of Feminist Cultural Studies* 9, 3, special issue on Women's Studies on the Edge (Fall 1997): 46–64.

Young, Robert. *White Mythologies: Writing History and the West*. London and New York: Routledge, 1990.

Zimmerman, Bonnie. "Lesbians Like This and That: Some Notes on Lesbian Criticism for the Nineties." In *New Lesbian Criticism: Literary and Cultural Readings*, ed. Sally Munt, pp. 1–16. London: Harvester/Wheatsheaf, 1992.

Zimmerman, Bonnie. "What Has Never Been: An Overview of Lesbian Feminist Criticism." In *The New Feminist Criticism: Essays on Women, Literature, Theory*, ed. Elaine Showalter, pp. 200–24. New York: Pantheon, 1985.

Zuckoff, Aviva Cantor. "Jewish Women's Haggadah." In *The Jewish Woman*, ed. Elizabeth Koltun, pp. 94–104. New York: Schocken, 1976.

Zumwalt, Nancy. "Exclusae Feminae." In *The Road Retaken: Women Reenter the Academy*, ed. Irene Thompson and Audrey Roberts, pp. 127–32. New York: The Modern Language Association of America, 1985.

Index

Abel, Elizabeth, 74, 83, 87, 183*n*20

Abraham, Julie, 52–53

Abzug, Bella, 84

Academic feminism: and activism, 4, 134, 195*n*37; and Judaism, 74, 80–81, 181*n*5; specialization, 9, 102–3, 151, 157, 158–59, 164, 185*nn*8, 9, 186*n*14, 198*n*7. *See also* Academic feminism, divisions within; Academic feminism, future of

Academic feminism, divisions within, 6–7, 8–10, 17, 114–15; attacks on older critics, 13–14, 114, 118, 188–89*n*10; and feminist misogyny, 150–51, 197*n*20; and future of feminism, 160–61, 163, 198*n*4; generational tensions, 18–19, 101–5, 114, 164, 187*n*2; hive metaphor, 7–8; and specialization, 102–3, 151, 186*n*14; status asymmetry, 101, 184–85*nn*6, 13. *See also* Racial divisions within academic feminism

Academic feminism, future of, 15, 19, 153–67; and activism, 164–65; advice, 166–67; and censorship, 163–64; and divisions, 160–61, 163, 198*n*4; and identity politics, 154,

155; and institutionalization, 161–62, 164–65; and interdisciplinarity, 158–59, 198*n*7; and poststructuralism, 154–55, 156, 197–8*nn*2, 3; and specialization, 156–60; supernova metaphor, 9, 159–60, 165, 167, 198*n*8; and theory, 163

Academy: humanities downsizing, 93–94, 98–9, 103–4, 130, 184*nn*4, 5, 185*nn*11, 12; postwar Jewish influx, 82–83. *See also* Female professors; Feminist literary criticism

Activism, 4, 6, 11, 15, 134, 164–65, 195*n*37

Adler, Rachel, 72, 73, 84

Aesthetics, 10, 46, 68, 163, 180*n*31

African-American female professors, 131, 184*n*3, 189*n*10

African-American feminists, 118, 124, 170*n*9, 189*n*12, 192*n*21. *See also* African-American female professors; African-American Studies; African-American women artists; Race

African-American Studies, 13, 21, 80, 87, 90, 163, 194–95*n*36

African-American women artists, 21–44; on assimilation, 22–24; on